THE BERLIN AIR LIFT

Part I: 21 June – 31 December 1948
Part II: 1 January – 30 September 1949

1952

HISTORICAL DIVISION
EUROPEAN COMMAND
KARLSRUHE GERMANY

Published by Books Express Publishing
Copyright © Books Express, 2011
ISBN 978-1-78039-507-4

Books Express publications are available from all good retail and online booksellers. For
publishing proposals and direct ordering please contact us at: info@books-express.com

Prepared by Elizabeth S. Lay of the Staff of the Historical Division, Headquarters, European Command.

W. S. Nye
Colonel, Artillery
Chief, Historical Division

FOREWORD

This volume consists of two monographs completed in six copies each at separate intervals as parts of the Occupation Forces in Europe Series. Part I was originally published in 1949 under the title, "The Berlin Air Lift, 21 June - 31 December 1948," and Part II in 1952 under the title, "The Berlin Air Lift, 1 January - 30 September 1949." The purpose of reproducing these studies in a single volume is to give a wider distribution to these histories which together cover the entire story of EUCOM ground support of the air lift. Parts I and II differ slightly in style and format as a result of changes adopted since Part I was originally published. No preface was written for Part I, but the remarks in the Preface of Part II apply generally to the entire volume.

Historical Division
Headquarters European Command

VOLUME I　　　　　　　　June 1952　　　　　　　NUMBER 5

CONTENTS

Special Studies Series. Prepared nonperiodically by the Historical
Division, Headquarters, European Command, for the purpose of increasing the availability of selected special studies and monographs
prepared by or under the supervision of this division and in coordination with other staff divisions of this headquarters as appropriate. The material presented herein does not necessarily reflect
official Department of the Army doctrine or accepted practices, but
is for information only. Local reproduction may be authorized upon
specific request to this headquarters. A limited number of additional copies may be obtained from the Historical Division, EUCOM,
APO 403, Phone Control Officer, Karlsruhe Military 2614.

Page

- iii -

THE BERLIN AIR LIFT
21 June-31 December 1948

1. Double Role of the Air Lift

The supply of Berlin Military Post by air began on 21 June
1948 following a series of restrictions placed on western traffic
by Soviet authorities and the refusal of General Lucius D. Clay,
United States Military Governor, to permit the search of Berlin-
bound U.S. military trains by Soviet inspectors. On that day
three planes landed at Tempelhof Air Base, Berlin, with 5.88 tons
of military cargo from Rhein-Main Air Base, near Frankfurt.[1] In
the next few days the task of supplying the military community was
almost eclipsed by the sudden requirement to supply all of Western
Berlin by air lift. On 24 June all rail traffic between the western
zones and Berlin was suspended.[2] On 25 June a Soviet order barred
movement of loaded Allied rail cars within Berlin, and the Soviet
authorities announced that they would supply no more food to the
city's western sectors.[3] The next day, 26 June, marked the official
beginning of Operation VITTLES, according to USAFE Headquarters, although Transportation Corps records indicated that the 82 tons
lifted on that date was military cargo, and listed 223 tons on
28 June as the first civil cargo received at Tempelhof. On that
day, word of the proposed supply of the civil population by air
reached EUCOM Headquarters and General W. B. Palmer, Director of
Logistics, directed the Quartermaster Depot at Giessen to move

---

[1]Stars and Stripes, 22 June 48, "Planes to Supply Berlin Yanks,"
daily Tonnage figures supplied by Operations Br, Trans Div, EUCOM.

[2]OMGG(US), Monthly Report of the Military Governor, June 1948,
No 36, p 8.

[3]Stars and Stripes, 25 Jun 48, "Russians Cut Power, Food Lines
in Berlin"; 26 Jun 48, "Capital Has 30 Days Stock Left," dateline
Berlin, 25 Jun; BMP, Rpt of Opr, May and Jun, p 67.

300 tons of food to Rhein-Main daily, beginning the following day, so that food shipments for the Germans could begin without delay. These stocks were transferred to the Germans and later replaced. No supplies of any sort were flown to Berlin on 27 June, the last Sunday taken as a holiday by air lift workers in 1948. On Monday, 28 June, General Palmer conferred with USAFE officials at Wiesbaden concerning the role to be played by EUCOM Headquarters and the technical services.[4] By 29 June the European Command was beginning to face up fully to the share of the ground forces in the most urgent single mission to confront the occupation since V-E Day.

Supplying the Occupation Forces by Air

2. Background of the Military Supply Lift

Although the supply of the military community at Berlin was soon lost sight of by the public, in view of the spectacular accomplishments of Operation VITTLES, it started as a separate operation and retained most of its distinctive features. It was a reply, moreover, to restrictions aimed principally at military rail operations. Interferences with U.S. military traffic between Berlin and the western zones was not an unfamiliar phenomenon in the spring of 1948, and even occasioned a brief air-lift rehearsal in April. Contrary to quadripartite agreements, the Soviet occupation authorities gradually endeavored to apply to military rail traffic between Berlin and the western zones the type of restrictions that might reasonably have been exercised only at an international frontier. Such encroachments on their rights met steady resistance from the western occupation powers.

a. Events in April. On 30 March, ten days after the Soviet walkout from the Allied Control Council, the chief of staff of the Soviet Military Government stated that new measures would have to be taken to control traffic passing through the western zones.[5] On 1 April the Soviets stated that military rail traffic through their zone was subject to search.[6] Rather than agree, the United

---

[4] Interview with Brig Gen W.B. Palmer, Dir, Log Div, EUCOM, 16 Dec 48.

[5] Stars and Stripes, 31 Mar 48, "Russ May Cut Berlin Routes," dateline Berlin, 30 Mar.

[6] BMP, Rpt of Opr, 1 Jul-30 Sep 48, Supporting Documents, Trans Br, "Historical Report Transportation Corps Airhead Tempelhof."

States authorities suspended military rail traffic between Berlin and the western zones and established a daily air lift.[7] The April lift of military supplies lasted only 11 days, although passenger travel and the outshipment of military freight and household goods continued to be by plane only.[8] On the night of 2-3 April a U.S. train was permitted to enter the Soviet Zone without being searched. Air supply of Berlin was suspended on 11 April and on 12 April military supply by rail was resumed, subject only to normal inspection of shipping documents.[9]

b. Events in May. During the April air lift it was agreed between U.S. and Soviet authorities that there would be an inspection at Helmstedt of documents only, and that U.S. Military trains could be cleared at that point.[10] Late in May, however, Soviet rail authorities raised the question of labeling all rail cars, military as well as civil, with the name of the siding at which the car was to be finally unloaded, and a list of the contents.[11] U.S. rail authorities took the view that military supplies could not be inspected. They agreed to furnish detailed lists of contents, but not to let the rail cars be opened.[12]

c. Events in June. Incidents in June, even before the final blockade, bore further witness to the Soviet intention to shackle western rail transport both at the border of the Soviet zone and in Berlin. Because the Soviet authorities controlled the Reichsbahn in Berlin, a Soviet lieutenant was permitted to supervise repair and maintenance of engines at the Anhalter Terminal, in the U.S. Sector. On 9 June this officer ordered the German dispatcher to send three engines into Soviet-occupied territory. Counter-orders were issued by the American Officer-in-Charge, and guards were kept on duty at the roundhouse until 15 June. On 11 June a military train was delayed at Brandenburg. On 15 June the Soviets closed the autobahn bridge across the Elbe River, forcing traffic to cross by ferry at Neigripp.[13] On 16 June the Soviet delegation

---

[7]Cable No CC-3692, COMNAVMED from COMNAVFORGER sgd SCHUIRMANN, 2 Apr 48; cable message to OMGUS for Chief of Staff from EUCOM sgd HUEBNER, 2 Apr 48, No 5-2869.

[8]Interview with Lt Col Bunker; BMP, Rpt of Opr, May and Jun 48, Supporting Documents, Trans Br, p 4.

[9]EUCOM, Deputy Commander in Chief's Weekly Staff Conference Report, No 14, 7 Apr 48, p 8; BMP, Rpt of Opr, 1 Jul-30 Sep 48, Supporting Documents, Trans Br, "Historical Report, etc."

[10]Interview with Lt Col C.S. Lewis, Rail Operations Officer, Trans Br, Berlin Military Post, 15 Feb 48.

[11]BMP, Trans Br, Memo to Col Bunting, 29 May 48, in BMP, Rpt of Opr, May and Jun 1948, Supporting Docs, Trans Br, Tab "A".

[12]Interview with Lt Col C.S. Lewis.

withdrew from the Allied Kommandatura of Berlin. Announcement of the western currency reform precipitated further acts hampering transport.[14] On 19 June, rail and highway travel to Berlin were blocked at the border of the Soviet zone although freight shipments by rail continued.[15]

d. Blocking of Military Rail Movements. On 20 June a Soviet officer asked to inspect contents of sealed cars in train "20 Han 307" on its arrival at Marienborn at 1738 hours. The train commander refused, ordering the train back at Helmstedt. On 21 June, upon orders of General C. K. Gailey, OMGUS Chief of Staff, the train returned to Marienborn. This was the day on which the Soviets ordered that no trains would be moved because of technical rail difficulties at and beyond Marienborn.[16] Finally, train 20 Han 307 was returned to Helmstedt at 2100, 22 June, the last U.S. military train to try to reach Berlin during 1948.[17] At the same time, high-level negotiations were required in Berlin to obtain permission to move some 300 rail cars from Anhalter Terminal to various U.S. depots for unloading following a Soviet ban on rail movements in the city. On 21 June, after some delay, the Soviets stated that U.S. cars then at the terminal could be moved through Reichsbahn switches to their destination. The emergency air supply plan for Berlin became effective the next day.[18]

3. Basic Planning

S-4 staff members at Berlin had long been aware of the precarious status of rail supply for the military forces at Berlin. Intensive planning was undertaken in February and March to foresee emergency requirements in the event that air supply became necessary.[19] This planning was so thorough that on 1 April a detailed memorandum, classified SECRET, was submitted to the Commanding

---

[13]BMP, Rpt of Opr, May and Jun 48, Supporting Docs, Trans Br, p 4; narrative pp 13, 67.

[14]OMGG(US), Monthly Report of the Military Governor, Jun 48 No 36, pp 1-2.

[15]Stars and Stripes, 20 Jun 48, p 1 "Russ Cut Off Auto, Rail Travel to Berlin," dateline Berlin, 19 Jun.

[16]Interview with Lt Col Lewis.

[17]IRS, Rail Operations Officer to Trans Officer, BMP, 21 Jun 48, "Report of Incident 20 June 1948 Train 20 Han 307," in BMP, Rpt of Opr, May and Jun 48, Supporting Docs, Trans Br.

[18]Interview with Lt Col C.S. Lewis, 15 Feb 49; Message from EUCOM, sgd HUEBNER, to CO, BMP, 22 Jun 48, Ref No SX-1246.

[19]Interviews with Maj L.F. Valiante, S-4 BMP, 11 Feb 49, and Lt Col C.S. Lewis, 15 Feb 49.

Officer, Berlin Command, describing the air lift needed to supply basic requirements and recommending other measures to meet the supply situation.[20] This study made a number of assumptions concerning the continuing responsibilities of the military at Berlin, basing of airplanes at Rhein-Main, control of motor transportation at the airhead, movement of cargo to depots, and the load capacity of the C-47 airplane (see Appendix I). Monthly supply requirements, by class and type, were listed in terms of short tons and cubic feet. The memorandum estimated that nearly 4,000 persons would need air transportation, either for duty or leave purposes, every month. Apart from Quartermaster Class I and medical supplies, requirements were based on minimum essentials. For these supply and passenger requirements it was stated that a maximum of fifty C-47 plane trips would be required daily. On 3 April the plan was forwarded to the Chief of Staff, OMGUS, and following its approval by General Gailey was sent to the Deputy Commander in Chief, EUCOM. On 5 April it was forwarded to the Logistics Division. On 7 April the following plan for airlift operations in the event of future interruptions of rail shipments was presented at the weekly staff conference of the Deputy Commander in Chief, European Command:

"1. USAFE will provide necessary aircraft and crews.

"2. The Chief of Transportation will reestablish TCP (Traffic Control Point) at Rhein-Main Air Base.

"3. All technical services will furnish the Chief of Transportation quantities, including weight and cubage, to be shipped to fill Berlin requisitions already submitted. The Chief of Transportation will call on technical services to ship supplies to Rhein-Main as required. Technical services will withhold from shipments such bulky or heavy items as they may believe to be nonessential and will report items withheld to Logistics Division, EUCOM, which will seek to clear cancellation of requirements for those items with Berlin Command.

"4. Berlin Command will forward new requisitions for supplies in addition to those already on requisition through the TCP by air pouch to the chief of services concerned, designating priority desired. Supplies on requisition before air freight movement is instituted will be given Priority II by EUCOM.

"5. Chiefs of technical services will expedite action on requisitions and when shipments are ready will notify TCP which will call forward in accordance with priorities established by Berlin on their requisitions, and the availability of aircraft. All shipments

---

[20] Berlin Command, OMGG(US), Memorandum for the Commanding Officer Berlin Command, OMGUS, sub: "Air Lift for U.S. Sector of Berlin," 1 Apr 48, sgd DeWitt Thompson, Lt Col, GSC.

from depots to Rhein-Main will be by truck, and the Chief of Transportation will provide necessary lift from depots to Rhein-Main as required.

"6. Each chief of technical service will designate an individual from his office who will be responsible for the expeditious handling of Berlin requisitions and insure that depots handle such requisitions on the highest priority."21

4. Lessons from the April Experience

Although the air lift of 1-11 April was only a "drop in the bucket" compared with Operation Vittles, it provided valuable experience for the Occupation forces. Air supply operations then undertaken were summarized in a cable dated 3 April, along with instructions to Berlin concerning the submission of requisitions in the event of continued supply by air. The plan detailed in this cable was approved by OMGUS on 8 April and it was this plan which was made effective on 22 June.22

a. Central Clearance of Cargo. The April lift showed, even with 80-tons a day, the importance of clearing all cargo through a central agency before letting it be flown, and of having all requirements screened by a single agency at Berlin, for priority.23

b. Transportation Operations. The Transportation Corps decided in April to operate its airhead transportation on a shuttle basis, with loaded trailers parked where they could be drawn on, as needed, to load the planes. The general lines of responsibility established in the April venture remained the backbone of plans for a subsequent military lift. After the April experience a number of officers were briefed on Transportation Corps operations, and two truck companies were kept alerted for possible air lift duty.

c. Interim Use of Surface Transportation. To prepare for a future emergency, the period between the April and June lifts was used to build up stock levels at Berlin and to ship out personnel and supplies due for evacuation.24 Early in April the Chief Engineer was directed to establish winter coal supplies, within available storage limits, at Berlin, and the services were directed to ship by rail all supplies covered by current requisitions from Berlin Command. Military coal shipments to

---

21EUCOM, Deputy Commander in Chief's Weekly Staff Conference Report, No. 14, 7 Apr 48, pp. 8-9.

22Cables No. SX-4053,EUCOM sgd HUEBNER to CG OMGG(US), 3 Apr 48; CC-3772,OMGUS sgd HAYS to EUCOM REAR, 8 Apr 48; SX-1246, EUCOM sgd HUEBNER to CG OMGUS; USAFE, RM Air Base, TCP No. 1, RMAB.

23Interview with Lt Col Bunker.

24BMP, Rpt of Opr, 1 Jul-30 Sep 48, Supporting Docs,"Historical Report,etc." Trans Br, pp. 1-2.

Berlin were increased from 67 carloads (1,451 tons) in March to 636 carloads (12,082 tons) in April.[25] Military supplies shipped by rail to Berlin totaled 523 carloads (6,020 tons) in May and 271 carloads (3,151 tons) in the first part of June, while military coal shipments totaled 525 carloads (10,443 tons) in May and 245 carloads (4,749 tons) in June. Motor convoys sent to Bremerhaven with troops scheduled for redeployment returned with Class I perishable supplies.[26] On 3 May, the Ordnance Branch in Berlin began evacuation of more than 300 vehicles over the autobahn. At Brunswick these vehicles were loaded on flat cars and shipped to Ordnance rebuild installations. Three hundred and thirty-five tons of selected line items, expedited by an Ordnance representative from Berlin, were received by rail during this period. Rebuild activities at Berlin were expanded, and reprocessing was begun on 200 tons of assemblies previously boxed for shipment to the U.S. Zone for rebuild.[27]

5. Start of Operations

With a basic plan for guidance and main procedures already established the June air lift swung quickly into operation. On 21 June EUCOM Headquarters received orders to start the supply of Americans in Berlin by air.[28] Already on 18 June Transportation Division, EUCOM, had established a traffic control point (TCP No. 1) at Rhein-Main Air Base and the 67th Heavy Transportation Truck Company, on 19 June, had delivered 200 tons from the Quartermaster Supply Depot at Giessen.[29] Fresh milk had been flown to Berlin on both the 19th and 20th of June.[30] On 21 June the Transportation Officer, Berlin, expanded the traffic control point at Tempelhof Air Base and established liaison with Logistics Division, EUCOM, and Rhein-Main Air Base. From an official 5.88 tons in three planes (C-47's) on 21 June the lift jumped to 156.42 tons in 64 planes on 22 June, when the Commanding General, United States Air Forces in Europe (USAFE), was directed to use "the maximum number of airplanes to

---

[25]EUCOM, DCINC's Wkly Staff Conf. Rept No. 14, 7 Apr 48, p.9. Berlin Command was redesignated "Berlin Military Post" effective 1 May by EUCOM GO No. 28, 17 May 48; Figures from Lt Col Lewis.

[26]BMP, Rept of Opr. May and Jun 48, narrative p. 37; interv with Lt Col Lewis.

[27]BMP, Ord Officer, Rept for the Chief of Ordnance, "Berlin Ordnance Blockade Airlift Operations," 1 Apr - 15 Sep 48.

[28]Interview with Gen Palmer.

[29]Lt Col William B. Bunker, "The TC in the Vittles Operation," Army Transportation Journal, Washington, DC, Nov - Dec 48, Vol. 4, No. 6, pp. 9-10.

[30]Information obtained by Olive Farmer, Operation Br, Trans Div, EUCOM, 9 Mar 49, from Maj A. P. Flannigan, TC, who organized the traffic control point on 18 June.

transport supplies to Tempelhof."[31]   For the rest of the week,
daily totals ran a little over 80 tons. On 28 June, when Tempelhof
counted its first "Vittles" tonnage, 120 planes brought 72.20 tons
of military and 222.75 tons of civil cargo during the 24-hour period
preceding 1200 hours.[32] On 29 June the Transportation Corps opened
TCP No. 2 at Wiesbaden Air Base,[33] sometimes referred to as "Y-80"
or "Erbenheim." On its opening day, Wiesbaden outloaded 94 planes
with three tons of civil and 238.63 tons of military cargo, while
Rhein-Main was shipping 98.45 tons of civil and 38.63 tons of military supplies.[34] By 30 June the air lift to Berlin had become primarily, in terms of scheduled tonnages, a civil supply operation.
But military cargo would continue to receive the highest priority
and the lift would remain essentially a military operation.

Supplying the Civil Population;
Transition to Operation "VITTLES"

6. Background and Planning

Air lift planning at EUCOM Headquarters from April to June 1948
was based on the assumption that only a military lift would be
needed.[35] In contrast to military freight, shipments of German-
owned flour, sugar, fat, cereals and meat, moving on German civil
waybills, were rarely delayed by the Soviets.

a. Interruptions to Normal Traffic. On 5 June two westbound
German trains carrying civil mail were stopped, however, and effective 15 June, following an order originally issued on 12 June
and temporarily rescinded, civil affairs coal trains were forced to
stop at Lichterfeld West instead of going to Anhalter Terminal to
unload.[36] On 19 June all passenger train and autobahn traffic to

---

[31]BMP, Rpt of Opr, May and Jun 48, narrative p. 6; Cable SX-
12053, EUCOM to USAFE, 22 Jun 48, sgd HUEBNER.
[32]Figures from Operations Br, Trans Div, EUCOM
[33]Information obtained by Olive Farmer, from Capt R. A.
Brausch, TC, who opened Traffic Control Point No. 2 on 29 June.
[34]Figures from Operations Br, Trans Div, EUCOM.
[35]Interview with Lt Col Bunker and General Palmer.
[36]BMP, Rpt of Opr, May and Jun 48.

Berlin were suspended, and Soviet inspections aimed at currency smuggling delayed both Allied and German freight shipments. Water transport required special Soviet permission. British Military Government officials complained to Soviet Headquarters on 19 June concerning delays to German freight shipments, while U.S. authorities suspended their military freight shipments to Berlin on 21 June. On 24 June the Soviets stopped all railroad shipments to Berlin, and on 25 June added that they would not supply food to residents of the western sectors.[37]

b. Military Anticipation of the Civil Lift. There is no readily available evidence of any logistical planning by EUCOM Headquarters for an air lift to supply Western Berlin. A cable from EUCOM to the Chief of Staff, dated 14 June, is one of the few indications that any possibility of a civil blockade was ever contemplated, prior to the event. An extract follows:[38]

Statement that the Elbe River Bridge needed repairs is believed to mean that the Soviets will use this excuse to stop all Berlin-bound Allied and German traffic through Helmstedt, the only Allied highway through to Berlin. Tightening of restrictions on coal trains believed to indicate that Soviets intend to prevent Western Powers from supplying Berlin by rail. If Soviets prevent rail and highway to Berlin only means of shipment will be by air. Unknown here whether air transport facilities exist for supplying German population in Western Sectors (of) Berlin (estimated 2 million) in addition to the Western Allied Forces in Berlin. The resulting deterioration in the food and fuel situation in Western Sectors (of) Berlin would probably cause Germans in Western Sectors to turn against Western occupation powers and make their position in Berlin untenable.

As late as 24 June, General Clay asked a Stars and Stripes reporter, "Do you think the Russians want to starve 2,000,000 Germans?"[39] The foregoing extract, taken with the reported statement of General Clay, indicate that any planning for a civil lift was going on at a very high level, and was being closely guarded against publicity.

---

[37]Stars and Stripes, 20 Jun 48, "Russ Cut Off Auto, Rail Travel to Berlin"; ibid., 22 Jun 48, "Planes to Supply Berlin Yanks"; ibid., 25 Jun 48, "Armed GI's Patrolling Streets"; ibid., 26 Jun 48, "Capital Has 30 Days Stock Left."

[38]Cable, USAFE in No 11135, EUCOM to C of S, US Army, 14 Jun 48, information copy to USAFE.

[39]Russell Jones, Staff Correspondent, Stars and Stripes, 25 Jun 48, "Clay Declares U.S. to Stay in Berlin."

7. The Decision for Air Transport

EUCOM Headquarters was not consulted with regard to the decision to supply civil Berlin by air. The task was first presented to the United States Air Forces in Europe. On 26 June, Lieutenant General Curtis E. LeMay, Commanding General, USAFE, cabled this message to the Deputy Chief of Staff for Operations, United States Air Forces:[40]

> 1. Development of situation in past few days in regard to supply of Berlin completely by air General Clay queried me yesterday as to my capabilities in this connection. My estimate to him was that my maximum sustained capability during good weather months is approximately two hundred twenty-five tons daily. General Clay further desired information as to action necessary to be taken in order to reach a sustained capability of five hundred tons daily and was advised that in addition to my present units, approximately thirty C-54 aircraft with two crews per aircraft would be necessary if this command were committed to such an operation.

> 2. In view of the above item (1) recommended that urgent consideration be given to the development of a plan to move a C-54 group to Europe immediately in the event additional air lift capabilities are requested by General Clay. I do not feel that a task force such as mentioned above could be creditably and efficiently carried out with a smaller force. At this end we will immediately complete a plan to accept (a) C-54 group. I further recommend that serious study be given to the possible conversion of the two troop carrier groups in my command at earlier dates than specified . . . . As mentioned in my recent letter of 22 June to General (Muir S.) Fairchild (USAF) and in view of the situation I have outlined above, the most urgent requirement of CINCEUR (Commander in Chief, European Command) is efficient modern air lift.

Operation VITTLES apparently grew out of the conference between General Clay and General LeMay on 25 June, for Stars and Stripes announced, in a news story dated Berlin, 26 June, that "The U.S. took to the air today to bring supplies for 2,500,000 Germans in Berlin through the Soviet blockade."[41] There is more satisfying proof that actual shipments for German consumption began, at least in tangible quantity, on 28 June. EUCOM Headquarters heard of the proposed civil lift on 26 June and had food supplies forwarded to Rhein-Main from

---

[40] Cable USAFE No UAX-3552, USAFE to C of S, USAF, 26 Jun 48. The cable is quoted as paraphrased and edited by Hist Sec, USAFE.

Giessen on the twenty-seventh, but not until 28 June did EUCOM and USAFE officials confer at Wiesbaden to map the outlines of future air-ground cooperation. The report of General Palmer, Chief of Logistics, to the Deputy Commander in Chief, EUCOM, at his staff conference on Tuesday, 29 June, summarized the plans of the Air Force, action taken on behalf of the Deputy Commander in Chief, and the situation existing on Tuesday morning.[42] The notes on which his report was based now have, to quote General Palmer, a "constitutional value." In succeeding months the operation set in motion on 28 June underwent continual expansion but remained essentially unchanged.

a. Plans of the Air Force. The conference at Wiesbaden on 28 June followed a conference between General LeMay and General Clay held Sunday at Berlin. General LeMay announced at the Monday meeting that he was going to send air freight to Berlin to maximum capacity, 24 hours a day, seven days a week, on a wartime basis, with no holidays. Four C-54 squadrons (52 airplanes) were on their way to Germany, to arrive about 5 July.

b. Action Taken by Director, Logistics Division. General Palmer reported on 29 June that to meet the plans announced by General LeMay, he had taken the following actions in the name of the Deputy Commander in Chief:

(1) Placed Lt. Col. M. M. Stone of Logistics Division on liaison duty with A-4.

(2) Directed the Chief of Transportation

(a) To organize Traffic Control Offices at Rhein-Main and Wiesbaden on a 24-hour, 7-day basis;

(b) To establish a Rail Regulating and Reconsignment Point in the Frankfurt yards;

---

[41]Stars and Stripes, 27 Jun 48, "Planes Ease Siege in Berlin." This item stated that "two B-17's landed at Tempelhof Airfield from Frankfurt with vitally needed medicines" and that other planes were "scheduled to arrive with foodstuffs to supplement the German diet." Lt Col E.G. Cooper, Supply Branch, Medical Division, EUCOM, stated in an interview on 2 March 1949 that any medical supplies for the civil population of Berlin must have come through BICO (Bipartite Control Office) or Military Government, since none were provided for the Germans by Medical Division, EUCOM, at that time.

[42]The following summary of these points is adapted from the report by General Palmer to the Deputy Commander in Chief, 29 June 1948, 1000 hours, copied from the handwritten notes of General Palmer on 17 December 1948.

To order in enough truck companies to handle 1200 tons daily without permitting any airplane to be delayed by waiting either to unload or load.

(3) Directed the Chief Quartermaster to deliver Monday night to Wiesbaden Air Field 220 tons of commissary supplies for Berlin Military Post.

(4) Requested General Clarence L. Adcock, U.S. Chairman, Bipartite Control Office:

(a) To deal with USAFE through the EUCOM Liaison officer:

(b) To establish shipping agents with the Transportation Corps Traffic Control Officers at both Air Bases on a 24-hour, 7-day basis.

(5) Alerted two DP (Displaced Person) labor service companies to move to Frankfurt Military Post for 24-hour 7-day loading and unloading.

(6) Alerted Brigadier General R. E. Duff, Commanding Officer, Frankfurt Military Post, to prepare for the following:

(a) Beginning in 3 days, to be prepared to quarter 800 officers and men in barracks on a hotel basis, with meals available 24 hours a day and bus service to and from the airfield 24 hours a day;

(b) To accept three extra truck companies at once;

(c) To accept two extra DP companies at once.

c. Situation on Tuesday Morning, 29 June 1948. On Tuesday morning there was enough Army and German freight at hand to meet shipping requirements through the next Friday. The EUCOM liaison officer was at work with USAFE and Frankfurt Post officials on the problem of hotel service for air crews. And on the major problem, that of getting German food supplies flowing into the air lift pipeline, EUCOM was doing "a lot of suggesting and explaining", since this was recognized as "fundamentally a BICO problem."

8. Implications for the Ground Forces

With the Air Force committed to a maximum flying effort, the support demanded of European Command installations and personnel began to be apparent. EUCOM would have to supply or work with the Air Force in supplying truck transportation and vehicle maintenance, quarters and accommodations for air crews, expanded air terminal facilities, communication, manpower for moving cargo, and other services, supplies, and equipment. At the start, EUCOM would have full responsibility for finding the cargo and getting it to the planes. Since the Bipartite Control Office (BICO) was not prepared to take the swift action necessary to divert large shipments to the air bases, Transportation Division temporarily assumed this task in addition to directing operation of the traffic control points at Rhein-Main and Wiesbaden. For several weeks, shiploads and trainloads of food were commandeered by Transportation Corps officials to keep the lift going. EUCOM was relieved of this emergency job on 28 July, when BICO took the responsibility for getting German food to the airports.[43]

Outline of Air Lift Operations to 31 December 1948

9. Main Lines of Organization

During the few days of strictly military air supply, only military agencies -- USAFE, EUCOM, S-4 Berlin, and the technical services -- had a part in the air lift. Upon the launching of Operation VITTLES, new tasks immediately fell to the Bipartite Control Office and the Office of Military Government, Berlin Sector (OMGBS). At the same time, the need began to develop for other agencies, especially to coordinate requests and shipping procedures.

a. Developments in Air Force Organization. On 29 June Brigadier General Joseph Smith was designated Project Commander for the Berlin Air Lift Operation and was given direct operational control over air lift activities of Wiesbaden, Rhein-Main, Keufbeuren and Tempelhof Air Force Bases.[44] An important development came on 29 July, when the Berlin Air Lift Task Force (Provisional) was created. Major General William H. Tunner was named Commander of the new unit on 30 July.[45] General Tunner was authorized to communicate directly with EUCOM regarding air cargo and the loading and unloading of aircraft. (See Appendix II). On 12 October, the

---

[43]Interview with General Palmer.

[44]Ltr, USAFE, sub: "Designation of Project Commander," 29 Jun 48, sgd S.S. KISSNER, Brig Gen, USAFE, C of S.

[45]USAFE, GO 59, 29 Jul 48; see Appendix 2.

.United States Air Force merged with the Royal Air Force in a Combined
Air Lift Task Force (CALTF) headed by General Tunner, Commanding
General, and Air Commodore J.W.F. Merer, RAF, Deputy Commander. The
British lift, named "Operation PLAIN FARE" had started on 28 June
following several days of increased flight service for British occu-
pation forces.[46] The merger aimed to achieve better utilization of
British and American resources. One important result was that United
States planes were allowed to fly coal from British zone airfields.
The combined directive establishing CALTF is attached as Appendix
III. The U.S. element of CALTF became First Air Lift Task Force on
14 November, by order of the Department of the Air Force.[47]

   b. The Berlin Air Lift Coordinating Committee. It was clear
from the beginning that civil and military aspects of Operation
VITTLES would need close coordination. In July, Major General
Charles P. Gross, Deputy Chief, Transport Group, BICO, was appointed
by General Adcock to coordinate all BICO responsibilities in the oper-
ation.[48] Through General Gross and his assistant, Mr. W. A. Fagan,
Chief of Movements Division, BICO Transport Group, informal coordi-
nation was achieved among representatives of the Air Force, Transpor-
tation Division, British Military Government, and BICO Transport,
Food and Agriculture, Coal and Commerce and Industry Groups.[49] The
Berlin Air Lift Coordinating Committee (BEALCOM) was established at
Frankfurt about the first of October, on oral instructions from
Major General George P. Hays, Deputy Military Governor, OMGUS, and
Major General N.C.D. Brownjohn, Chief of Staff and Deputy Military
Governor, British Element. Its main function was to coordinate and
supervise all movements of supplies to the airfields, a task of
"moving the right trains and carrying the right supplies at the
right time to the right airfield."[50]

   c. The Air Lift Staff Committee (Berlin). At Berlin there was
a comparable need for coordination among agencies requesting shipments
by air. The coordinating committee there, like BEALCOM, came into
being largely without the aid of written instructions. Some three
weeks after the beginning of the lift, the British and United States

   [46]Hq, CALTF, Spec Order No 31, 12 Oct 48; Stars and Stripes,
16 Oct 48, "US, Britain Merge on Lift"; The Christian Science Monitor,
10 Dec 48 (Reuters); Stars and Stripes, 23 Jun 48.

   [47]Information from Hist Sec, FALTF, Hq, CALTF, 27 Jan 49.

   [48]Ltr, 28 Jul 48, W.B. Palmer to Maj Gen C. L. Adcock, US Chairman BICO.

   [49]Lt Col Bunker, "The TC in the Vittles Operations," p 10; interview with William A. Fagan, Chairman, BEALCOM, 14 May 48.

   [50]Interview with Mr. Fagan; General Gross as quoted in The
Christian Science Monitor, 13 Nov 48, "Teamwork Keeps Berlin Air
Lift Flying," p 6.

military governors of Berlin agreed on coordination of British and U.S. policies, and Mr. A. W. Moran, Deputy Director of OMGBS was appointed to represent the United States side. When the Combined Air Lift Task Force was set up, General Hays stated that no instructions would be sent to CALTF unless completely coordinated. At this time a letter from Colonel Howley, Director, OMGBS, to the British and French commandants led to the formal establishment of the Air Lift Staff Committee.[51] This committee met each month to fit the requirements of the various requesting agencies into the forecast of total tonnage to be lifted by CALTF the following month.

d. The Atterberry-Betts Area Command. On 6 December the Air Force established a new unit, the Atterberry-Betts Area Command, "to provide logistic support and assure the highest standard of discipline" for all personnel billeted in Atterberry and Betts Barracks, an area formerly used to house infantry and other units stationed in Frankfurt.[52] Up to this time, Frankfurt Military Post had provided complete support for air lift personnel billeted at Frankfurt. Although much of this basic support continued, the new unit took over such important functions as food service, billeting, and motor vehicle transportation for all VITTLES personnel assigned to the Atterberry-Betts Area.

e. The Berlin City Government. Two levels of the civil administration at Berlin had a part to play in connection with the air lift. The Magistrat was the consignee for civil food and coal shipments, and dealt directly with OMGBS concerning civil affairs supplies and the movement of industrial goods. The Bezirk governments -- six in the United States Sector, four in the British, and two in the French -- were responsible for supplying laborers upon request of the Manpower Branch, OMGBS.[53]

10. Working Relationships

Cooperation, not command, marked the working relationships of all the services and agencies working together in Operation VITTLES. Between the Air Force and EUCOM there was no question of command in regard to the air lift; both were concerned to act in accordance with the wishes of the Commander in Chief. Only in a few cases, as

---

[51] Interview with Mr. Moran.

[52] Ltr, 61st Troop Carrier Wing (H) Rhein-Main Air Force Base, AI O 57, US Army, sub: "Establishment of Atterberry-Betts Area Command," to Lt Col James D. Campbell, 61st Troop Carrier Wing (H) sgd Walter S. Lee, Col, USAF, 6 Dec 48.

[53] Interview with Mr. Moran.

of units within Berlin Military Post or under EUCOM Headquarters, were lines of command clearly discernible. Many questions arose during 1948 as to the respective responsibilities of the participating agencies but these were worked out through conference and agreement. Colonel Arthur V. Winton, Deputy Director of Logistics Division, was charged with the task of insuring cooperation between air and ground elements.[54] On 28 July 1948, Colonel H. S. Crain was designated EUCOM Liaison Officer with the United States Air Forces and assigned to General Tunner's staff. Between BICO and EUCOM there was no question of a supreme command, although resort to command channels, had they existed, might sometimes have been tried as a shortcut to agreement. Instead, major problems were threshed out at meetings of BEALCOM. Because of the distance between the two headquarters and the sketchy organizational ties connecting them, comparative independence of EUCOM marked the air lift activities of Berlin Military Post.[55]

11. Operating Responsibilities

The essential functions of USAFE, EUCOM and BICO in the air lift were clear and distinct. The Air Forces had the task of flying as much cargo as possible, EUCOM was to assist by moving cargo from the railheads to the airfields and loading it into the planes under the supervision of Air Force loading technicians, and BICO was responsible for procuring civil supplies and assuring their delivery to the appropriate railheads. During the first few weeks EUCOM, better prepared to deal with the emergency, performed a share of the tasks later assumed by BICO. On 27 July a conference was held at Heidelberg to settle certain points, and the following agreements resulted:[56]

> (1) The U.S. Army authorities are not responsible for any of the following matters, as to all of which the civil authorities are responsible, and as to all of which BICO is the agent for transmission of information to the military authorities.
>
> (a) Determination of the total requirement for supplies which are to be air-lifted for the German population of Berlin.
>
> (b) The procurement of such supplies.

---

[54]Interview with General Palmer.

[55]Interviews with Mr. Fagan and with Colonel Winton, 23 Feb 49.

[56]Ltr, 28 Jul 48, Brig Gen W.B. Palmer, to Maj Gen C.L. Adcock.

(c) The allocation of such supplies respectively to British and American air lifts.

(d) The movement of such supplies forward to the airbase at such a rate as to insure that the available air lift is completely utilized.

(e) The delivery of the supplies to railheads in proper quantities of proper components and in proper condition for loading on airplanes.

(2) The Military authorities are responsible for the following.

(a) The U.S. Air Force will air lift supplies to Berlin within its capabilities.

(b) The U.S. Army, Europe, will:

1 Provide motor transportation to move the air lift cargo from railheads to airplanes.

2 Provide labor to handle cargo between railheads and airplanes.

3 Exercise the functions of a regulating officer in calling cargo forward to the railheads.

As the air lift expanded and became more complex, responsibilities had to be further clarified.

12. Control of Cargo

The process of controlling cargo involved nearly every agency taking part in the lift. On 28 June USAFE furnished the first tonnage estimate to the Director, Logistics Division, showing a proposed increase from 450 tons daily on 30 June to 1500 tons daily on 10 July.[57] This meant that military requirements could be met without difficulty. The real problem lay in meeting civil requirements, particularly for coal. On 30 June civil stocks in Berlin comprised approximately 25 days' supply of flour, 81 days' sugar, 19 days' meat, 56 days' fat supply, 18 days' potatoes, 54 days' cereals, 19 days' milk, and 18 days' coffee. The lift beyond that allocated for military supplies was used for civil

---

[57]USAFE Historian, from Log of Operation Vittles, 30 Jul 48, Berlin, Air Lift Task Force, Camp Lindsay.

cargo, and throughout the year an effort was made to keep the military supply lift at a minimum.[58]

a. Submission of Requirements. At Berlin, the Berlin Military Post S-4 examined and consolidated all military requirements before submitting them to the Air Lift Staff Committee. This committee studied both military and civil requirements and submitted its findings, in the form of allocations of daily tonnages and priorities, to BEALCOM. BEALCOM in turn decided how many tons of each item would be shipped, and from what airports. The Combined Air Lift Task Force aided by submitting estimates of its monthly lift from airports in the United States and British zones. The shipping schedule finally prepared by BEALCOM therefore took account of amounts requested by Berlin, location and characteristics of air bases, availability of storage facilities, supplies and transportation, and the estimated tonnage to be flown by the Air Force.

b. Allocations. The initial allocation of air lift for United States and French military supplies was 50 tons per day. On 7 July the Bipartite Control Office cabled OMGUS that USAFE was expected to lift 1200 tons of civilian supplies, 25 tons of French, and 25 tons of United States military supplies daily, beginning 10 July. The British lift was estimated at 600 to 700 tons daily. On 19 July the United States allocation was raised to 100 tons per day, to include 50 tons of pierced steel plank and 25 tons of asphalt. On 5 August revised allocation provided for 80 tons daily for U.S. military airfield construction in Berlin and 50 tons of other U.S. military supplies. The French allocation continued at 25 tons. On 15 September the United States allocation rose to 135 tons daily for airfield construction materials and 57 tons for other supplies. On 23 September it was changed to 345 tons, to include 250 metric tons of solid fuels, and the French allocation was raised to 105 tons, to include 80 tons of solid fuels.[59] At the end of December the air lift was taking 250 tons daily for U.S. military use and 85 tons for the French.[60]

c. Shipments from Berlin. From April on, all military supplies and household goods shipped from Berlin were sent by air. Close control was exercised over such shipments when Operation

---

[58]Planning paper, "Air Lift to Berlin, Requirements and Capabilities," 14 Jul 48, from files of Log Div, EUCOM, and interview with Mr. Moran.

[59]BMP, Rpt of Opr, 1 Jul-30 Sep 48, Supporting Docs, S-4 Br, p 3; Cable No FMPC 296, BICO to OMGUS, for Hays; OMG for Berlin Sector for Howley; Berlin Sector for Willard, 7 Jul 48.

[60]Interview with Col Hall S. Crain, EUCOM Liaison Officer, Hq, Air Lift Task Force, 22 Dec 48.

VITTLES began, since only an estimated 60 tons could be outshipped daily, without reducing the incoming load.[61] On 9 August representatives of USAFE, Tempelhof Air Base and Berlin Military Post met to consider ways of reducing outshipments to a minimum. Items to be outshipped by Berlin Military Post on a routine basis were estimated at 41 tons daily, with bulk tonnage for outshipment amounting to 1,268 tons. To increase incoming cargo, future outshipments were limited to 33.5 tons (daily routine) and 493 tons (bulk).[62] On 26 August the Commanding Officer, Berlin Military Post, appealed to the Chief of Staff, OMGUS, concerning an embargo placed by the Air Force on outshipments from Berlin, on 21 August. By August 26, household goods, Civil Affairs industrial goods and other approved items awaiting shipments on a routine basis aggregated 1,050 tons.[63] Routine outshipments resumed about the first of September. Within the first week of July the problem had arisen of flying German economy products out of Berlin. The Air Force agreed to start carrying industrial products out of Berlin on 8 July, at the rate of about 500 tons per month. These shipments, which later amounted to several hundred tons weekly, were also under the coordinating control of BEALCOM.[64]

    d. <u>Loading at Planeside</u>. The problem of assigning responsibility for the transfer of supplies from truck to plane remained partially unsolved at the end of 1948. Up to 31 December, the Air Force was regarded, at Rhein-Main and Wiesbaden, as responsible for moving the truck load to the proper aircraft. In practice this responsibility tended to be shared by the air and ground forces, with the pilot in any case making a final check to see that the load was properly tied down. An airman known as a "flight clerk" or "traffic technician" directed the backing of the truck to the plane, and was responsible for the loading, distribution of cargo in the plane, tiedown, and manifesting.[65]

13. Equipment and Facilities

    At the beginning of the air lift, USAFE was ready to carry an estimated 225 tons daily.[66] A larger lift meant more planes, more trucks, and more airfields. It also meant learning how to use the

---

[61]Cable No FMPC 296, BICO to OMGUS, 7 Jul 48.

[62]BMP, Memo to C of S, OMGUS, sub: "Outshipments by Airlift," 12 Aug 48 from Robert A. Millard, Col, Sig C, Commanding.

[63]BMP, Memo for the C of S, OMGUS, sub: "Embargo on Outshipments," 26 Aug 48, from Robert A. Millard, Col, Sig C, Commanding.

[64]USAFE, Office of the Historian, from draft, "Air Supply of Berlin in 1948"; The Christian Science Monitor, 13 Nov 48.

[65]Interviews with Lt Col Bunker and with Maj E.A. Guilbert, Hq, CALTF Traffic Sec, 27 Jan 49.

available equipment to best advantage and reckoning with special handicaps imposed by local circumstances.

a. **Airplanes.** Four types of plane were employed during the first six months of the lift. These were the C-47, capacity 3.5 tons, the C-54 Skymaster, capacity 10 tons, C-74 Globemaster, capacity 19 tons, and the C-82, capacity 5 tons. Only C-47's were at hand when the lift began. On 2 July seventeen C-54's arrived at Rhein-Main.[67] During August and September a C-74 made 23 flights to Berlin, carrying 2,674 pieces of freight weighing 834,491 pounds. Much of the cargo was heavy engineering equipment. On 15 September five C-82's joined the lift, making 78 flights to Berlin with 760,411 pounds during the next two weeks. Thirteen private automobiles were shipped out of Berlin by the C-74 and 130 private and Ordnance vehicles were brought out by the C-82's.[68] While both C-47's and C-54's were engaged in the lift, "blocks" of flying time were assigned so that only one type of plane would take off during a period of several hours. C-47's ceased to take part in the lift on 1 November. At the end of the year, over 200 C-54's were committed to Operation VITTLES.[69]

b. **Airfields.** Tempelhof Air Base, in the U.S. Sector, and Gatow in the British, were the only fields available in Western Berlin at the start of the lift. The inadequacy of airport facilities at Berlin gave rise to an Engineer Corps construction program of breathtaking scope. The design of each airfield affected the procedures used by Transportation Corps in loading and storing supplies. Rhein-Main and Wiesbaden were the only fields in the U.S. Zone used for Operation VITTLES. As a tactical field, designed with scattered hardstands instead of a central parking strip, Rhein-Main was poorly adapted to "mass-production" loading procedures. At Wiesbaden, on the other hand, the Transportation Corps learned that a consolidated loading point provided better traffic control and lessened the likelihood of accident and pilferage.[70] In addition

---

[66] Cable, USAFE No UAX-8552, Gen Curtis E. LeMay, CG, USAFE, to Lauris Norstad, USAF, 26 Jun 48.

[67] Interview with Maj E.A. Guilbert; Hist Sec, USAFE, from "Log of Operations Vittles, 30 Jun-30 Jul," Berlin Air Lift Task Force.

[68] BNT, Rpt of Opr, 1 Jul-30 Sep 48, Supporting Docs Trans Corps (Tempelhof) pp 8-9.

[69] Stars and Stripes, 2 Nov 48, p 12; information from Maj E.A. Guilbert, 22 Mar 49.

[70] Interview with Lt Col M.A. Darragh, Operations Br, Trans Div, EUCOM, 6 Jan 49.

to these two fields, British zone bases at Celle, Fassburg, Wunstorf, Schleswigland, Fuhlsbuettel, and Luebeck were being used by CALTF at the end of 1948. Finkenwerder, a base for flying boats, was used by the British during the summer and fall of 1948.[71]

  c. <u>Operational Problems Affecting the Ground Forces</u>. Loading procedures were subject not only to limitations of plane capacity and airfield design but to restrictions affecting Air Force operations between the western zones and Berlin. The restriction of traffic to three air corridors and the scarcity of landing facilities made the exact timing of take-offs vital to air supply operations. Loading and unloading therefore had to be geared to the timetable of the Air Force. Weight and balance of cargo were additional factors demanding careful adherence to Air Force standards. Light bulky cargo, such as noodles, had to be "married" to heavy cargo, to insure the right balance in flight. It was learned, in time, that sacks of coal to be flown to Berlin could not be allowed to vary from 80 to 150 pounds when they were all supposed to weigh the same amount. Unless they weighed within three or four pounds of the stated figure, the safety of the plane might be jeopardized.[72] Even apart from limitations of sheer bulk or weight, not all types of cargo could be carried on board all types of planes. Because of its peculiar tendency toward "deliquescence," or gradually becoming liquid, salt could be carried only in the bomb bays of bomber planes or by flying boats, presumed to be comparatively immune to the effects of salt water.[73] Fortunately for Berlin menu-planners, both types of plane were included in the British Lift.

  d. <u>Ground Transport and Loading Equipment</u>. Most of the half-million or so tons flown to Berlin during 1948 traveled part of the way on a man's back. Sacks of coal and flour could be lifted from a truck and stowed inside a plane more satisfactorily by manpower than by mechanical means. Lt. Col. Bunker of EUCOM Transportation Division has summarized air lift experience with materials-handling equipment as follows:[74]

    While the use of mechanical materials-handling
    equipment for loading has been tried, particular-
    ly for handling bulk and heavy items, such as
    asphalt drums, pierced steel planking and similar
    commodities, it has been found that the critical
    time factor makes the use of hand labor mandatory.

---

[71]Information from Major Guilbert, 22 Mar 49.

[72]Interview with General Palmer.

[73]Interview with Lt Col Bunker.

[74]Army Transportation Journal, Nov-Dec 48, "The TC in the Vittles Operation," p 10.

The average 10-ton C-54 aircraft can be loaded
with normal commodities in 25 minutes, and with
pierced steel planking--the most awkward bulk
commodity handled--in 40 minutes. Special e-
quipment cannot be operated on this tight a
schedule even if it were available in sufficient
quantities to handle the job. Fork-lifts and
similar equipment are used only in loading particularly heavy items such as the Engineer construction machinery which has been handled
primarily in C-74 and C-82 aircraft. Experience
in the operation at Berlin has also proved that
the use of this equipment is equally impractical
for fast unloading operations. Mantime for unloading 20,000 pounds of cargo from a C-54 plane
to a 10-ton truck by a stevedore crew is about
12 minutes.

On 26 July airlift officials decided to concentrate the military
lift and German industrial lift at Wiesbaden, leaving the more
easily-handled civil supplies to be shipped from Rhein-Main.[75] At
the two Rhein-Main railheads, one located on the base and the other
at Zeppelinheim, coal and flour were loaded from railcars into 10-
ton trailers, (actually 6-ton semi-trailers) by six-man teams. Ten-
man crews were used in loading at planeside, where supplies had to
be lifted chest-high to the floor of the plane, and carried some
distance inside the plane.[76] At Wiesbaden, fork lifts were used to
handle cargo items weighing several hundred pounds.[77] At Berlin the
emphasis was on rapid unloading. Tin-covered wooden chutes were
used for a time, to move coal and flour from planes to trucks. The
tin often broke, however, and eventually hardwood chutes were provided by the Engineers, with far better results. Whereas the tin-
covered chutes had required replacement at the rate of at least one
daily, it was found that only one or two hardwood chutes had to be
replaced per month.[78] Although lighter trucks were used to some
extent at Wiesbaden and Tempelhof, the 10-ton trailer combined with
the 4-5 ton tractor was accepted as standard equipment for moving
cargo to and from the airplanes.

---

[75]USAFE, Hist Sec, from "Log of Operations Vittles, 30 Jul 48."

[76]Interview with Lt Col Edward T. Whiting, Labor Supervision
Sec, FMP, 24 Jan 49.

[77]Interview with Capt E. C. Winkler, Trans Officer, Wiesbaden
Air Base, 4 Feb 49.

[78]Interview with Lt Col John U. Schiess, Operations Officer,
Trans Br. BMP.

14. Manpower

Operation VITTLES made heavy and unforeseen demands on every type of manpower available to the Army in Germany. So far as members of the Armed Forces were concerned, it meant in many instances a heavier workload and added duties rather than a complete change of assignment. Certain infantry companies, transportation truck companies, and labor supervision units, and a few men from the Ordnance and Engineer units, were assigned in direct support of the lift. But the military posts and nearly every division at EUCOM Headquarters felt the burden in terms of more reports, more projects, and more intensive activity in many lines. On the military side, therefore, it is not possible to compute the amount of labor devoted to support of the lift, although some estimate will be given in a later section dealing with the work of the technical services. Most of the labor employed in lift operations, however, was provided by Displaced Persons and Germans.

a. Organized Labor Units. The first organized labor unit assigned to the lift at Frankfurt, the 4060th Labor Service Company (Lithuanian), under the 38th Labor Supervision Company, served at Rhein-Main continuously from 22 June to 31 December. On 1 January 1949 this company was assigned to Wiesbaden, where the workload was considered a little lighter. The 8958th Labor Service Company (Polish), first under the 1839th Labor Supervision Company and later under the 523d, started with VITTLES on 30 June. The 2958th Labor Service Company was activated on 29 June, starting work under the supervision of the 503d on 2 July. Other labor service companies joined the lift at Rhein-Main and Wiesbaden as follows: the 8957th, under the 501st Labor Supervision Company, on 10 July; the 4052d (Polish), under the 38th Labor Supervision Company on 10 August; the 4543d (Polish), under the 36th Labor Supervision Company on 7 July; the 7441st (German), under the 7380th Labor Supervision Company, and the 2905th (German), under the 7881st Labor Supervision Company, on 24 August; and the 8512d (Polish), under the 54th Labor Supervision Company, fully committed on 1 July. All of these companies remained with Operation VITTLES throughout the rest of 1948. The 4041st Labor Service Company (Polish), from Hanau, serving under the 35th Labor Supervision Company, worked from August until September, while other companies were being collected. Five companies were housed at Eschborn, three at Zeilsheim, and one at Frankfurt. These laborers worked 384 on a shift at Rhein-Main, and 170 on each shift at Wiesbaden. One ton per man per hour was the standard work rate for crew members loading trucks from railcars. In addition to a daily ration of 2900 calories received at camp, members of these labor services units received an Army meal on the airfield. At the beginning of the lift they worked eight hours on and sixteen hours off, but this was later changed to the more satisfactory hours of 12 on, 24 off, with one day off per week.[79]

b. German Labor at Tempelhof. No labor service units were available for airhead operations at Berlin but the Magistrat agreed to supply German labor if the Army would provide supervision. On 30 June 1948, 600 Germans came to work at the Transportation Corps Air Head, Tempelhof, and were assigned to three shifts of 200 men each. During the next three months the number rose to four shifts of 500 each.[80] The average number of Magistrat-employed workers at Tempelhof, per shift, for each month from July to December 1948 was as follows: July-134; August-399; September-438; October-328; November-529; December-443.[81] As the year ended, Transportation officials were reducing the number of laborers and trucks engaged in airhead operations, at the same time that more efficient methods were being reflected in the handling of increased tonnages. Being on the receiving end of the lift, airhead officials at Tempelhof had to be ready to unload, without notice, up to 25 or even 30 planes an hour. On the average, each laborer handled only 2.10 tons, the equivalent of about 40 sacks of coal per eight hours. During 95 percent of the time, therefore, more laborers were on hand than necessary, but during an unpredictable five percent of the time, it was essential to have the full number. In December, laborers at Tempelhof handled 24 percent more cargo than ever before, with 24 percent fewer trucks and a reduction of 22 percent in personnel.[82] At Tempelhof, Germans were employed as truck drivers. Drivers and stevedores were supervised by trained enlisted "boss-checkers" drawn from local Constabulary and infantry troops.[83]

c. Labor for Construction Projects at Berlin. Construction of two new runways at Tempelhof and a new airfield at Tegel, in the French Sector, was accomplished with German labor supplied by the Berlin Magistrat. At peak activity, the Tegel project employed German foremen and sub-contractors, as well as 17,000 laborers, of whom more than half were women.[84]

d. "VITTLES" Labor in the European Command. Apart from the thousands supplied by the Magistrat at Berlin, and the hundreds

---

[79]Interview with Lt Col Whiting.

[80]Interview with Lt Col Schiess, 14 Feb 49; BMP, Rpt of Opr, May and Jun 1948, Supporting Docs, Trans Br; ibid., 1 Jul-30 Sep 48.

[81]According to Lt Col Schiess, figures from July to October are the best available, but not to be regarded as completely accurate. Later figures are based on accurate records.

[82]Interview with Lt Col Schiess.

[83]Interview with Lt Col George McClintic, Exec Officer, Trans Br, BMP, 17 Feb 49.

[84]Interview with Lt Col C.R. Rain, Engr Br, BMP, 15 Feb 49.

regularly employed in Ordnance units, Engineer units, technical
service depots and other Army installations, the number of Germans
hired in direct support of Operation VITTLES increased during the
fall and winter. By the end of July, Operation VITTLES had added
3,599 to the 30 June 1948 EUCOM ceiling for local personnel in
Germany. On 1 September USAFE reported 2,431 Germans employed on
the air lift and Frankfurt Military Post reported 2,594, a total of
5,025. On 1 December, Germans employed in Operation VITTLES were
reported as follows:

USAFE	4,491
Frankfurt Military Post	2,506
Heidelberg Military Post	40
Berlin Military Post	136
Total	7,173

The total for 1 January was 7,494, including 50 Germans employed by
Bremerhaven Port of Embarkation.[85]

15. Cargo Requirements and Tonnages

When the lift began, U.S. military supplies in Berlin were sufficient for 30 days or longer. Accustomed to reporting on the status
of supplies, the military encountered no great difficulty in defining
future requirements and estimating necessary air lift. Control over
civil supplies was exercised by OMGUS.[86] The Air Lift Staff Coordinating Committee and the coordinating group which preceded it re-
frained from figuring total civil requirements. Instead the committee took the view that as much civil cargo would be flown as the
lift could carry. Starting from a 30-day supply level at the end
of June, food stocks were gradually raised to a 40-day supply, then
lowered to a 30-day level so that maximum amounts of coal could be
brought in. A Stars and Stripes article honoring the lift at the
end of its first six months stated that Western Allied Commanders
had estimated a 4,500-ton daily maximum as necessary to feed and
warm Berlin. Early in July the Logistics Division, EUCOM, placed
monthly maintenance requirements for Berlin at 750 tons for United
States Forces, 750 for French military support, and 90,560 tons for
civil supply, including 30,060 tons of food, 59,000 tons of hard
fuel, and 11,500 tons of petroleum products. Thanks to the air
lift, civil food stocks were better balanced at the end of the year

[85]EUCOM, Deputy Commander in Chief's Weekly Staff Conference
Report, No 30, 27 Jul 48, p 6; ibid., No 38, 21 Sep 48, p 4; ibid.,
No 51, 21 Dec 48, p 6; ibid., No 4, 25 Jan 49, p 7.

[86]BMP, Rpt of Opr, 1 Jul-30 Sep 48, Supporting Docs, S-4 Br,

than at the beginning of July.[87] During November, the individual
normal ration in Western Berlin was raised to 1,882 calories per
day, an increase of 274 calories over the October ration.[88]

a. Developments Affecting Cargo Operations. Expansion of the
air lift involved several developments affecting cargo operations.
On 7 July the first civil coal was hauled by plane to Berlin. The
next day work started on a new runway at Tempelhof.[89] On 23 July
the first load of some 5,000 displaced persons to be evacuated from
Berlin arrived at Rhein-Main.[90] On 22 August, three squadrons of
C-54's began flying coal from Fassberg, in the British zone.[91]
Construction of Tegel Air Field began on 9 August,[92] and a formal
agreement concerning the field was signed by Lieutenant General
Curtis E. LeMay, Commanding General of USAFE, and the Military
Governor of the French Sector, Berlin, on 25 August (Appendix IV).
On 26 August a newly-built land pier was put into use at Tempelhof
Air Base as a point for transferring incoming civil affairs cargo
from Army trailers to German trucks. A further step to conserve
Army fuel and transport was taken on 6 September, when a privately-
owned coal train of one engine and 28 coal cars began moving Civil
Affairs coal from Tempelhof to the Vaubeka coal yards. Four box
cars were added on 10 December to haul gasoline and diesel oil to
the Esso petroleum dumps.[93] Shipment of coal by air for U.S. military use began on 15 October, and coal shipments for the French
started the next day.[94] Twenty-four Navy planes joined the lift on
26 October. On 5 November, lift planes started using Tegel Air Base.
In December the opening of Celle to United States planes gave air
lift C-54's a base within 131 miles of Berlin.[95]

---

[87]Interview with A.W. Moran; Memo "Air Lift-Berlin" sgd C.A.
HIBBERT, Maj, GSC, Log Div, undated.

[88]OMGG(US), Rpt of the Military Governor, Nov 48, p 10.

[89]Interview with Capt W.S. Hart, Engr Br, BMP, 15 Feb 49.

[90]USAFE, Hist Sec, from "Log of Operations VITTLES, 30 Jun to
30 Jul 48," Hq, Berlin Air Lift Task Force.

[91]Stars and Stripes, 28 Aug 48, p 2; "C-54's Pace Air Lift
Carriers."

[92]EUCOM, Deputy Commander in Chief's Weekly Staff Conference
Report, No 37, 14 Sep 48, p 8.

[93]BMP, Rpt of Opr, 1 Jul-30 Sep 48, Supporting Docs, Hist Rpt,
TCAHT. (The report for the following quarter (p 123) states that
delivery of coal by rail to German coal yards began on 2 Sept).

[94]EUCOM, Deputy Commander in Chief's Weekly Staff Conference
Report, No 42, 19 Oct 48, p 8.

[95]Stars and Stripes, 28 Oct 48; 6 Nov 48; 26 Nov 48.

b. Reporting of Lift Tonnages. When considering figures on the air lift it is necessary to note that there was at first no uniform system of reporting tonnages. The British lift was reported in long tons, the United States lift in short tons, and German economy cargo in metric tons. Some figures represented net and others represented gross tons. Although BICO did not include personnel in its tonnages, passengers were included in USAFE figures on the air lift.[96] The Transportation Corps, accustomed to basing daily rail figures on the hours from 0001 to 2400, acceded to the Air Force preference for a reporting period from 1200 to 1200. Daily tonnage figures, as reported at the end of 1948, are in net tons and take account of all cargo leaving the ground for Berlin up to 12 noon of the day reported.[97]

c. Cargo Tonnages to 31 December 1948. On 27 December 1948, the Stars and Stripes carried a front-page headline, "Lift, 6 Months Old, Tops 700,000 tons." According to the accompanying story, the total lift carried by British and American planes from June to 26 December was 700,172.7 tons. Daily tonnages flown from the U.S. Zone to Berlin from 21 June to 31 December 1948, totaled approximately 330,000 tons, or 42,597 plane-loads. Appendix V gives a detailed summary of monthly tonnages lifted to Berlin in U.S. aircraft, thus including cargo lifted from British zone bases in U.S. planes. This table shows the amount of each type of supply, both military and civil, lifted by U.S. planes. Such cargo totaled over 500,000 tons as of 31 December. Outbound cargo, similarly listed, is summarized in Appendix VI. The following tonnages were received at Tempelhof Air Base during the second half of 1948; July-38,713; August-63,515; September-61,638; October-61,158; November-48,521; and December-64,730. Outbound cargo from Tempelhof was as follows: July-1,311; August-1,754; September-2,090; October-2,525; November-1,924; and December-3,968.[98]

---

[96] Interview with Col Hall S. Crain, EUCOM Liaison Officer, Hq, CALTF, 22 Dec 48.

[97] Interview with Lt Col Schiess.

[98] Ibid.

16. Logistics Division and the Technical Services

Principally through its Logistics Division and the liaison officer representing that division at Headquarters, CALTF, in Wiesbaden,
the European Command Headquarters at Heidelberg shared in planning
the support to be given to Operation VITTLES by the ground forces
in Europe and controlled the manner in which that support was forth-
coming. In all of the work ascribed to the technical services,
therefore, the coordinating, guiding and often compelling role of
Logistics Division is to be discerned. Basic policies of these
services reflected the coordinating influence of the Logistics
staff. But measures applying these policies were put into practice
by the technical services and their field installations. EUCOM support of the air lift is therefore considered here primarily with regard to support rendered by the technical services, at EUCOM
Headquarters, at the air bases, and at military post level. The
"abnormal" requirements imposed by the air lift may best be considered as part of the support rendered by the individual services.

17. Transportation Support

Transportation was the key service afforded the air lift by
the ground forces. Within the U.S. Zone, the EUCOM Transportation
Division acted as the right arm of the Air Force by setting up and
maintaining traffic control points at Rhein-Main and Wiesbaden Air
Base. At Berlin, where the Post Transportation officer acted compa-
rably in establishing the Transportation Corps Air Head Tempelhof
(TCAHT), EUCOM exercised only indirect control. In addition to
keeping in close touch with operations at Rhein-Main and Wiesbaden,
Transportation Division directed its field staff, during the first
weeks of Operation VITTLES, to work with OMGUS and German rail officials in diverting civil cargo to railheads at Wiesbaden and
Rhein-Main.[99] Transportation Division assigned more vehicles and
drivers as lift tonnages increased, and was continuingly concerned
with the provision of personnel and improvement of equipment, organization and procedures to support the lift.

18. Transportation for Rhein-Main and Wiesbaden

All Transportation units serving Rhein-Main and Wiesbaden were
under the operational control of the Chief of Transportation. The
line of command was from Colonel C. DeWitt, Jr., Chief of

---

[99]Lt Col Bunker, "The TC in the Vittles Operation," p 10.

Transportation, and his Operations Officer at Heidelberg through the Officer-in-Charge, Transportation Traffic Control Point, Rhein-Main, to Lt. Col. H. Y. Chase, Commanding Officer of the 24th Transportation Truck Battalion and thence to the company commanders. TCP No. 2, at Wiesbaden, was under the supervision of the Transportation officer-in-charge at Rhein-Main. Up to the last week of December a liaison officer from the 24th Battalion endeavored to plan hours of work, routes, maintenance and other activities for all truck units working at Rhein-Main. At that time, concurrently with an approved increase in truck companies, a six-officer Truck Operations Section was created. The new unit, directly subordinate to the Transportation officer-in-charge, was expected to provide effective on-the-job supervision and coordination of all truck company activities on the field.[100]

a.   Transportation Units.   By the end of 1948, six heavy truck companies grouped in the 24th Transportation Truck Battalion were assigned to Operation VITTLES.[101] These were the 66th, brought from Munich; the 67th, from Giessen; the 68th, from Mannheim; the 76th from Nuernberg; and the 70th and 84th, already in Frankfurt area when the lift began.

b.   Cargo-Hauling Operations.   The Rhein-Main Air Base was divided diagonally from northeast to southwest by a single runway paralleled on both sides by taxistrips edged with individual hardstands, each the assigned and numbered parking place of a particular aircraft. (See Appendix VII). On either side of the field was a parking lot used by the Transportation Corps. One parking lot accommodated enough vehicles to load up to 20 planes per hour, the maximum rate at which take-offs were possible from the runway, so the other lot, on the east, was used to hold trailers loaded with reserve sacks of coal. Rhein-Main was served by a railhead newly constructed on the southeast side of the base, and a railhead nearby at Zeppelinheim (formerly called Lufthaven). Cargo was loaded into trailers at the railheads, covered with tarpaulins, and driven to the main parking lot on the west side of the airfield. Here were maintained an active line and a reserve line of trailers loaded with coal, gasoline and food.[102] A third line, the "ready line" was composed of tractors with loaded trailers attached. Tractors at the front of this line kept their motors idling and their loading crews on hand, ready to start whenever the control tower notified

---

[100]Interview with Lt Col A.B. Evans, Trans Traffic Control Point, Rhein-Main, 28 Dec 48.

[101]Interview with Lt Col H.T. Chase, CO, 24th TT Bn, Frankfurt, 21 Jan 49. The 69th and 83d TT Companies replaced the 66th and 84th on airfield duty during January 1949.

[102]Interview with Lt Col Evans.

the dispatch point that an airplane was about to land and take on a load for Berlin. At Rhein-Main, tractors averaged 43 miles per day, on the air base. Vehicles at Wiesbaden averaged 12 miles per day. Estimated total mileage on the air bases, to 11 January, was 1,215,000 miles.[103]

c. Vehicles and Drivers. From June through August, two truck companies worked at Rhein-Main and one served the Wiesbaden Air Base. Each company was equipped with 48 tractors and 96 trailers. In September, Rhein-Main was given 268 trailers and 144 tractors. By the end of December, Rhein-Main was using three companies and one platoon, with 192 tractors and 268 trailers. Wiesbaden continued to employ one company.[104] At least twenty-eight tractors were needed on the ready line, loading planes; ten were assigned to Zeppelinheim railhead; and ten more served the railhead on the base.[105] Eleven or twelve percent of the vehicles were usually in field maintenance.

d. Driver Responsibilities. Each truck driver was permanently responsible for the same tractor. With that tractor he might bring as many as fifteen trailers to planeside during a single day. At the beginning of each shift, company commanders received orders as to the number of vehicles needed at different points and platoon leaders briefed their drivers accordingly.[106] During the first six months of the lift even third-echelon maintenance was performed by drivers and mechanics assigned to Operation VITTLES. A combined organizational maintenance shop was set up on the air base, where drivers brought their tractors daily for grease and oil checks, to keep batteries in order, and to perform other maintenance tasks.[107] The most serious responsibility of the drivers was the handling of their equipment. Skill and constant carefulness were needed to hook on to loaded trailers, back up to planes, cross the busy taxiways, and steer their heavy trucks safely through the fog and mud characteristic of Rhein-Main Air Base during the fall of 1948.

e. Equipment. The Transportation Corps learned through hard experience the shortcomings of the equipment it was forced to use in support of the air lift. Most of the available vehicles had seen six years of service in Europe. The 10-ton trailer with tractor, a typical long-range vehicle, had not been intended for

---

[103] Interview with Lt Col Chase.

[104] Ibid.

[105] Interview with Lt Col W.E. Schoenfeld, Chief, Mtr Trans Sec, Operations Br, Trans Div, EUCOM, 6 Jan 49.

[106] Interview with Lt Col Chase.

[107] Interview with Lt Col Evans.

around-the-clock short hauls over high-crowned dirt and gravel roads.[108] Trailer beds warped as a result of too frequent uncoupling. The standing gear of the trailer had been built for use on hard standings, not mud. But since tractors and trailers had to be used, they were gradually modified to withstand the special kinds of hard treatment afforded them at Rhein-Main.[109] All of the cabs were winterized with solid tops and doors supplied by Ordnance and put on by the truck companies. Spotlights were installed for night operations. Steel braces were added at the front end of the trailers where the stakes were not strong enough. Steel plates were built around the standing gear to keep the front of the trailer from sinking into the mud. Steel guards were placed in front of air hoses to protect the air brake couplings on the front end of the trailer.[110] To consult with EUCOM transportation officials on the overcoming of various mechanical difficulties the Transportation Corps Board sent an engineer to Germany. As a result, the Transportation Corps gathered information of value in the future designing of equipment.[111]

f. Maintenance. Truck companies assigned to loading operations at Rhein-Main and Wiesbaden were given 10-day periods in "rotation rehabilitation status" at the end of each 30-day period at the airfield.[112] This time was spent at the company areas, resting and working on vehicles. Organizational maintenance shops were located in the kasernes where truck troops were billeted. The 24th Battalion Maintenance Shop at Rhein-Main was also used for organizational maintenance. Field maintenance was performed by a shop of the 559th Ordnance MAM Company at Rhein-Main.[113] Field maintenance for truck units billeted at Mainz-Kastel, in the Wiesbaden Area, was also performed at Rhein-Main.[114] To lessen wear and tear on vehicles, hard standings at the air base were improved; vehicles were left at Rhein-Main instead of being driven to unit motor pools after work, saving about 30 miles of daily travel; and Transportation and Ordnance officers made weekly inspections to appraise maintenance efficiency.[115] Every month, 20 to 25 engines were sent out for rebuild.

---

[108]Ibid.

[109]EUCOM, Deputy Commander in Chief's Weekly Staff Conference Report, No 3, 18 Jan 49, p 11.

[110]Interview with Lt Col Schoenfeld.

[111]Lt Col Bunker, "The TC in the Vittles Operation," p 53.

[112]Interview with Lt Col Darragh.

[113]Interview with Lt Col Chase; EUCOM, Deputy Commander in Chief's Weekly Staff Conference Report, No 3, 18 Jan 49, p 10.

[114]Information from Lt Col Bunker, 7 Mar 49.

g. <u>Working Conditions</u>. During the first six months of the air
lift, drivers assigned to lift operations at Rhein-Main and Wiesbaden
had a morale-testing job. For six months, their shifts were 12 on
and 12 off, seven days a week, the "off" hours including, for most
of this period, time spent driving to and from work. A battalion
club system provided recreation at the different kasernes, and at
Edwards Area, home of the battalion headquarters, the mess hall was
open all night long. Termination of enlistments tended to create a
critical driver shortage later in 1948. Confronted with the urgent
need for their services, many drivers reenlisted, deferring stateside
furloughs so that the air lift would not suffer. As the result of
a training program which converted light truck drivers to heavy
drivers, truck companies at Rhein-Main and Wiesbaden were able to
change to shifts of 12 hours on and 24 hours off, beginning 27 December.[116]

h. <u>Training</u>. Driving a tractor with a semi-trailer called
for skill developed through weeks of special training. Such
training was given at Kitzingen Basic Training Center, at the
Transportation Corps Training Center at Hammelburg, and by the 3d
Transportation Truck Battalion, charged with the training mission
for heavy drivers, at Giessen. Mechanics were trained at the
Ordnance School at Eschwege.[117]

19. <u>Transportation at Tempelhof</u>

At the start of the June air lift the small Transportation
Corps unit which had been handling outgoing cargo at Berlin was
rapidly expanded into the Transportation Corps Air Head Tempelhof
(TCAHT). On 23 June a captain was placed in charge of unloading
operations. Two days later 18 enlisted men from the 7798th Traffic
Regulation Detachment and 5 officers were added to the staff. On
29 June, Major C. S. Lewis was charged with coordinating Transportation Corps activities in connection with the lift. Effective
30 June, 110 enlisted men were placed on temporary duty with the
7798th Traffic Regulation Detachment, to help with airhead operations.[118] Six hundred Germans went to work for TCAHT the same
day. Early directed to plan on handling 4,500 tons per day,[119] the
air head organization rapidly expanded its personnel and sought ways

---

[115]EUCOM, Deputy Commander in Chief's Weekly Staff Conference
Report, No 3, 18 Jan 49, p 11.

[116]Interview with Lt Col Chase.

[117]Ibid.

[118]BMP, Rpt of Opr, May and Jun 48, narrative p 68, and
Supporting Docs, Trans Br.

[119]Interview with Lt Col Lewis.

of conserving vehicles and gasoline. A cargo transfer point was
built so that German vehicles could pick up Civil Affairs cargo at
the edge of the airfield. At first such cargo was hauled to
warehouses by U.S. trucks. A coal ramp was constructed so that
rail cars of the Neukoeln Mittenwalder Kleinbahn could be loaded
with coal on the base, and an engine and cars were hauled to the
rail line on German moving equipment.[120] In the face of rising
tonnages, it was found possible to cut the number of trucks in
loading activities from 108 in July and August to 102 in November
and 79 in December.[121] Close study of operating problems was begun
in November so that maximum savings in manpower and equipment could
be achieved.

a. Cargo-Hauling Operations. Planes arriving at Tempelhof
came in from the eastern side of the field, landed on a runway
leading almost due west, and taxied to a wide paved apron curving
around the northwest corner of the field. (See Appendix VIII).
Loading and unloading operations took place in a concentrated,
assembly-line type of operation, a truck going out from the ready
lines along the hangars to meet each plane as it stopped behind a
"follow-me" jeep on the apron. Enlisted men trained as boss-
checkers supervised the movement of the truck, examined the manifest and checked the cargo against it, directed the backing of the
truck against the plane and the placing of blocks to prevent it
from hitting the plane, supervised the work of the stevedores,
turned in a signed copy of the manifest to an officer "cargo
director", and were responsible for the movement of the truck to
the proper hangar or unloading point. At the start of operations,
trucks were held in three sections or "ready lines" between the
apron and the hangars. Four eight-hour shifts were organized, each
supervised by an officer-in-charge who was aided by three officer
cargo directors. Each cargo director had charge of a section consisting of ten work crews comprised of one enlisted boss-checker
and 12 German stevedores each. A fourth officer, serving as
warehouse supervisor, controlled a section of 15 enlisted cargo
checkers and 120 German stevedores. Crews of six stevedores and
2½-ton trucks were used for unloading C-47 planes. Later, all
trucks were grouped in a single section near the little white
house which served as headquarters for TCAHT. With the building
of the land pier for Civil Affairs cargo, such cargo could be unloaded by Army trucks within half a mile of planeside. Later in
the year delivery to Quartermaster warehouses was placed on a
24-hour basis, ending the practice of using up to 50 trucks for

---

[120] Interviews with Maj L.F. Valiante, S-4 Br, BMP, 11 Feb 49,
and Lt Col Lewis.

[121] Interview with Lt Col Schiess.

storage of Quartermaster supplies at the air base overnight.[122]
Truck mileage in support of the lift was estimated at about 385,000
miles up to 31 December. The truck accident rate was one for every
22,284 miles.[123]

b. Personnel. American and German civilians, supervised by
an administrative officer from Transportation Branch, maintained
transportation records at the TCAHT office. Motor officers and
enlisted truckmasters from the 7807th Motor Transportation Battalion
were responsible for the discipline and training of drivers, inspection of the loading of trucks and formation of convoys carrying
military supplies to local depots, and supervision of preventive
maintenance and refueling. Neither the Air Force nor the Transportation Corps had men enough available to supervise the hundreds of
Germans working for the Transportation Corps Air Head at Tempelhof,
and on 5 August, Companies I and E from the 3d Battalion, 16th
Infantry, were given this work. On 18 October men of the 3d Battalion were relieved by the 16th Constabulary Squadron, which provided 96 enlisted men for aircraft unloading and 14 enlisted men
as outloaders, with seven officers as supervisors. On 16 November,
there were 12 Transportation Corps, and 12 Constabulary officers
and 252 enlisted men assigned to the transportation mission of the
air lift.[124] After a careful analysis of the airhead organization,
two lieutenant colonels were removed from shift supervision and
detailed as executive officer, in charge of administration personnel, and fiscal and accounting matters, and operations officer,
responsible for the operation of TCAHT and the control of motor
vehicles. The system of having separate labor groups to unload
cargo from the planes and to transfer it from the trucks was
discontinued, with a resultant saving of 456 laborers. Use of the
same crew for both operations cut down turnabout time for the
trucks and reduced pilferage. At the end of the year, each of the
four shifts was working on the same around-the-clock pattern of
eight-hour shifts, mounting to 40 to 48 hours each week.

c. Operational Problems. Efficient loading and unloading to
meet Air Force timing without harm to equipment or cargo was the
constant concern of the Transportation Corps Air Head Tempelhof.
With all kinds of cargo coming, much of it requiring the use of a
fork lift, Tempelhof crews could not hope to equal the records of

---

[122] BMP, Rpt of Opr, 1 Jul-30 Sep 48, Hist Rpt, TCAHT, BERLIN;
Rpt of Opr, 1 Oct-31 Dec 48, p 122.

[123] Interview with Lt Col Schiess.

[124] BMP, Rpt of Opr, 1 Jul-30 Sep 48, Supporting Docs, Hist Rpt,
TCAHT; ibid., 1 Jul-30 Sep 48, S-4 Br, p 2; ibid., 1 Oct-31 Dec 48,
pp 122 and 124.

crews unloading only coal at Gatow and Tegel. Coal unloading time
at Tempelhof averaged 12-15 minutes per plane, although a 12-man
team by back-breaking effort unloaded a plane in five minutes and
45 seconds during Air Force Day, 17-18 September. Pilferage was
not excessive, but absenteeism became a serious problem.[125] Incor-
rect manifesting of loads from Rhein-Main and Wiesbaden, and in-
accuracy in marking military ("Chicago") and civil ("New York")
cargo called for continuing alertness on the part of cargo checkers.

d. Support of Air Lift Construction Projects. The construction of two additional runways at Tempelhof Air Base called
for additional transportation support. During the summer 42 10-ton
trucks and 42 2½-ton dump trucks were dispatched to the air head for
use in runway construction. During the fourth quarter of 1948
some 89,000 gallons of gasoline were diverted by Berlin Military
Post to Transportation and Engineer activities for unloading and
construction operations in support of the air lift.[126] Transportation officials worked closely with the Engineers and the Air Force
to provide transportation for asphalt and other supplies flown to
Tempelhof for use in the construction of Tegel Airfield.

e. Maintenance. Maintenance of vehicles received special
emphasis at Berlin, since trucks were old and the replacement of
parts by air was not easy. At the request of the Motor Transport
Officer the Berlin Military Post Ordnance Officer established a
maintenance company at Tempelhof in June. Vehicles used in the air
lift and in runway construction were given organizational and field
maintenance, and also were refueled, at the air base. Vehicles
were returned to the 7807th Motor Transportation Battalion shop for
the 6000-mile check.[127]

20. Engineer Support

Engineer support was directed mainly at the construction of
increased airfield facilities at Berlin and the provision of satisfactory accommodations for personnel brought to the Frankfurt area
to take part in the lift. Additional support was provided at Rhein-
Main and Wiesbaden Air Force Bases, at Oberpfaffenhofen Air Force
Sub-Depot, and at military posts throughout the U.S. Zone.[128]

---

[125] Interview with Lt Col Schiess.

[126] BMP, Rpt of Opr, 1 Jul-30 Sep 48, Supporting Docs, Hist
Rpt, TCAHT; ibid., 1 Oct-31 Dec 48, p 125.

[127] Ibid., May and Jun 48, Supporting Docs, Trans Br; ibid.,
1 Jul-30 Sep 48, Supporting Docs, Hist Rpt, TCAHT.

[128] EUCOM, Engr Div Rpt, "Engineer Participation in Operation
VITTLES," 9 Nov 48, Tab C.

a. Projects. Of 72 projects approved for VITTLES in 1948, USAFE was the construction agency for 50, nine were assigned to Berlin Military Post, two to Frankfurt Military Post, two to Wetzlar for repair of a runway at Fritzlar and construction of a radio range station at Fulda, and the rest, for recovery of pierced steel planking (PSP) and pierced aluminum planking (PAP) at various airfield sites, to Augsburg, Wetzlar, Nuernberg, Regensburg, and Wurzburg. Thirty-one projects had been completed by the end of 1948.[129] Engineer personnel in the U.S. Zone supervised the recovery of 582,900 panels of pierced steel and aluminum planking, including 1,259 tons PAP and 14,632 tons PSP, for various airfields supporting Operation VITTLES. VITTLES projects included 1,058,000 manhours, for emergency requirements, under a separate budget, during July and August. Projects under construction on 1 November included 14,000 manhours approved for Augsburg Military Post, 728,000 for Berlin, 36,000 for Wurzburg, and 737,000 for USAFE, totaling 1,515,000.[130] For seventy-seven projects approved up to 10 January 1949, 2,339,359 manhours were allotted.[131]

b. Personnel. Early in July, 110 enlisted men and three officers from the U.S. Zone were placed on temporary duty at Berlin to aid in VITTLES construction work. By 20 October the number on temporary duty had been reduced to 83.[132] On 1 October, 217 enlisted men and 14 officers, assigned or on temporary duty, were directly employed on airfield construction, equipment assembly and maintenance, operation of equipment, and supervision of construction labor at Berlin. During the peak of activities at Tegel, Americans were supervising 17,000 German laborers per day.[133] No command-wide increase in Army personnel was authorized. Those left to carry on the normal mission did so by dint of individually assuming heavier workloads.

---

[129] EUCOM, Engr Div, Spec Rpt, "Status of Operation VITTLES Construction Projects (10 Jan 49)."

[130] Engr Div Rpt, "Engineer Participation in Operation VITTLES," 9 Nov 48, Tab A, 1 Dec 48; EUCOM, Deputy Commander in Chief's Weekly Staff Conference Report, No 35, 31 Aug 48, pp 8-9; ibid., No 48, 30 Nov 48, Appendix "B".

[131] Engr Div, Spec Rpt, "Status of Operation VITTLES Construction Projects (10 Jan 49)." This total included 5,800 manhours allotted for three of the five projects approved after 31 December 48, but did not include allotments of manhours for 12 of the 72 projects approved during 1948.

[132] EUCOM, Deputy Commander in Chief's Weekly Staff Conference Report, No 45, 9 Nov 48, p 6.

[133] Engr Div Rpt, "Engineer Participation in Operation VITTLES," 9 Nov 48, Tab A.

21. Engineer Shipments to Berlin

The outstanding Engineer projects undertaken by Berlin Military Post were the building of two new runways at Tempelhof and the construction of Tegel Air Base. Air shipments for these projects included, to 14 September, 3,300 tons of asphalt, 3,300 tons of pierced plank, and 650 tons of construction equipment.[134] By 1 December they comprised 5,562 tons of asphalt (2,062 from depot stocks and 3,500 from the U.S.), 671 tons of heavy equipment from Hanau Engineer Depot and various military posts, and 438 tons of general Engineer supplies and 67 tons of spare parts from depot stocks, a total of 6,738 tons, exclusive of pierced plank shipments. Depot personnel disassembled the heavy equipment at Hanau, delivered it to the airfield, helped load it aboard planes, reassembled it at Berlin, serviced and tested it, and turned it over to the Berlin Post Engineer. This equipment included 18 tractors, 10 motorized graders, 20 motorized road rollers, 4 crushing and screening plants, 10 scrapers, 10 asphalt distributors (six 165-gallon and six 1,250 gallon), nine generators (15-100 KW) and two searchlight generators.[135] By 9 November, 81 pieces of heavy equipment had been shipped to Berlin, while 23 were in use at Rhein-Main.[136]

22. Construction at Tempelhof

It was soon evident that the existing runway at Tempelhof was incapable of handling for long the heavy traffic demanded by operation VITTLES.

a. The "First" Runway. On 8 July the Berlin Military Post Engineer Branch received a request to build a new runway at Tempelhof. Construction started the same day,[137] and was completed early in September. Costs of the runway were estimated, in dollars, at $97,175.62 for labor, $98,923.76 for equipment, and $16,117.00 for supplies, a total of $212,216.38. The project required 136,545 manhours, including 44,388 worked by the Engineer Corps and 92,157 worked by Germans supplied by the buergermeister.[138] This first runway was built with pierced plank.

---

[134] EUCOM, Deputy Commander in Chief's Weekly Staff Conference Report, No 37, 14 Sep 48, p 8.

[135] Engr Div Rpt, "Engineer Participation in Operation VITTLES," 9 Nov 48, Tab A, 1 Dec 48.

[136] EUCOM, Deputy Commander in Chief's Weekly Staff Conference Report, No 45, 9 Nov 48, p 6.

[137] Interview with Capt Hart.

[138] Interview with Lt Col Rain.

b. The "Second" Runway. Work on asphalt runway at Tempelhof was started on 23 August to provide adequate facilities for the coal lift.[139] By 3 September some 4,400 feet of sub-grade had been graded for the runway and the first course of brick rubble had been laid for 2,700 feet.[140] This runway opened for operations on 30 November, giving the air base three parallel runways. The project involved construction of 5,250 feet of runway 140 feet wide, with some 7,000 feet of taxiway. Because of the limited lift available for bringing construction supplies to Berlin, deliveries of asphalt and other materials to Rhein-Main and Wiesbaden had to be planned so as not to create a storage problem at the airfields, but without risking a delay in the work going forward at Berlin.[141] As of 31 December, costs for this runway were estimated in dollars at $222,897.33 for labor, $160,739.86 for equipment, and $2,911.55 for supplies, a total of $386,684.74. The project required 347,525 manhours, of which the Engineers supplied 63,931, and Germans paid by the buergermeister supplied 283,594.[142] Throughout the fall it was necessary to divert construction materials from other projects throughout the U.S. Zone, so that VITTLES construction projects could be completed.[143]

c. Other Construction. Other Berlin Military Post Engineer projects at Tempelhof included construction of taxiways, building of a truck ramp and land pier, and the installation of truck-weighing scales.[144] USAFE was responsible for the installation of marker and approach lighting.

23. The Construction of Tegel Air Base

Planning for a complete new airfield at Tegel in the French Sector of Berlin began in July and actual work on the field started on 4 August.[145] The field was formally dedicated on 5 November,

---

[139] EUCOM, Deputy Commander in Chief's Weekly Staff Conference Report, No 37, 14 Sep 48, p 8; interview with Capt Hart.

[140] EUCOM, Deputy Commander in Chief's Weekly Staff Conference Report, No 37, 14 Sep 48, p 8.

[141] BMP, Rpt of Opr, 1 Oct-31 Dec 48, p 121.

[142] Interview with Lt Col Rain.

[143] Engr Div Rpt, "Engineer Participation in Operation VITTLES," 9 Nov 48, Tab E.

[144] Ibid., Tab C.

[145] Interview with Capt Hart; EUCOM, Deputy Commander in Chief's Weekly Staff Conference Report, No 37, 14 Sep 48, gives 9 August as the first day of construction work at Tegel.

when a C-54 plane bearing Lt. General John K. Cannon, CG, USAFE, and Major General William H. Tunner, CG, CALTF, made the first official landing. On 1 December the field was opened for operations. By 20 December, Berlin Military Post had practically completed its share of the construction.[146]

a. Specifications. Plans for Tegel Air Base called for a runway 5,500 feet long and 150 feet wide, warm-up aprons, 2,400 feet long and 100 feet wide, taxiways, 2,600 feet long and 60 feet wide, and an unloading apron 2,200 feet long and 400 feet wide, all with a minimum thickness of 21 inches of asphalt macadam. An estimated 190,000 cubic yards of compressed brick and 40,000 cubic yards of crushed rock were to go into the field. Some 8,000 feet of 20-foot wide roads, a fire station, a control tower, and administration building, 4,500 linear feet of water mains, 6,000 linear feet of primary electric lines, and an emergency 150kw generator plant were also needed to make the field operational.[147] Appendix IX shows the plan of Tegel Air Base.

b. Division of Responsibility. USAFE, the Berlin Military Post, the French authorities, and local German officials worked together for the success of this vast project. USAFE was responsible for technical specifications, installation of high intensity lighting, and air operations. The Berlin Military Post Engineer was responsible for planning, construction, supply and supervision. French authorities had custodial responsibility for the field and provided labor through local German officials.[148] Construction of the primary phase of Tegel Airfield by Berlin Military Post was approved by the EUCOM Engineer Division as Project No. 1067 on 31 July 1948.[149]

c. Operations, Labor and Equipment. By the end of September Tegel was the scene of construction work involving thousands of men and women, and large scale land-leveling, rock-crushing, asphalt-pouring, and building operations. On 29 September, the first shift (2200 to 0600 hours) employed 418 laborers, 20 trucks, 8 bulldozers and 11 rollers. All heavy equipment and some of the trucks were handled by enlisted men. The second shift (0600 to 1400 hours) employed 8,149 laborers, 304 trucks (219 brick and 85 dirt),

---

[146] Stars and Stripes, 6 Nov 48, BMP, Rpt of Opr, 1 Oct-31 Dec 48, p 121; interview with Lt Col Rain.

[147] Engr Div Rpt, "Engineer Participation in Operation VITTLES," 9 Nov 48, Tab E.

[148] Ibid.

[149] Engr Div, Spec Rpt, "Status of VITTLES Construction Projects, (10 Jan 49)."

- 39 -

8 bulldozers, 9-rollers, (one-16T, one-12T, two-10T, two-8T, and three-5T), 1 roller (7-ton, caterpillar-drawn), 1 grader, 3 clamshells and 2 carryalls. The third shift (1400 - 2200 hours) employed 8,459 laborers, 313 trucks (222 brick and 88 dirt), 7 bulldozers, 15 rollers (including two 7-ton rollers), 4 clamshells, 1 grader, 3 carryalls, 1 asphalt distributor, with 6-ton truck, and one U.S.-type stonecrusher. In this work picture enlisted personnel gained as much Engineer experience in six months as they might ordinarily have received in six years.[150]

d. Estimated Costs and Manhours. Tegel runway costs up to 20 December were estimated in dollars at $5,353,044.35 for labor, $786,037.06 for equipment, $171,756.21 for supplies, a total of $6,310,837.62. Appropriated dollar costs accounted for $317,195.00 of this amount. The cost in Deutsche marks was DM 20,140,330.67. Engineer manhours expended on the project totaled 91,479, including 3,218 from Engineer troops, 1,135 from Department of the Army civilians, 75,620 on the Engineer payroll, and 11,506 furnished on contract. Buergermeister employees worked 8,872,518 manhours, making a grand total of 8,963,997 worked by all taking part.[151]

24. Engineer Responsibilities in the Frankfurt Area

At Frankfurt, Engineer support of air lift operations was partly in the form of support for truck companies and labor service units brought into the area to aid the lift. Packing and crating of household goods shipped by air to and from Berlin was an added task occasioned by the blockade of Berlin but not directly in support of the lift. This task required the work of 30-35 officers, enlisted men and displaced persons. A transit storage shed was built at Rhein-Main for the Transportation Corps, early in the summer. But the main responsibility resulting from air lift operations, and in support of them, was the provision of housing for approximately 5,000 Air Force and Navy personnel. In providing the foregoing types of support and in its packing and crating activities, Frankfurt Military Post Engineer Section daily employed about 100 men.[152]

25. Quartering of VITTLES Personnel

Soon after the lift began the Air Force presented its requirement for a central area near Rhein-Main where it could house a

---

[150] Interview with Lt Col Rain.

[151] Ibid.

[152] Interview with Lt Col C.P. Fortney, Operations, Engr Sec, FMP, 29 Jan 49.

large number of its men. Frankfurt Military Post thereupon provided Betts Area as quarters for about 1,000 men. Within 10 days,
however, Air Force requirements jumped from 1,500 to 5,000, and
the 18th Infantry, back from Karlsruhe on the strength of an agreement that Atterberry Area (adjoining Betts) would not be requested
by the Air Force, was moved to Mannheim.[153] The biggest problem
during this period was to get a firm statement from the Air Force
as to its requirements. Establishment of Atterberry-Betts Area
Command on 6 December and the subsequent channeling of requests for
repair and maintenance through a single "utilities officer" appointed
by the Area Commander achieved some clarification on this point.

a. Survey of Accommodations. On 22 November a board appointed
by EUCOM completed a survey of living accommodations needed to provide 100 square feet per officer and 70 square feet per airman for
VITTLES personnel stationed at Rhein-Main. The board determined
that by 1 January 1949 the Air Force would need 1,561 officer
spaces and 6,200 spaces for airmen. Spaces available on 22 November
numbered 1,227 for officers and 4,112 for airmen. Space for 237 officers and 2,063 airmen was to be provided by 1 January through
the release of the remaining portion of Atterberry Barracks, construction of additional housing at Rhein-Main Air Force Base, and
the rehabilitation of five private homes in Neu Isenburg and Buch-
schlag. Frankfurt Military Post was allotted 23,000 DM to cover
installation of plumbing and provisions of hot water in each of
the eight Romney type mess halls at Atterberry which were to be
used as barracks.[154]

b. Progress in Meeting Requirements. An inspection was made
by top EUCOM officials and representatives of Rhein-Main, USAFE
and Frankfurt Military Post on 8 December to determine whether the
European Command was doing all it should to accommodate the personnel of the air lift task force. In a memorandum to the Deputy
Commander in Chief, EUCOM, General Carter B. Magruder, Deputy Chief
of Staff, pointed out that the recommendations based on the survey
of 22 November were in process of rapid fulfillment.[155] The in-
specting party found, however, that the standards for officers'
billets were not high enough. The decision was made that three
barracks in Atterberry Area should be converted to hotel-type rooms

---

[153]Ibid.; EUCOM, Deputy Commander in Chief's Weekly Staff
Conference Report, No 49, 7 Dec 48, p 17.

[154]EUCOM, Deputy Commander in Chief's Weekly Staff Conference
Report, No 49, 7 Dec 48, pp 16, 17.

[155]EUCOM, Memorandum for the Deputy Commander in Chief, EUCOM,
sub: Inspection of Airlift Task Force Accommodations in Frankfurt,
10 Dec 48, sgd Carter B. MAGRUDER, Maj Gen, GSC. Deputy C of S.

and furnished with easy chairs, rugs, wall lights and wardrobes. The Frankfurt Military Post Engineer Section was given 30 days for this work, and completed the project within the time allowed. Other Engineer accomplishments at the area included the building of a service club, a ration breakdown point, an officers' mess, a beer hall and a chapel in the Romney huts in the area.[156] On 21 December a follow-up inspection was conducted by Logistics Division to determine progress made since 8 December. A report of this inspection listed the following achievements: (1) in Betts Area, a service club and crafts shop (in Romney hut) 90% completed and in operation; the beer club completed and operating; the library installed in a permanent building and the Romney hut planned for it made available as billets; (2) the officers' mess project in Atterberry Area 60% completed; (3) installation of plumbing to make adequate barracks in eight Romney huts postponed on request of the Air Force; (4) installation of electric wall plugs in officers' rooms 50% completed.[157] Not until January was a 400,000 Deutsche mark project, authorizing rehabilitation and conversion of buildings for VITTLES personnel at Atterberry and Betts Areas, approved by Engineer Division, EUCOM.[158] Under this project Frankfurt Military Post Engineer Section was to provide a permanent-type service club in Betts Area, a bowling alley, a snack bar and a crafts shop.

c. Provision of Individual Quarters. In addition to remodeling and refurbishing Atterberry and Betts barracks for VITTLES personnel, Frankfurt Military Post Engineer Section provided 160 sets of quarters in Frankfurt, Hoechst, Griesheim and Heddernheim for married officers and billeted 180 Air Force and Naval officers in bachelor officers' quarters.[159]

26. Winterization Projects

Long before the end of the summer, EUCOM and the Air Force had to plan the special measures needed to continue Operation VITTLES under winter conditions. After a survey of Rhein-Main and Wiesbaden Air Bases in August it was estimated that necessary winterization projects for the winter 1948-1949, would require 116,000 manhours and would cost DM 580,000. Approved Army and Air Force winterization projects in progress at Rhein-Main at the end of October included improvement of hardstands and taxiways, building of second and third

---

[156]Interview with Lt Col Fortney.

[157]EUCOM, Deputy Commander in Chief's Weekly Staff Conference Report, No 52, 27 Dec 48, p 6.

[158]Engr Div, Spec Rpt, "Status of Operation VITTLES Construction Projects (10 Jan 49)."

[159]Interview with Lt Col Fortney.

echelon tractor maintenance shops, a truck drivers' shelter and Transportation Corps control offices, and winterization of tents for aircraft loading personnel.[160]

27. Ordnance Support

The major role of Transportation Corps in Operation VITTLES gave a correspondingly vital role to Ordnance. Ordnance support was focused on the two ends of the lift, involving special problems of vehicle maintenance both at Berlin and in the U.S. Zone. But Ordnance installations throughout the U.S. Zone shared in the urgent task of meeting Berlin's Ordnance requirements quickly so that lift operations in Berlin would not risk delay. As of 9 November the 1182 Ordnance vehicles directly supporting Operation VITTLES on a 24-hour basis were found to require 118 rebuilt vehicles, 732 rebuilt tires, and 659 tons of spare parts and supplies above normal per month.[161]

28. Ordnance Operations in the Frankfurt Area

At the end of 1948, three of the six Ordnance companies at Frankfurt Military Post were supporting VITTLES.

a. Units. The Ordnance Service Center at Heddernheim, operated by the 7865th Ordnance HAM Company, was the supply point for all parts and major items needed at Frankfurt. Up to 1 November, when the 559th Ordnance MAM Company arrived at Rhein-Main from Munich, the men of the 7865th worked seven days a week on the heavy vehicles used at Rhein-Main. The 656th Ordnance MAM Company, at Oberursel, repaired jeeps, sedans and three-quarter ton vehicles. When the 559th Ordnance M.M Company arrived, on 1 November, it took on responsibility for field maintenance at Rhein-Main and provided detachments at Mainz-Kastel and Fraunheim to give additional support to organizational shops.[162]

b. Maintenance Problems. Of the 300 tractors used at Rhein-Main and Wiesbaden over 200 had to be replaced completely or to have their engines replaced. A large number of the 555 trailers had to be repaired and rebuilt. Wear and tear on these vehicles was estimated at twice the normal for tractors and four times the normal amount for trailers. Coal, for example, had to be loaded

---

[160]EUCOM, Deputy Commander in Chief's Weekly Staff Conference Report, No 45, 9 Nov 48, pp 7-8.

[161]Ibid., p 7.

[162]Interview with Lt Col Walter H. Freeman, Exec Officer, Ord Sec, FMP, 28 Jan 49.

forward in the trailer so that the other end could slide under the plane door. This forward loading brought too much weight on the landing gear. One thousand plates to keep landing gears from sinking into the mud were manufactured by the 7865th.[163]

c. Personnel. The 559th Ordnance MAM Company consisted of two officers and 40 enlisted men. The Ordnance Service Center (7865th Ordnance HAM Company) consisted of six officers and 117 enlisted men, and employed three United States civilians, 327 Germans, and the 8090th Labor Service Company (Lithuanian), used in supply work. To keep up with maintenance demands these units worked seven days a week. By 30 November they had furnished 230,000 manhours in support of Operation VITTLES.[164]

d. Costs. To 30 November costs of Ordnance labor, supplies and equipment provided by Frankfurt Military Post for the air lift amounted to approximately $650,000. Costs for December were estimated at an additional $130,000.[165]

29. Ordnance Operations at Berlin

At Berlin, Ordnance faced the added problem of having to rely on the air lift for all incoming supplies. Short of permitting complete replacement of vehicles, this proved an advantage rather than a handicap, and air supply combined with improved procedures to produce unprecedented efficiency in Berlin Military Post maintenance operations.

a. Preparation for Blockade. As pointed out earlier (paragraph no. 4), Berlin Military Post Ordnance Branch took advantage of the period 11 April to 21 June to evacuate vehicles requiring rebuild, to expedite the shipment of line items from the U.S. Zone to Berlin, and to expand Ordnance rebuild facilities at Berlin.

b. Flow of Supplies. Before 1 April, Ordnance supplies amounted on the average, to 111 tons inbound and 103 tons outbound, by rail, per month. Between 12 April and 21 June, Berlin Ordnance received 335 tons of selected line items from Command depots and evacuated 350 vehicles by autobahn. The rebuild shop at Berlin worked to resupply the local depot and it also performed top overhaul on vehicles while they were receiving other essential maintenance. On 21 June the Ordnance depot had an over-all 30-day stock level. Requisitioning procedures placed in effect by Berlin Military Post on 22 June based priorities for Berlin shipments on

---

[163] Ibid.
[164] Ibid.
[165] Ibid.

immediate needs. All Ordnance requisitions, from 23 June on, were based upon needs of vehicles awaiting parts or shop space in unit or field shops. Since depots throughout the Command coordinated to fill Berlin requisitions on first priority, the "turn-around" time on requisitions for Berlin Ordnance was reduced from about two months to five days. Needed parts arrived from Command depots while a requisition was being submitted to the local depot and the vehicle was being scheduled for shop space. The increased tempo of maintenance resulting from stepped-up supply procedures made it possible to surmount a 42 percent reduction in personnel without loss in production. Air shipments to replenish depot stocks began on 27 August. On 22 September the S-4 Branch of Berlin Military Post increased the allocation of air lift available to Ordnance Branch, to permit shipment of an estimated 150 tons over a 35-day period. By 15 October 113.8 tons of supplies had been received. During the period 16 October to 15 November the depot received 156 tons of parts and assemblies and shipped 124 one-quarter ton vehicles and 28 sedans to the U.S. Zone.[166]

   c. Maintenance Activities. As a result of Operation VITTLES, Berlin Ordnance had to assume responsibility for more than its usual echelon of maintenance.[167] In the face of unusual conditions and demands, the Ordnance Officer tried to keep Ordnance support of the lift a normal operation, on a normal basis.[168] A team of one officer and 20 enlisted men was moved to Tempelhof to perform field echelon repair (unit replacement) on air lift vehicles. In its first ten days of work, this group completed more job orders, including complete overhauls, than ever accomplished previously by any 150 Germans employed by Ordnance at Berlin. Rigid inspection of driver maintenance plus driver cooperation brought maintenance deficiencies to a lower point than ever before. From 16 September to 15 October the field shop completed 442 vehicles job orders. On 15 November, 180 vehicles were on job order, 65 were in the shop being worked on, and 49, with all supplies on hand, were awaiting shop space. A month later the field shop had 86 vehicle job orders from using units and 104 from the depot unserviceable stock pool. During the first six months of the lift the contact team at Tempelhof completed 1,101 vehicle job orders. Awareness of the emergency caused by the blockade was recognized by the Ordnance

---

   [166]BMP, Ord Officer, Rpt for the C of Ord, "Berlin Ordnance Blockade Airlift Operations," 1 Apr-15 Sep 48; ibid., 16 Sep-15 Oct 48; ibid., 16 Oct-15 Nov 48.

   [167]BMP, Rpt of Opr, 1 Jul-30 Sep 48, Rpt, Hq 7783d Ord Bn, p 5.

   [168]Interview with Lt Col Martin F. Shaugnessy CO, 7783d Ord Bn, (Post Ord Officer).

Officer as a factor stimulating the using units to achieve top efficiency in the care and maintenance of their vehicles.[169]

d. Manpower. The 7783d Ordnance Battalion had an assigned strength of about 20 officers and 260 enlisted men. At the end of June the battalion was employing 504 Germans, including 302 assigned to shops and 121 at the Depot. In July the allocation for German personnel was reduced to 304.[170]

e. Maintenance Costs. A study of costs on 194 vehicles used in direct support of the air lift, not covering overhead, estimated $8,824.64 for labor and $41,089.32 for parts, a total of $49,913.96, or an average of $257.28 per vehicle.[171]

30. Signal Support

The Signal Corps was responsible for maintaining Signal Corps items common in use by the Air Force and supplying equipment to expand the radio, telephone and teletype communications needed by the air lift. Although no individual was assigned entirely to Operation VITTLES, hundreds within the Signal Corps were spending from 10 to 50 percent of their time supporting the lift.[172] Traffic and supply activities increased approximately 7 percent as a result of the air lift. This increase, equivalent in manhours to the fulltime work of several hundred military and civilian workers, was actually spread among many more as extra work added to their regular duties.

a. Main Types of Support. Signal support was reflected in the following developments:

(1) the establishment of a large number of high grade circuits in the Zone;

(2) a sizeable increase in facilities between the U.S. Zone and Berlin;

---

[169]BMP, Ord Officer, Rpt for the C of Ord, "Berlin Ordnance Blockade Airlift Operations," 1 Apr - 15 Sep 48; ibid., 15 Sep - 15 Oct 48; ibid., 16 Oct - 15 Nov 48.

[170]BMP, Rpt of Opr, 1 Jul - 30 Sep 48, Rpt, Hq, 7783d Ord Bn; ibid., May and June 48.

[171]BMP, Ord Officer, Rpt of the C of Ord, "Berlin Ordnance Blockade Airlift Operations," 1 Apr - 15 Sep 48.

[172]Interview with Lt Col L. P. Jacobs, Plans and Intelligence Br, Sig Div, EUCOM, 2 Mar 49.

(3) an increased load on the Signal Depot, especially in the number of high priority, "hurry-up" requisitions;

(4) an increased traffic load on the entire communications system; and

(5) a considerable increase in engineering work on EUCOM and Air Force projects.[173]

b. Equipment and Supplies. During the first six months of the lift, about $250,000,000 worth of Signal Corps equipment was procured and turned over to the Air Force as a result of Operation VITTLES. Equipment and contract project costs chargeable to the lift amounted to over 1,000,000 DM.[174] To 9 November, 24 tons of equipment had been furnished and 9 teletype and 28 telephone circuits had been established for Operation VITTLES. The cost of equipment used on Signal projects to bolster the communications system because of the lift was approximately $106,000.[175] Radio beacons and air-ground communication sets were the outstanding items furnished the Air Force. Every project of concern to VITTLES was given highest priority by the EUCOM Signal Division.[176]

31. Quartermaster Support

Quartermaster support consisted mainly of subsistence, clothing and equipment for VITTLES personnel and supplies of petroleum products for air and ground transport used in the lift. Subsistence and other supplies for United States personnel stationed at Cello and Fassberg in the British zone were forwarded by Bremerhaven Military Post. Although no Quartermaster personnel were assigned directly to the lift, approximately 15 percent of QM operations at Frankfurt were regarded as directly or indirectly supporting Operation VITTLES. Laundry service was 25 percent in support of VITTLES, and laundries at Dorheim and Darmstadt were authorized larger staffs to insure 72-hour service for lift personnel. Mirrors, wall lockers, mattresses and pillows were supplied for men living at the Atterberry-Betts Area.[177] At Berlin, incoming supplies had to be received

---

173Ibid.

174Ibid.

175EUCOM, Deputy Commander in Chief's Weekly Staff Conference Report, No 45, 9 Nov 48, p 7; interview with Lt Col Jacobs.

176Interview with Maj E.H. Johnson, Procurement and Distribution Br, Sig Div, 20 Jan 49.

177EUCOM, Deputy Commander in Chief's Weekly Staff Conference Report, No 45, 9 Nov 48, p 7; ibid., No 52, 27 Dec 48, pp 7-8; telephone interview with Maj W.D. Sperry QM Sec, FMA, 24 Jan 49.

24 hours per day, and checking procedures were more complicated under air-supply conditions, but there was no direct support of the lift comparable to that at Frankfurt. Over 400,000 duffel bags were supplied by Quartermaster Division, EUCOM, on a one-time basis, for lifting coal to Berlin.[178]

a. Petroleum Products. Aviation gasoline for the lift was shipped by rail tank cars to Rhein-Main and Wiesbaden, and direct from Farge to Celle and Wiesbaden. At the airfields it was pumped into servicing units or storage facilities. Separate accountability was maintained for aviation and Ground Forces gasoline. Because of the thousands of extra gallons required for planes flying the lift, storage facilities at Farge were modified to hold more aviation-type gasoline.[179]

b. Cost of Quartermaster Support. Measured in terms of its cost, Quartermaster support, from the beginning of the lift to 31 December 1948, amounted to $1,681,229.18 for subsistence; $11,661 for office supplies; $104,569.10 for regular supplies; $10,794.45 for the cost of warehouse equipment; $1,686,616.10 for cost of clothing and equipment; $12,826.81 and DM 89,193 for repair labor; $24,246.28 for supplies and parts; $59,572.50 for laundry and supplies; $781.29 and DM 94,570 for laundry and labor; $16,151.40 and DM 209,934 for personnel; and $4,030.00 for mortuary services, as well as large amounts for petroleum, oil and lubricants.[180]

[178]EUCOM, Deputy Commander in Chief's Weekly Staff Conference Report, No 45, 9 Nov 48, p 7; interview with Maj Buchanan, QM Div, EUCOM, 2 May 49; interview with Col F.B.L. Myer, QM, BMP, 16 Feb 49.

[179]Interview with Lt Col V.H. Moore, Chief, POL Sec, Supply and Procurement Br, QM Div, EUCOM, 20 Jan 49.

[180]IRS, EUCOM, Office of the Chief, QM Div, to Hist Div, EUCOM, sub: "Quartermaster Support of Berlin Airlift," 11 Mar 49, sgd Q.L. Kendall, Lt Col, QMC, Chief, Comptroller Br, inclosures 1-11, "Estimated QM Cost of Airlift."

32. Effects on Berlin Military Community

The shift to air supply had an immediate effect on the Berlin military community. Official transportation was organized into a system of official taxi stands, gasoline for private automobiles was rationed, bus lines were revised, electric power was cut off daily from 0830 to 1800 and from 2300 to 0630, billeting areas were resurveyed, and troops and headquarters were consolidated to conserve supplies and equipment. Within the next three months, gasoline rationing was tightened from five gallons per week to five per month and bus lines were contracted as personnel moved from outlying districts.[181]

33. Effects on Supply Procedures

Reliance on air supply forced the Berlin Military Post to state its requirements for supply in terms of weight and cubage when submitting requisitions. Gradually the process of determining military requirements for Berlin became a fairly routine task for S-4, but no military supplies could be flown in until assigned a priority by this office, which coordinated all military requirements for the post.[182] The technical services continued to function satisfactorily under air-supply conditions. The Engineer Branch reported that air shipment had no serious effect on the variety or quantity of supplies received. Ordnance Branch found its requisitions filled far more quickly by air, thanks partly to the speed of air transport and partly to the improved service given by Ordnance depots in view of the blockade.[183] The Quartermaster submitted requisitions for clothing, food, office supplies and other items monthly, through S-4, and was in communication with the depot at Giessen daily. Quartermaster supplies frequently came in small lots by air, making their handling a little more difficult than when shipped in large quantities by rail, but the allocation of 1,600 tons per month provided adequate stocks. Only a few types of supply, including Engineer airport construction material, were below a 30-day level as of 1 October. Army solid

---

[181]Interview with Maj L.F. Valiante, S-4, BMP, 11 Feb 49; BMP, Rpt of Opr, May and Jun 48; ibid., 1 Jul-30 Sep 48, S-4 Rpt, and Trans Br Rpt.

[182]Interview with Maj Valiante.

[183]BMP, Rpt of Opr, 1 Jul-30 Sep 48, Supplementary Docs, Engr Br Rpt, p 2; interview with Lt Col Shaugnessy.

fuel stocks in Berlin on 1 October totaled 10,017 tons, or about 32 days' supply at the estimated January 1949 consumption rate.[184]

34. Command-Wide Impact

There is no way of measuring exactly the effect of Operation VITTLES on Army projects and operations throughout the European Command but a few effects can be cited. Most of the heavy Transportation units were moved to Frankfurt and replaced by increased use of German drivers and rail transportation. Labor service companies and Engineer personnel were moved from other duties to Operation VITTLES without any question of replacement, simply because the air lift was given the highest priority of all EUCOM activities.

35. Estimates of Cost

Any estimates of the cost of Operation VITTLES should be prefaced by some explanation of the extent of which air lift support was provided by hundreds who were being paid by the Army, and who would have been used for some other work had there been no air lift. This is especially true, of course, of Army personnel and equipment. Direct support of Operation VITTLES to 13 December 1948 was estimated at $5,147,984, plus DM 21,543,739, while support given to USAFE by EUCOM for direct ground support by USAFE was estimated at $12,099,437 plus DM 11,369,349.[185] Transportation Corps estimated its costs to 31 December, in dollars, at $3,379,698.40.[186] Engineer support to 1 November was estimated at 2,000,000 DM from Engineer funds, 4,600,000 DM from GARIOA (Government and Relief in Occupied Areas) funds, and 45,000 from Engineer (ESA) appropriated funds.[187]

36. Training and Experience Values

The air lift also had its values. On the human side, it was the means of giving food and warmth and courage to over two million people. On the political side, it bulwarked the American government's policy of living up to its commitments and holding to the rights it had fought for. In its military aspect, the aspect

---

[184]Interview with Col Myer; EUCOM, Deputy Commander in Chief's Weekly Staff Conference Report, No 42, 19 Oct 48, p 8; ibid., No 41, 12 Oct 48, p 6.

[185]Interview with Col A.V. Winton, Deputy Director, Log Div, EUCOM, 23 Feb 49.

[186]Information from Operations Br, Trans Div, EUCOM.

[187]Engr Div, Spec Rpt, "Engineer Participation in Operation VITTLES," 9 Nov 48.

with which the European Command was directly concerned, it provided unprecedented peacetime opportunities for developing better air-ground coordination in air-supply operations, afforded an occasion to test and improve equipment used by the Transportation and Engineer Corps, proved an occasion for intensive experience in airfield construction, and showed how a military community could continue to function satisfactorily under the limitations of air supply.

Headquarters Berlin Command
Office of Military Government for Germany (US)
Berlin, Germany
APO 742, US Army

1 April 1948

MEMORANDUM FOR THE COMMANDING OFFICER, BERLIN COMMAND, OMGUS

SUBJECT: Air Lift for US Sector of Berlin

I. Problem:

To determine the amount of air lift in terms of C-47 cargo and transport planes, to provide complete air lift for the support of the US Sector of Berlin.

II. Assumptions:

a. That the US and Allied strength of Berlin is to remain approximately constant.

b. That the support now being rendered by the military to Military Government, and other agencies will continue.

c. That all personnel travel will be confined to duty travel or permanent change of station travel. (Except persons going on leave from Berlin).

d. That no rail transportation will be available within the US Sector of Berlin.

e. Cargo and transport planes to be used will be based on Rhein-Main, and will carry sufficient fuel and lubricants for the round trip to Berlin.

f. All motor cargo transportation from the air head to present DPs will be under the control of the Transportation Officer, Berlin Command.

g. POL DP will be established at Tempelhof for the Quartermaster, in lieu of RTO SO.

h. A provisional depot company from each of the supply services to be established at Tempelhof in a hangar provided for that purpose.

i. That the normal cargo load of the C-47 aeroplane is four thousand (4,000) pounds, increasable to six thousand (6,000) pounds under favorable flying conditions; that the controlling factor is weight. With the exception of heavy items such as POL, normally the bulk which may be accommodated by a C-47 aeroplane will not reach its weight capacity.

III. Requirements per month by class and type of supply in terms of US tons (2,000 pounds) and cubic feet.

Class and Type	Tons	Cubic Feet
Special Service Supplies and Equipment	10	1,836
Ordnance	78	3,120
Medical Supplies	8	1,800
Signal Supplies and Official Signal Messenger Service	2.5	408
Mail (Air Mail and First Class)	19	8,500
(2d, 3d, 4th Class, PP, Newspapers and Periodicals)	200	50,000
Engineer Class II and IV Supplies	748	42,145
Quartermaster Class I (Perishable)	362	14,501
Class I (Fresh Milk)	147	5,900
Class I (Non-Perishable)	742	29,369
Class II	95	3,800
Class III (85,000 gals)	300	17,000
Class IV	2	80
Class VI	74	7,500
Post Exchange Supplies	170	21,000
Total	2,957.5	206,959

IV. Average requirements for inbound travel of personnel per month:

a. Duty 460 (Air): 2,843 (Rail) - Total . 3,303

b. Leave 161 (Air): 521 (Rail) - Total 682

Aggregate - 3,985

V. Discussion:

a. In consideration of the supply problem, requirements have been studied in two phases:

(1) Normal consumption based on experience factors in this area.

(2) Minimum essentials necessary in the conduct of requisite activities, and the maintenance of high standards of health, sanitation and morale.

The requirements presented in Section III above, with the exception of Quartermaster Class I and Medical Supplies, are in the category of minimum essentials. The exceptions, that is Quartermaster Class I and medical supplies, have been listed based on the normal rate of consumption. It is appreciated, however, that in the event of limited availability of aerial transport, all requirements as listed could be curtailed to a limited degree without seriously affecting the desired standards. This was the major factor in determining the priorities indicated hereinafter.

b. As of this date, there are on hand in local stocks, Quartermaster Class III (POL) supplies in the following quantities (gallons):

Gasoline MT - 72	1,218,054
MT - 80	40,212
MT - 100	121,943
Diesel Oil	44,864
Kerosene	43,666
SAE-10	9,005
SAE-30	4,850
SAE-50	486
SAE-90 (Lub)	2,868
Grease #1	1,958
#2	2,620
#3	373

c. The normal consumption of gasoline in Berlin for ground use, including that for privately owned vehicles, is 440,000 gallons. Normal air consumption is 65,000 gallons. Air consumption is of no moment at this time, since all planes refuel in the Zone. We have, therefore, a total gallonage for ground use of 1,380,209. This does not include that stored at Tempelhof Air Field. At normal consumption rate, we have approximately three (3) months supply. By rationing gasoline for only minimum essential use, I believe we could stretch this over a period of six months. There is therefore no immediate problem of POL.

d. Class I supplies are on hand for forty-five (45) to sixty (60) days. Class VI supplies are on hand for fifteen (15) to thirty (30) days. Medical supplies are on hand for thirty (30) days. PX supplies are on hand for from thirty (30) days to six (6) months (Cigarettes four months). Signal supplies are on hand for thirty (30) days. Engineer supplies are on hand for thirty (30) days. Ordnance Class II and IV are on hand for forty-five (45) days.

VI. Air Lift required:

To provide air lift on the basis set out above, will require a maximum of fifty (50) C-47 plane trips per day.

VII. Recommend Priorities:

1. Medical Supplies
2. Mail
3. Class I (fresh milk)
4. Essential Travel
5. Signal Supplies
6. Sanitary utility and PX Supplies
7. Office Supplies
8. Ordnance, Class II and IV
9. Class VI
10. Quartermaster Class II and IV
11. Special Service

POL (The priority to be established as the situation develops - see below).

An initial air lift of twenty-five (25) tons per day is in operation. USAFE will step up as we desire, assuming there is no interference with corridor or landing rights. I have been in contact with Chief, Supply Branch, Logistics Division, Headquarters EUCOM (Rear). All outstanding requisitions have been cancelled; automatic supply has been instituted. EUCOM (Rear) will ship what we ask for. Cable report of the supply situation existing in Berlin, together with requests for shipment will be dispatched late to-day. It may not be necessary to curtail any of the requirements stated in Section III. It will be noted that Section III includes transportation of POL. I do not believe that we should air lift POL for the time being. If as the situation develops, it appears that it will be necessary, we can start.

VIII. Recommendations:

a. Although we are assured of adequate supplies by air lift, I see no reason why we should continue to ship luxury PX items,

Engineer construction materials and so forth, into Berlin. I think we should immediately start on the rationing of gasoline. A separate recommendation will be submitted on this point. I do not recommend any rationing in food supplies at this stage. However, the Quartermaster will be instructed to restrict sale in commissary of critical items such as canned milk, on the 'so many per customer' basis. It may or may not be necessary to ration food supplies later.

b. Recommend that the priorities stated above be approved as the basis for air lift. Stock levels will be watched closely and modifications in the above priorities will be recommended if such become necessary.

Tel: Berlin 44897

DEWITT THOMPSON
Lt Colonel, GSC (sgd w/initials
DWT)

30 July 1948

SUBJECT: Instructions to Commander, Airlift Task Force
(Provisional)

TO: Major General William H. Tunner
Headquarters, United States Air Forces in Europe
APO 633, US Army

1. You are designated as Commander, Airlift Task Force (Provisional). The mission of the Airlift Task Force is to provide airlift to Berlin and such other places as may be directed by the Commanding General, USAFE.

2. You will exercise direct operational control of personnel and equipment allocated to your Task Force at:

a. Wiesbaden (Y-30), Rhein-Main, Tempelhof Air Force bases, and such other airbases as may be designated in all matters pertaining to this mission.

b. Oberpfaffenhofen and any other depots available to this command and engaged in the progressive heavy maintenance of transport aircraft (not including depot maintenance).

c. The Air Traffic Control Center at Frankfurt and any other such centers which may be established incident to your mission.

3. You will exercise operational control over all aircraft using the Frankfurt-Berlin air corridor and the air space allocated to your mission in any other corridor.

4. You are authorized to communicate directly with the following agencies in any other matters indicated:

a. Military Air Transport service for MATS personnel, aircraft, and equipment which have been or may be assigned to your Task Force.

b. EUCOM in respect to air cargo, loading and unloading of aircraft.

B/L Hq. USAFE, Subject: "Instructions to Commander, Airlift Task Force (Provisional), to Maj Gen William H. Tunner, dtd 30 Jul 48

5. Respective station, wing base, or group commanders will remain entirely responsible for administrative details incidental to this operation and will retain their normal station, wing base, or group commander responsibilities.

6. You will keep the Commanding General, USAFE, regularly advised as to the status of this project and will make known to this headquarters any needs you may have for its successful accomplishment.

7. You are authorized to organize and maintain at 11 Taunusstrasse, Wiesbaden or such other place as may be specifically designated, a headquarters to assist you in the performance of your mission.

8. Reference is invited to the inclosure, General Orders No. 59, Headquarters, USAFE, dtd 29 Jul 48.

BY COMMAND OF LIEUTENANT GENERAL LEMAY:

1 Incl
  GO #59 (dup)

A TRUE COPY:

/s/ Cecil L. Reynolds
/t/ CECIL L. REYNOLDS
  Captain, USAF
  USAF Historian

A. W. KISSNER
Brigadier General, USAF
Chief of Staff

AIR HEADQUARTERS
BRITISH AIR FORCES OF OCCUPATION (GERMANY), UNITED STATES
AIR FORCES IN EUROPE, ROYAL AIR FORCE
C/O B.A.O.R.1.

                APO 633
                U.S. ARMY

SUBJECT: Letter Directive for Combined USAF-RAF Airlift Task Force

TO: Major General William H. Tunner, US Air Forces

1. By agreement with the Air Officer Commander-in-Chief, British
Air Forces of Occupation, announcement is hereby made of the establishment of Headquarters, Combined Airlift Task Force. Major
General William H. Tunner, USAF, is designated Commander thereof
and shall be located in Wiesbaden for the time being, Air Commodore J. W. F. Merer, No. 46 Group, R. A. F. is designated Deputy
Commander and will be located at Buckeburg. The Combined Airlift
Task Force shall be organized generally along the lines indicated
in the attached organizational charts.

2. The purpose of this organization is to merge the heretofore coordinated, but independent, USAF-RAF Airlift efforts in order that
the resources of each participating service may be utilized in the
most advantageous manner. Its primary mission is to deliver to
Berlin, in a safe and efficient manner, the maximum tonnage possible, consistent with the combined resources of equipment and personnel made available.

3. Matters of policy and emergency planning of mutual concern to
USAFE and BAFO, and effecting the Combined Airlift Task Force, will
be agreed upon by the Commanding General, USAFE and the Air Officer
Commander-in-Chief, BAFO prior to dissemination as combined USAFE-
BAFO directives. Matters not covered by combined policy directives
and requiring immediate action will be noted upon by the Commanding
General, Combined Airlift Task Force and information of action will
be forwarded expeditiously to USAFE and BAFO with request for future
guidance. Routine matters related to base logistics and personnel
administration, singularly peculiar to either USAFE or BAFO, will
be handled as heretofore; that is, directly with the air base concerned. Each of these major commands will provide complete support
at bases used solely by its own operating forces, and each will be
responsible for administrative functions at bases within its own

- 59 -

Zones or Sectors when such bases are utilized operationally by air units of the other. The Task Force will monitor this support and advise USAFE and BAFO Headquarters of any deficiencies which adversely affect the mission of the Task Force.

4. The major functions of the Combined Airlift Task Force shall be generally operational in nature rather than administrative. The Commanding General, is given command over all U.S. units and operational control of R.A.F. units to which aircraft are assigned and which are directly engaged in the Airlift effort. He is granted the authority to direct Wing, Base and Station Commander, as a first priority mission, to provide within the limits of their capabilities administrative and logistical support for his operating units. He is further granted the authority and responsibility to regulate **all** air traffic entering or leaving the air-space utilized by Airlift aircraft in the delivery of supplies to Berlin, subject to such policies as may be jointly issued from time to time by USAFE and BAFO. He is also empowered to direct the operational aspects of those elements of air traffic control agencies, facilities and services assigned to support the Airlift in order to insure their proper contribution to the Airlift. He will keep the Commanding General, USAFE and the A.O. Cin C. BAFO informed as to the program of the Airlift effort, and as to major difficulties encountered in the accomplishment of his mission.

5. Normal channels of communication for Airlift Task Force are through USAFE or BAFO Headquarters; however, authority is granted for the Commanding General, Combined Airlift Task Force to communicate directly with the following on matters indicated.

    (a) EUCOM, EAOR and BICO relative to supplies being transported to and from Berlin, including but not limiting to maintenance of backlogs, safe and expeditious handling of supplies of airports, and management of cargo handlers.

    (b) Headquarters Military Air Transport Service and R.A.F. Transport Command relative to personnel, technical and training matters.

/s/ A.P.N. Saunders
SIR ARTHUR P.N. SAUNDERS,
    AIR MARSHAL
AIR OFFICER COMMANDER-in-CHIEF

/s/ Curtis E. LeMay
    CURTIS E. LEMAY
Lieutenant General, USAF
    Commanding.

A G R E E M E N T

This agreement entered into this 25th day of August, 1948, between the Military Governor of the French Sector, Berlin, Germany, and the Commanding General, U.S. Air Forces in Europe, Wiesbaden, Germany, for the construction and use of an airfield at Schiessplatz Tegel, French Sector, Berlin, Germany, hereinafter called the Tegel Air Base, witnesseth that the parties hereto do mutually agree as follows:

I. CONSTRUCTION:

 a. The French Military Governor agrees to turn over to the US Air Forces in Europe the area known as Schiessplatz Tegel, French Sector, Berlin, Germany, for the construction and operation of an air base.

 b. Tegel Air Base will be constructed by the United States Berlin Military Post Engineers in conformity with the plans and specifications prescribed by the United States Air Forces in Europe.

 c. The French Military Governor agrees to aid this construction by putting at the disposal of the Berlin Military Post Engineers in such quantities as can be made available, such items as are requested by them; these items to include construction equipment, trucks, German manpower, construction material, etc. The procurement of these items and agreements of the amounts to be supplied will be arranged through the respective French and American Military Governments.

 d. It is highly desirable that the transmitting tower of Radio Berlin and the adjacent uncompleted steel tower be dismantled and that the buildings now occupied by personnel of Radio Berlin, north of these towers, be requisitioned for the administrative and operational use of the Tegel Air Base. This will of course depend on the political situation in Berlin and will be the subject of future discussion and agreement.

 e. In the event of the lifting of the transportation blockade between Berlin and the Western Zones, the American authorities do not commit themselves to complete the construction of the airfield. The French authorities could proceed with the work if they see fit to do so and the American authorities, without making any commitment, will study the situation and decide whether it would be possible for them to place at the disposal of the

French engineers the material already on the premises, particularly the steel plates.

II. COMMAND JURISDICTION.

a. The French authorities will assume command of the Tegel Air Base and it will be placed under French colors upon the completion of construction by the Berlin Military Post Engineers; however, the American authorities will have the right to fly the American flag on one of the buildings in their area.

b. The Command authority mentioned in paragraph IIa above will assume all the normal military obligations incident to the operation of a military post, including but not limiting thereto, the following:

(1) Security and safeguarding of Tegel Air Base.

(2) Maintenance of roads.

(3) Repair of buildings, maintenance of utilities (water, power, telephones, etc.).

c. A French Base detachment will be stationed on the field to service the French airplanes. The Commanding Officer of this detachment will assume command for the security of the airfield and perform the liaison between the French and American authorities.

III. OPERATIONAL CONTROL.

a. The United States Air Forces in Europe will assume all operational control and responsibility in regards to airplanes and airdrome operations.

b. Upon the deactivation of Headquarters, Airlift Task Force (Provisional), the Operational control responsibility will revert to the French Military Government within a delay as short as possible but not to exceed 90 days from date of such deactivation.

c. In case of a new blockade, the operational control of the airfield will revert to the American authorities within five (5) days according to the conditions specified in this paragraph III: Operational control should be delegated to the American authorities at any time by agreement between the two parties hereto.

d. During operational control by the US Air Forces in Europe, French Airplanes will have the right to utilize the Tegel Air Base without charge of landing or other fees.

e. Military Naval and Marine Corps airplanes of the
United States Government will have the right for all time to use
the Tegel Air Base without charge of landing or other fees by the
French Military Government.

f. The following activities are to be considered as subject to Operational Control:

    (1) Operation of all classified equipment.

    (2) Operation of Ground Control Approach.

    (3) Operation of code rooms, deciphering and
        enciphering devices.

    (4) All factors relating to the command, control
        and administration of American Nationals,
        including the security, safeguarding, and
        military policing of the American area of
        the airfield.

    (5) All supply, maintenance and repair of
        American-owned aircraft and component
        parts, facilities, equipment, etc.

    (6) Cargo handling.

    (7) Handling passengers of the American airplanes.

    (8) Weight and balance for the American airplanes.

    (9) American motor pool.

   (10) Maintenance of runways, lighting facilities.

   (11) Flight operations.

   (12) Navigation and briefing.

   (13) Tower and flight activities.

   (14) Communications (except where it applies to
        Para IIb(3).

   (15) Radio maintenance.

   (16) Weather forecasting.

g. Authority is granted to base such American aircraft at the Tegel Air Base as is deemed necessary by the Commanding General, United States Air Forces in Europe.

h. French military personnel will be invited to participate as observers in operational functions.

IV. ADMINISTRATIVE:

a. Suitable space in the Camp Napoleon, or any other location accepted by the American authorities, will be provided for approximately five American officers and one hundred American airmen to include sleeping quarters, messing and bathing facilities, and such office space as is necessary.

b. The administration and discipline of the American troops will be exercised by the senior American officer stationed at Tegel Air Base.

c. The American troops will abide by all the French rules and regulations in force in the Camp Napoleon.

d. Respective grades of American officers, non-commissioned officers and airmen will be allowed their respective privileges in the Camp Napoleon in regards to recreation and clubs.

e. The American military force will supply all of its own requirements of bedding, food, supplies, etc.

f. Medical services for the United States Troops will be provided by the United States authorities.

g. French religious services will be extended to American personnel, provided, however, that a suitable place will also be provided for religious services by the United States chaplain.

h. Because the assignment of buildings to be constructed for or occupied by the personnel to be assigned to Tegel Air Base cannot yet be determined, no agreement can be made at this time as to control, but the French and American authorities will occupy such buildings or parts of buildings as are necessary to their respective Command or Operational jurisdictions.

i. Drivers of American vehicles will respect and observe the traffic code and regulations of Tegel Air Base, and will be subject to the control of French Military Police, who will report all violations by United States personnel to United States authorities for appropriate disciplinary action.

j. Authority will be granted to operate a snack bar in one of the operational buildings.

k. The United States Air Forces in Europe will be granted authority to hire either American, French, or German civilian personnel through either the American or French Military Governments.

V. SUPPLIES:

a. United States Air Forces in Europe will supply the necessary equipment for the operational control of the field. This equipment will be inventoried and attached to this agreement as annex.

b. All supplies and equipment necessary for the billeting of American troops in the Camp Napoleon will be withdrawn upon the withdrawal of American troops.

c. All communications and navigational aid equipment will be installed by the United States Air Forces in Europe to permit the opening and operation of the Tegel Air Base. All such equipment will remain in the property of the United States Air Forces in Europe.

d. Motor vehicle fuel and oil will be issued to American vehicles from the French Motor Pool if desired by United States Forces in Europe and will be replaced in kind by the United States Air Forces in Europe at frequent intervals.

e. Authority will be granted to install tanks or such equipment for the servicing of airplanes with gasoline and oil, if considered necessary by US Air Forces in Europe, and this service will be extended to French airplanes on the same basis as is contained in the agreement now in force at the Tempelhof Air Force Base. However, nothing in this agreement will be considered binding for the US Air Forces in Europe to furnish gasoline or oil to French airplanes if it is considered unnecessary to make such installation.

f. If and when operations of Tegel Air Base are turned over to French jurisdiction, all communications and navigational aid equipment installed by the United States will be removed by US Air Forces in Europe. The French Military Governor agrees either to undertake to replace this equipment and accomplish the installation of the French equipment within ninety (90) days after the turnover of control to the French Military Government or to open negotiations for the purchase or the renting of such equipment. This 90-day period will permit continuous operation of the field.

g. All permanent installations of the Airfield such as buildings, runways, taxiways, and parking aprons will be left as they are and will be transferred to the French authorities free of charge upon withdrawal of American troops from Tegel Air Base.

VI. REIMBURSEMENTS.

In consideration of the material and money expended by the United States Government or its agencies, upon the construction and maintenance of the Tegel Air Base, the French Military Governor will not charge the US Air Forces in Europe, the United States Government or its agencies any fees for services rendered except as follows:

a. Through agreement between the respective military governments.

b. When matters arise which may be deemed important enough to be the subject of further discussion by either party to this agreement.

VII. GENERAL.

The French Government does hereby forever release and discharge the United States, its agencies, agents, and or military, civilian or contract personnel acting within the scope of their employment, for any and all liabilities, claims or demands of any nature of character whatsoever arising out of or from any act, omission, negligence, quality of supplies, services rendered, or any cause whatsoever, in connection with the use of the Tegel Air Base or facilities by the United States Air Forces in Europe, excepting such liabilities, claims, or demands as result from the wilful misconduct of any agencies, agents, military civilian or contact personnel of or under contract with the United States.

IN WITNESS WHEREOF these presents are subscribed by General de Brigade Jean Ganeval, Military Governor of French Sector, Berlin, Germany, and Lieutenant General Curtis E. LeMay, Commanding General, United States Air Forces in Europe, Wiesbaden, Germany, this 25th day of August, 1948.

CURTIS E. LEMAY	JEAN GANEVAL
Lieutenant General, USAF	General de Brigade
Commanding General, United States Air Forces in Europe, Wiesbaden, Germany	Military Governor of Berlin, and Commanding General of French Troops in Berlin, Germany

Tonnages Lifted to Berlin in U.S. Aircraft Between 21 June 1948 and Noon 31 December 1948

Inbound Cargo	21-30 Jun	1-31 Jul	1-31 Aug[1]	1-30 Sep[2]	1-31 Oct[3]	1-30 Nov[4]	1-31 Dec[5]
AF Supply	—	—	—	—	—	—	102.9
QM Class I	862.43	524.89	1,542.61	1,140.55	1,191.0	975.1	817.8
QM Class I (Perishables)	78.11	50.49	23.24	52.52	282.2	648.9	368.2
QM Class III	—	135.82	47.18	79.32	1,288.8	1,392.7	1,698.3
QM Class II & IV	—	34.69	56.79	274.99	389.0	115.1	114.1
Engr Class II & IV	—	56.71	357.07	645.66	208.2	192.7	164.6
Engr (Air Force)	—	873.18	1,769.81	2,922.83	2,468.7	774.6	882.5
Ord II & IV	—	7.20	91.58	105.97	105.7	87.4	81.6
Medical	.60	7.55	12.49	10.43	—	26.0	7.3
Signal	—	2.02	14.85	—	18.6	17.0	25.8
EES	—	2.43	28.78	68.87	76.1	136.7	266.8
Special Services	—	—	.41	2.05	—	5.6	13.1
US Mail	38.45	82.88	83.74	130.58	129.2	138.3	192.8
Miscellaneous	9.85	37.27	50.67	86.42	77.2	173.2	86.1
CA Food	622.05	24,763.37	18,934.20	23,751.69	26,328.5	20,966.7	35,604.9
CA Coal	—	13,907.08	42,891.89	65,396.70	69,927.9	52,135.4	67,492.9
CA Mail	—	14.72	3.48	—	—	—	—
CA Medical	—	1.25	17.91	36.72	63.5	42.5	98.9
CA Miscellaneous	—	—	154.09	503.35	364.8	770.9	1,459.9
US Coal	—	—	—	—	4,159.1	—	—
Engr Coal	—	—	—	—	—	4,716.2	4,090.5
French Coal	—	—	—	—	1,191.8	1,816.4	1,826.9
French Miscellaneous	—	673.31	541.09	600.62	827.9	492.1	853.6
	1,611.49	41,174.86	66,621.88	95,809.27	109,098.2	85,623.5	116,249.5

(1) Hq EUCOM, DCINC's Wkly Staff Conf.No.37, 14 Sep 48, p.7. (2) BMP, S4 Mthly Rept "Airlift Cargo," September 1948. (3) Hq EUCOM, DCINC's Wkly Staff Conf No. 46, 16 Nov 48, p.8. (4) Ibid., No. 50, 14 Dec 48, p.8. (5) Ibid., No. 12, 22 Mar 49, pp. 10 - 11.

Note: Figures for June - November collected by Lt R. P. Boehner, formerly of Historical Division, Hq EUCOM.

Tonnages Lifted From Berlin in U.S. Aircraft Between 21 June and Noon 31 December 1948

Outbound Cargo	21-30 Jun	1-31 Jul[1]	1-31 Aug[1]	1-30 Sep[2]	1-31 Oct[3]	1-30 Nov[4]	1-31 Dec[5]
QM Class II & IV	235.29	84.37	86.12	93.580	269.9	119.5	48.6
Medical	—	.50	.50	—	—	—	—
Engr Class II & IV	48.40	2.30	23.55	13.046	32.9	12.4	136.5
Household Goods	141.61	351.30	280.12	567.982	361.7	166.6	224.9
Ord Class II & IV	32.88	13.61	6.31	—	33.2	45.2	88.2
Signal	13.54	21.47	—	48.207	5.6	3.6	5.6
Air Force Materials	—	.70	6.27	—	4.9	18.6	26.2
Documents and OMGUS Office Equipment	—	86.42	223.65	28.808	33.3	—	20.2
Misc Frt (ACT)	9.28	136.36	86.76	79.674	71.0	4.8	65.3
US Mail	20.57	50.31	45.30	130.915	47.5	35.0	47.6
Misc Frt	76.33	48.09	—	80.682	—	62.2	11.6
Private Vehicles	—	—	5.23	227.673	209.5	104.3	40.7
War Dead	—	—	.95	—	—	—	—
French	—	—	1.50	68.098	69.0	51.6	51.3
CA Industrial Items	—	558.69	321.81	298.171	521.6	572.0	1,036.3
CA Mail	—	12.49	25.36	71.382	161.2	281.9	1,172.1
CA Newspapers	—	—	—	—	.2	.2	—
CA Baggage	—	—	—	—	120.2	—	.7
	577.90	1,366.61	1,113.43	1,707.218	1,941.7	1,477.9	2,975.8

(1) Hq EUCOM, DCINC's Wkly Staff Conf No. 37, 14 Sep 48, pp. 7 - 8. (2) BMP, S4 Mthly Rept, "Airlift Cargo," September 1948. (3) Hq EUCOM, DCINC's Wkly Staff Conf No. 46, 16 Nov 48, p. 9. (4) Ibid., No. 50, 14 Dec 48, pp. 8 - 9. (5) Ibid., No. 12, 22 Mar 49, p. 11.

Note: Figures for June - November collected by Lt. R. P. Boehner.

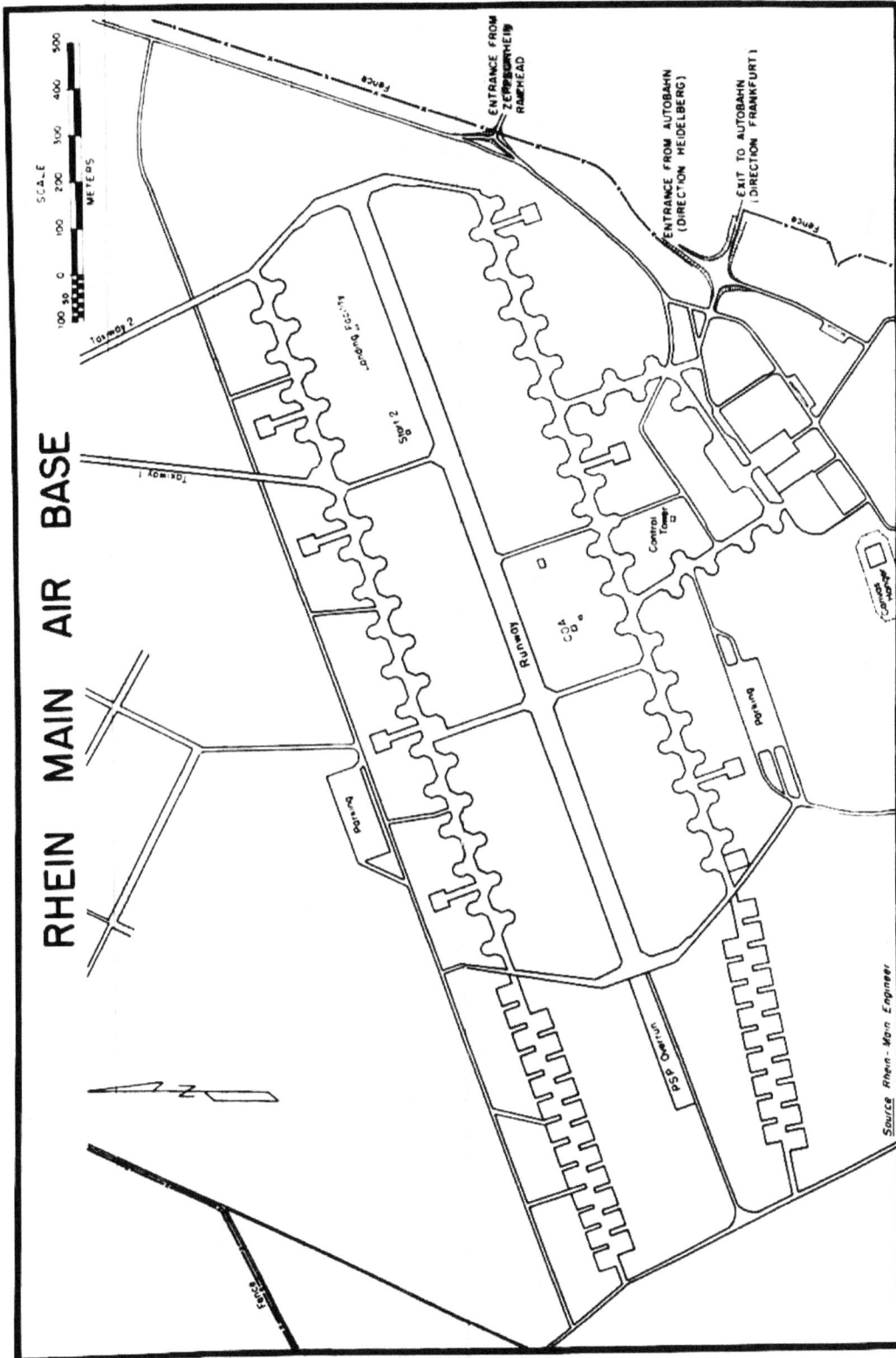

RHEIN MAIN AIR BASE

ENTRANCE FROM ZEPPELINHEIM RAILHEAD

ENTRANCE FROM AUTOBAHN (DIRECTION HEIDELBERG)

EXIT TO AUTOBAHN (DIRECTION FRANKFURT)

Fence

Fence

Fence

SCALE

METERS

Taxiway 2

Loading Ramp

Start 2

Taxiway 1

Control Tower

COA

Runway

Parking

Parking

PSP Overrun

Source Rhein-Main Engineer

TEMPELHOF — AIRBASE

PLOT – PLAN
AFTER CONSTRUCTION

Scale

FEET

0 200 400 600 800 1000
   100 300 500 700 900

CEMETERY

RIFLE RANGE

PAVED APRON

HANGARS & OFFICES

Source: Copied from plan prepared by Hq BMP, Office of the Engineer, as revised to 30 December 1948

- 70 -

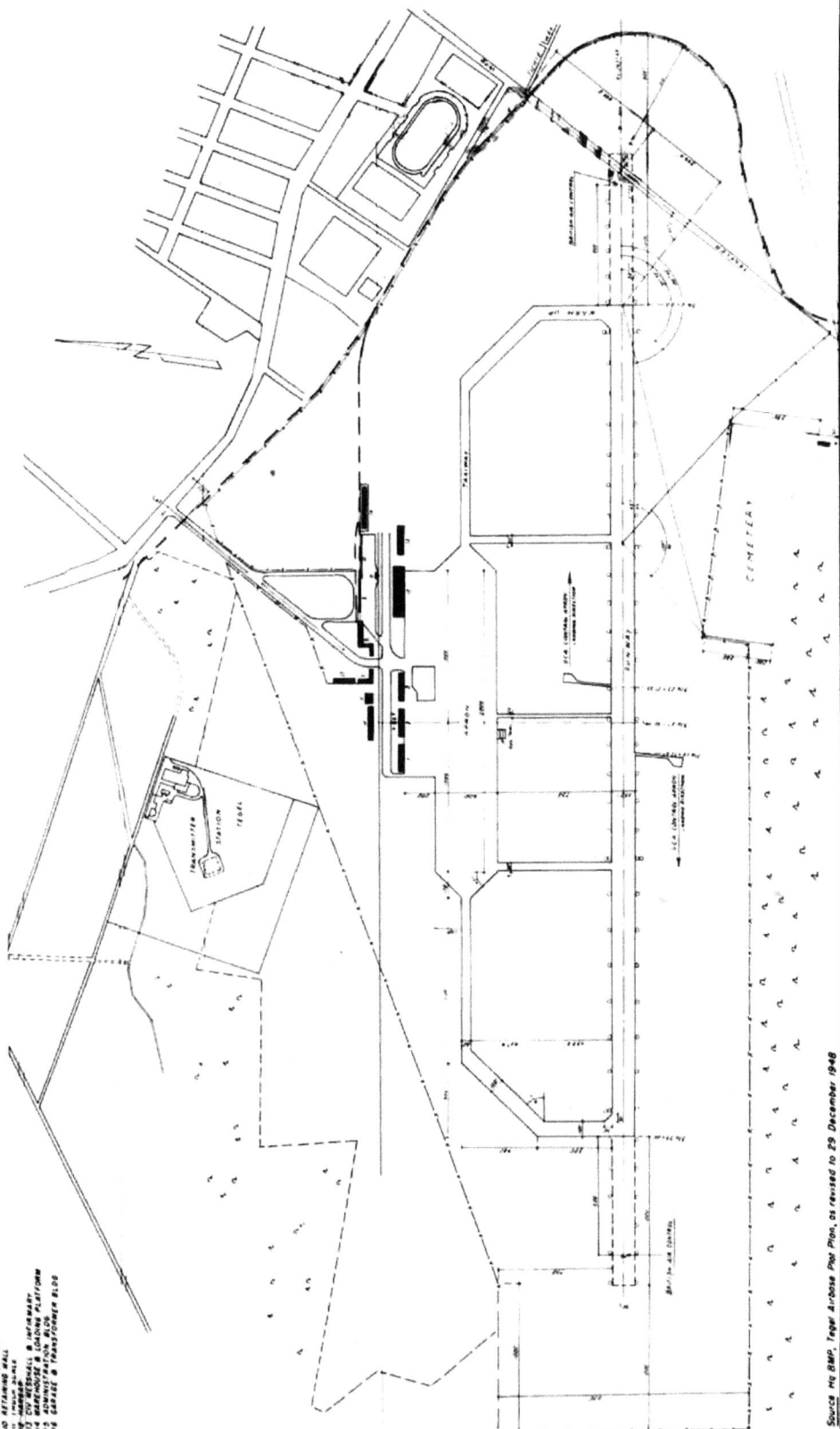

TEGEL AIRBASE

— PLOT PLAN —

SCALE 1:4,000

LEGEND

1. ADMINISTRATION BLDG. FRENCH
2. ADMINISTRATION BLDG.
3. UTILITIES BLDG.
4. CONTROL TOWER
5. ELECT. STATION
6. BOILER HOUSE
7. BREAD HOUSE
8. FRENCH ADMINISTRATION BLDG.
9. LOADING PLATFORM
10. RETAINING WALL
11. HANGAR
12. DINING HALL & INFIRMARY
13. CPT. BARRACKS & LOADING PLATFORM
14. WAREHOUSE & LOADING PLATFORM
15. ADMINISTRATION BLDG.
16. GARAGE & TRANSFORMER BLDG.

Source: HQ BMP, Tegel Airbase Plot Plan, as revised to 29 December 1948

PART II

1 January – 30 September 1949

The object of this study is to provide a record of both
the action taken and the experience gained by the European Command
in the Berlin air lift. It supplements an earlier monograph, "The
Berlin Air Lift, 26 June - 31 December 1948," published in the
spring of 1949.

The Berlin air lift of 26 June 1948 to 30 September 1949 had
two purposes. Initially it was intended to maintain American,
British, and French occupation establishments in Berlin in the
face of Soviet restrictions on military rail and highway transport to Western Germany. Its second objective was to support the
inhabitants of Western Berlin pending the re-opening of normal
transportation channels. Both of these purposes were achieved
with notable success.

As a history of the part played by the European Command in
the air lift this monograph, like the earlier study, is concerned
primarily with the role of the ground forces in providing ground
support.

In scope this study has been limited to the airlift role of
Headquarters, European Command, and its subordinate units and
agencies. The activities of other agencies taking part in the
lift -- primarily the United States Air Forces in Europe (USAFE)
and various organizations of the military government -- are outlined only to the extent necessary to provide background for the
role of the ground forces. The role of the United States Air
Force has been extensively recorded and illustrated in official
publications of that organization; classified monographs and
reports issued by the Historical Office, USAFE, provide detailed
coverage of air operations involved in the lift and careful
analysis of problems relating to supply, maintenance, and personnel.
Trade publications have provided both narrative and pictorial
coverage of the lift, while noting the experience of the air
force with various commercial products. Background developments
in Berlin are described in Decision in Germany by General Lucius
D. Clay and in Berlin Command by Brig. Gen. Frank Howley. Berlin
Bastion, by Lowell Bennett, provides an account of everyday life
in Berlin during the blockade. These studies have not been concerned with ground force support of the lift.

Most of the material on which the study is based had been
obtained from interviews with staff members and the study of

records of Headquarters, USAFE, and Headquarters, First Air Lift Task Force, in Wiesbaden; Headquarters, European Command, in Heidelberg; Headquarters, United States Army Airlift Support Command, Frankfurt; Frankfurt Military Post; Berlin Military Post; the Office of Military Government, Berlin, and Office of the High Commissioner for Germany, Berlin Element; and the Bipartite Control Office, Frankfurt. The patience and courtesy shown by staff members of these agencies have made the research for this study pleasant as well as possible. For opportunities to observe at first hand the ground-force support of operations at Rhein/Main, Tempelhof, and Wiesbaden airfields the author is particularly indebted to officers of the Transportation Corps. Acknowledgement of a further opportunity for first-hand contact with lift operations must be made to the respective Air Force and Navy crews in whose planes the author "flew the lift" in February 1949.

Contents

Appendixes

Tables

Charts

Maps

Plans

Graphs

CHAPTER I

Introduction

1. Continuing Need for the Air Lift

The beginning of 1949 brought no change in the conditions
which had required the support of western Berlin by air since
the end of June 1948.[1] Within those six months the lift, known
to Americans as "Operation VITTLES" and to the British as "Operation PLAINFARE,"[2] had grown from a few shipments of flour in a
handful of C-47's to an aerial supply operation involving eleven
airfields, hundreds of planes and pilots, the labor of many

_____

[1]For an account of airlift operations during 1948, with
emphasis on ground force support, see EUCOM Hist Div, OCCUPATION
FORCES IN EUROPE SERIES, 1948 - 1949, The Berlin Air Lift, 21
June - 31 December 1948 (Frankfurt, 1949). SECRET. Referred
to hereafter as "The Berlin Air Lift - 1948." Air Force aspects
of the lift are treated in two USAFE Historical Section monographs:
USAFE and the Berlin Airlift 1948, Supply and Operational Aspects
(Wiesbaden 1949); and USAFE and the Berlin Airlift 1949, Supply
and Operational Aspects (Wiesbaden 1950). Both SECRET. Berlin
Airlift, A USAFE Summary, published by USAFE (RESTRICTED), presents a comprehensive analysis. Another valuable reference is
A Report on Operation Plainfare (The Berlin Airlift), 25th June
1948 - 6th October 1949, by Air Marshal T. M. Williams, C.B.,
O. B. E., M. C., D. F. C., Commander in Chief, British Air Forces
of Occupation, prepared by BAFO, issued by Air Ministry, April
1950. RESTRICTED.

[2]This title replaced the British code name "Operation Carter
Paterson" (referring to a well-known motor transport firm) in July
1948. British planning for air supply of the military establishment in Berlin had used the code name "Knicker."

displaced persons and Germans, and a wide supporting organization of military units and personnel. Such expansion had permitted the carrying of 143,438 short tons to Berlin in British and American planes during the month of December 1948, an amount sufficient to meet minimum coal requirements and to allow adequate stockpiling of food. But still greater tonnages were demanded to meet the goals set by Allied and German authorities to safeguard Berlin politically and psychologically as well as economically. Lacking any indication of an approaching change in Soviet behavior at Berlin, the three western powers had no choice, at the beginning of 1949, but to make the lift an increasingly powerful weapon of occupation policy. The record for 1949 shows that they were able to do this, bringing airlift tonnages to impressive new totals in April and in May, at which time the blockade came to an end, and again in July, when the lift was being devoted primarily to building up coal reserves against any future contingencies which might beset western Berlin.

2. Developments in 1949

For the first three months of 1949 the lift went quietly ahead, surmounting the hazards of fog, rain, snow, and ice in the air, and of mud on the ground, particularly in the unpaved areas of the field at Rhein/Main. Combined British and U.S. lift tonnages for Berlin rose from 143,438.1 short tons in December to 171,959.2 in January,[3] fell slightly to 152,240.7 in February,[4] and rose to 196,160.7 in March.[5] On 15 April, beginning at twelve noon, the entire airlift team put its strength into a planned performance that brought 12,940.9 short tons into Berlin by air within 24 hours.[6] Meanwhile, since 15 February, United States Ambassador-at-Large Philip C. Jessup had been conferring informally at Lake Success with Jacob A. Malik, Soviet delegate to the United Nations, with a view to ending the blockade and opening the way for a meeting of the Council of Foreign Ministers.[7] Toward the end of April the pace of these discussions quickened, and the Soviet desire to lift the blockade became clear.[8]

---

[3]USAFE, History of Headquarters United States Air Forces in Europe, Jan 49, p. 27. SECRET.

[4]Ibid., Feb 49, p. 14. SECRET.

[5]Ibid., Mar 49, p. 14. SECRET.

[6]Ibid., Apr 49, p. 43. SECRET.

[7]The Washington Post, April 27, 1949, "Jessup Talks With Malik on Germany Are Divulged," p. 1, col. 8.

[8]The Christian Science Monitor, May 3, 1949, "US Imposes Stiff Terms," p. 1, col. 6 - 8.

On 5 May the Big Four agreement of 4 May on the lifting of the blockade was announced,[9] and one minute after midnight on 12 May, by order of Gen. Vassily I. Chuikov, Soviet Militar Governor in Germany, all transport, trade, and communication services between the eastern and western zones were restored.[10] Counter-blockade measures were cancelled at the same time by order of the three western commandants.[11] The general feeling of relief which followed the lifting of the blockade was marred, however, by a strike of western Berlin rail workers which began 21 May and lasted until 28 June, bringing rail traffic with the west to a standstill.[12] The rail strike, like the blockade imposed in June 1948, was complicated by questions of currency reform and the failure of the occupying powers to reach agreement on a single currency for all Germany. Not until 1 July 1949 was rail freight traffic with the western zones restored. By the end of July, western Berlin had a 109-day food reserve, a 230-day reserve of coal for public utilities and a 95-day reserve of coal for all other purposes,[13] and phase-out plans for the airlift could be stepped up, to sharply reduce tonnages for the month of August. The last load of coal was delivered from Rhein/Main to Tempelhof on 30 September, the final day of the lift.[14]

3. Outline of Airlift Organization

The organization built up during the summer and fall of 1948[15]

9(1) Ibid., May 7, 1949, "Berlin Land Routes to Reopen," p. 1, col. 4 - 6. (2) Lucius D. Clay, Decision in Germany (New York, 1950), p. 390. (3) The Stars and Stripes, Eur. ed., May 5, 1949, p. 1.

10The Christian Science Monitor, May 13, 1949, "First Allied Train Into Berlin: One Run, No Hitch, No Errors," p. 1, col. 5 - 8.

11Order BK/O (49) 92 of the Kommandatura. Brig Gen Frank Howley, Berlin Command (New York, 1950), p. 263.

12OMGUS, Mthly Rept of the Mil Gov, No. 47, May - Jun 49, pp. 3 - 5. UNCLASSIFIED.

13Ibid., No. 49, Jul 49, p. 7. UNCLASSIFIED.

14(1) USAASC R/M Det, Sum Rept Tonnage Movements (mimeographed rept). (2) Chart, Rhein/Main, Sep 49. UNCLASSIFIED. In EUCOM Trans Div file 73, USAASC.

15The Berlin Air Lift - 1948, pars 9 - 11. SECRET. Additional information on the organization for the air lift, most of it classified RESTRICTED, is given in Observers' Report, OPERATION VITTLES, Washington DC, 16 Feb 49, Annex 4, Command Relationship and Organization.

sufficed, except for a later concentration of control over ground-force support in the Frankfurt-Wiesbaden area, which materially improved the operating efficiency of such support. This organization, as it existed after the creation of the United States Army Airlift Support Command (USAASC), (see paragraph 14 below) on 6 April 1949, is pictured in Chart 1. As of 1 January 1949 various types of ground support, which will be discussed in detail in later chapters, were being furnished by Berlin Military Post, Frankfurt Military Post, and several staff divisions of Headquarters, European Command, including the Engineer Division, Ordnance Division, Signal Division, and Transportation Division, as well as by British and French occupation authorities at Berlin and the British Rear Airfield Supply Organization (RASC) in the British Zone.[16]

4. Cooperation Among Agencies

The success of the air supply operation depended on maximum flying by the Air Force, efficient loading and unloading by the Army, and timely procurement and delivery of supplies by the Bipartite Control Office (BICO) and the German agencies working under its supervision.[17] These three organizations worked together on a cooperative basis, seldom going out of technical channels to find solutions for joint problems arising out of airlift operations. At Berlin there was continuing cooperation between the Office of Military Government (Berlin Sector) (OMGBS) and Berlin Military Post (BMP) with regard to airlift operations. Except for submitting their requirements to the Air Lift Staff Committee, Berlin Military Post officials dealt directly with the technical services and their depots in the U.S. Zone on routine supply matters, clearing through European Command headquarters at Heidelberg only on major matters. Relations between USAFE and BICO, on the one hand, and the ground force elements in support at Wiesbaden and Rhein/Main on the other, were simplified and improved by the absorption of these elements into the U.S. Army Airlift Support Command.

---

[16]Mimeographed paper, The Rear Airfield Supply Organization at Celle. In EUCOM Trans Div file 3, USAASC.

[17]The Berlin Air Lift - 1948, pars. 10, 11. SECRET.

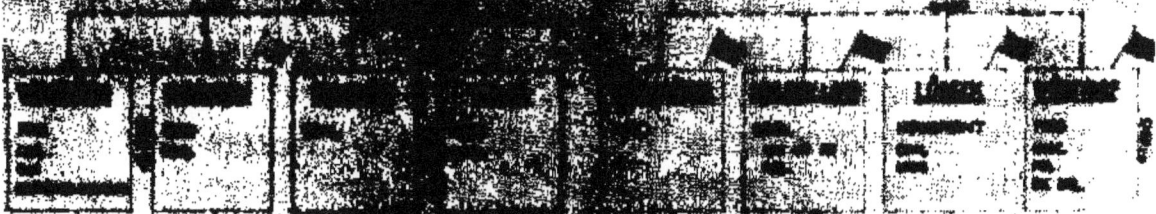

5. Main Difficulties Affecting Airlift Operations

Several main difficulties affected airlift operations. Aside from the sheer bulk of cargo requirements, some types of cargo, such as power plant equipment, gasoline, and salt presented special handling problems. The total amount thereof was negligible when compared to the total airlift tonnage. Air operations were affected by limited airfield facilities and timed corridor flying, winter weather conditions lasting into March,[18] by turnover of operating personnel and rotation of maintenance personnel, shortages of aircraft spare parts and equipment,[19] and by unfavorable loading and unloading conditions. At Berlin, military government officials were concerned by what they considered a lack of information and orientation on the part of participating enlisted and officer personnel as to the purpose and significance of the lift,[20] by losses through pilferage, and by the need for better coordination on the part of all agencies responsible for the movement of civil supplies. The work of BICO was handicapped so that delays were occasioned where cargo was not actually available due to the lack of food storage facilities on some of the zonal airfields, the lack of standardized package sizes, types and weights, lack of cooperation between the German agencies concerned with the lift, shortcomings on the part of German firms supplying and transporting food procured for Berlin[21] and the necessity for coordinating, without being able to control, the activities of German firms providing food and coal for West Berlin. Ground force support operations were affected by weather conditions, shortages of trained personnel and suitable equipment, and the need for meeting unpredictable take-off and landing schedules (partly forced on the Air Corps by the necessity for maximum flying in all good weather). A key factor in the proper loading of the planes was the standardization of packaging so that weight was evenly distributed, the plane filled to capacity, but not over loaded. Overloading was the major cause for crashes.

---

[18]USAFE, History of Headquarters United States Air Forces in Europe, Mar 49, p. 14. SECRET. In EUCOM Hist Div Docs Br.

[19]Ibid., Feb 49, p. 27. SECRET. In EUCOM Hist Div Docs Br.

[20]Interviews, E. S. Lay, EUCOM Hist Div, with Mr. C. A. Dix, Transport Advisor, Trans Div, HICOG BE, 23 Jun 50, and with Mr. Leon J. Steck, C/HICOG BE Trade and Program Br, 20 Jun 50. CONFIDENTIAL.

[21]See Appendix A, "Berlin Airlift," Summary by N. L. Smith, BICO, 24 Aug 51. CONFIDENTIAL.

6. Equipment and Facilities

The basic material needs of the airlift operation were planes, trucks, and airfields.[22]

a. Airplanes. By 1949 the 1st Air Lift Task Force (FALTF), comprising the U.S. elements in Combined Air Lift Task Force (CALTF), was assigned some 200 C-54's (capacity 10 tons), while five C-82's (capacity 5 tons) were available as needed. The British 46th Group, with headquarters first at Buckeburg and later at Luneburg, utilized 38 Yorks, 52 Dakotas, 14 Hastings, and 36 civil aircraft.[23] During the first six months of 1949 the average number of FALTF C-54 aircraft in commission increased from 117.67 in January to 131.03 in April, 132.29 in May, 133.79 in June, and 137.62 in July, while the C-82 average varied from 1.42 in January to 3.06 in May.[24] On 4 May a C-97A "Stratocruiser" joined the lift, taking part until 24 May, when it was grounded as a result of damage received while landing at Gatow.[25] By early May, when the blockade was lifted, approximately 380 British and American aircraft were assigned to the lift.[26]

b. Airfields. As of 1 January 1949 the following eleven air bases were being used by airlift planes: Tempelhof, Gatow, and Tegel at Berlin; Rhein/Main and Wiesbaden in the U.S. Zone; and Celle, Fassberg, Fuhlsbuettel, Luebeck, Schleswigland, and Wunstorf in the British Zone.[27] The location of these airfields and of the flying boat base at Finkenwerder (used until December 1948), is shown on Map 1.

---

[22]See The Berlin Air Lift - 1948, par. 13. SECRET. For the role of navigational aids and other technical equipment essential to Air Force operations in the lift, see Air Force monographs.

[23]CALTF Compt Sec, Operational Summary for period ending 1200, (mimeographed), 23 Jan 49. RESTRICTED.

[24]CALTF, Stat Sum, Jul 49, p. 4. RESTRICTED.

[25]USAFE monograph, USAFE and the Berlin Airlift 1949, Supply and Operational Aspects, p. 150, and History of Hq USAFE, Jun 49, p. 53. SECRET.

[26]OMGUS PIO, 10 May 49, OMGUS 5-D-18, release of airlift story prepared by USAFE.

[27]Observers' Report, Annex 5, Appendix A, describes airfield facilities in the western sectors of Berlin and in the U.S. Zone, giving data on runways, height above sea level, radio and radar, and night flying facilities. For information on fields in British Zone, see BAFO, Report on Operation Plainfare. RESTRICTED.

Map 1

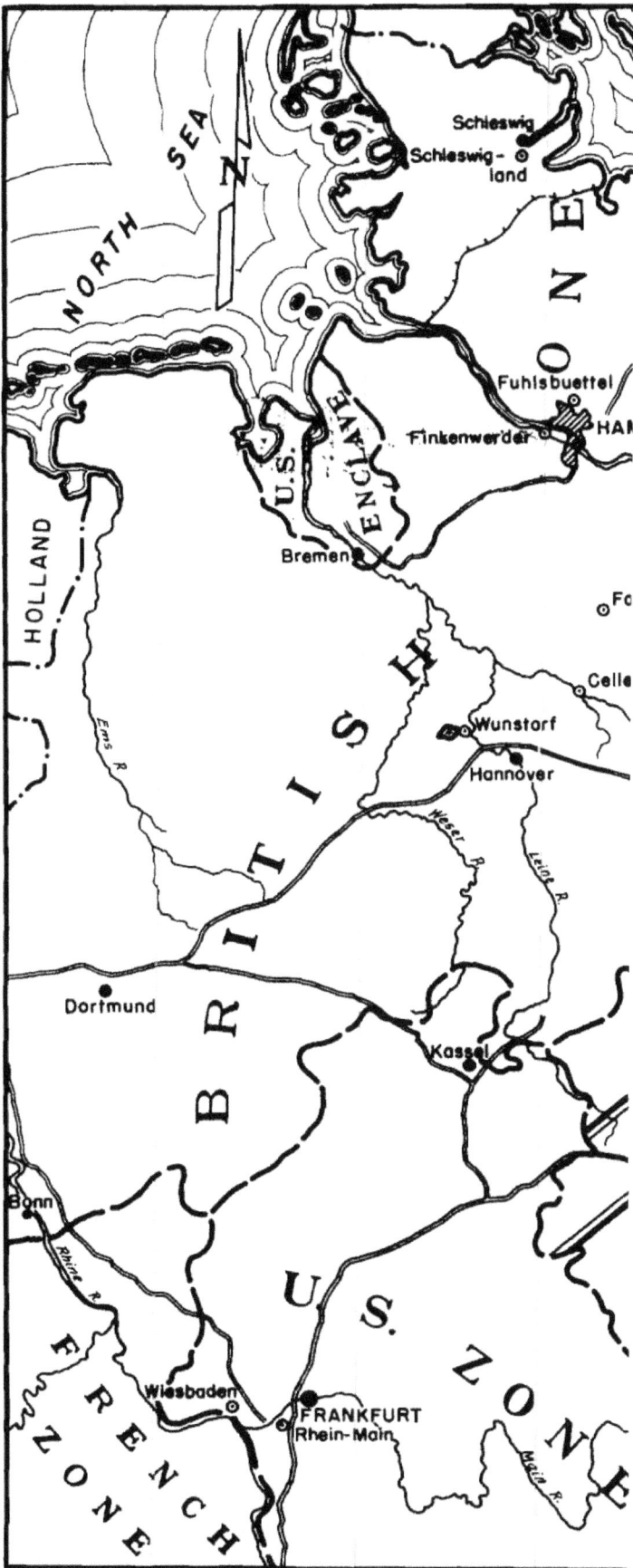

7. Limits on Airlift Expansion

The air lift as developed during the spring of 1949 was more than adequate to supply the minimum needs of western Berlin. Nevertheless it did not move as much cargo as the city had previously received by water, rail, and road transport. As the lift developed from a small to a large operation many of the initial limiting factors were overcome. But other limiting factors continued to restrict the amount of cargo which could be flown into Berlin in any given period of time. The group of Army observers who visited Germany early in 1949 to study airlift operations listed the following factors as limiting any cargo lift by air:

(1) The width of the available air lanes.

(2) The radius of the allowable takeoff, landing, loading and unloading areas.

(3) The aircraft availability.

(4) The surface transportation available for loading and unloading.[28]

By the spring of 1949 it had been demonstrated that planes and trucks and airfields were not the ultimately critical factors in the Berlin lift. A more critical limiting factor was the density of the air traffic over Berlin. Each arriving plane required its own minimum allotment of time and space to effect a landing. Given enough planes to fill a full schedule of landings, there was no reason for trying to put more planes in the air. Further expansion of the lift therefore lay in the utilization of planes with greater cargo-carrying capacity. The lift demonstrated the need for a load-carrying compartment or "air pod" which could be loaded at leisure and readily attached to and detached from the air frame. Such a "pod" could be loaded in advance and held near the loading ramps of hardstands. This development would help to decrease the amount of time spent by planes on the airfield, lessening the risk of their destruction at airheads in time of war and avoiding the many problems encountered in loading as performed in the Berlin airlift. Loading could also be handled more easily if planes had powered landing gear wheels so that they could move over terrain other than prepared hardstanding. A further step of practical value for purposes of loading and unloading

---

[28]DA, Observers' Report, Operation VITTLES, Washington DC, 16 Feb 49, p. 23. RESTRICTED (Over-all classification CONFIDENTIAL).

would be the development of wings that could fold back so the plane could move up roads, a development which would further lessen the hazards of loading under tactical conditions.[29]

8. Planning for Long-Run Operations

The Berlin lift started as a short-run demonstration of air supply potential during which current difficulties relating to Berlin were to be ironed out and settled. Subsequent experience showed that plans for a long-term operation, such as the lift turned out to be, must make provision for rest and repairs, factors not necessarily involved in a short-term operation.[30] Provision in planning must be made for maintenance and replacement of equipment used, example: trucks, trailers, and certain shop equipment. Rehabilitation and construction of shop facilities, roads, messes, and billets must be provided within the funds budgeted and made available for this specific mission. Plans should provide for ways and means of settling claims that may arise from such operations.

9. Advance Study of Airlift Logistics

The lift showed the possibility of mass movement of personnel and supplies between widely-separated points by air transport and of the establishment of airheads during war. Prior to the lift there were no logistical data available to Headquarters, European Command (EUCOM) to indicate the limitations and possibilities of an air lift for large-scale movements of military forces and supplies. The logistical data for the Berlin lift had to be implemented on a day by day emergency basis. The daily lift capacity was built up, and goods were shipped to Berlin, without the benefit of any advance logistical planning data. With the facts of the Berlin lift and other airlift operations conducted by the Army available, development of statistical data for guidance in future operations might well be undertaken in advance, using modern machine-calculating methods. Set up in accordance with key logistical data worked out in advance, and used by teams of trained technicians, such machine methods could turn out within a matter of hours the vital logistical data needed in effecting the movement of any given forces or supplies into any airhead. Following the lift, Engineer Division experts pointed out that technical staffs equipped with modern calculating machines were already in use by the Air Force on classified projects (set up by Remington Rand). It was estimated

---

29 Interv, D. S. Lay, EUCOM Hist Div, with Mr. Fred G. Scherrer, EUCOM Engr Div Ctl Br, 29 May 51. UNCLASSIFIED. And 25 Oct 51. RESTRICTED.

30 Interv, E. S. Lay, EUCOM Hist Div, with Brig Gen W. B. Palmer, Dir EUCOM Log Div, 16 Dec 48.

- 8 -

that advance development of logistical data with the aid of machines would make available within hours or minutes the results which might otherwise require the labor of highly-qualified staff officers over a period of months.[31]

10. Achievements

The general achievements of the air lift were summarized by General Lucius D. Clay, Commander in Chief, EUCOM, at the close of the operation as follows:

(1) The airlift demonstrated that air transport can be run on schedule just as any form of transport. It developed a technique comparable in its exactitude with the long-established railroad and steamship systems.

(2) It advanced by many years experimentation in various forms of equipment such as ground control landings, etc.

(3) It demonstrated the value of definite traffic patterns over an entire route instead of just at airports, to achieve maximum cargo use.

(4) Experience in these and other techniques would be of the greatest value in both civil and military operations in the future.

(5) The United States and Britain had developed from this experience staff officers having the know-how to run vast air operations with confidence and skill that did not exist before.[32]

---

[31] Interv, E. S. Lay, EUCOM Hist Div, with Mr. Fred G. Scherrer, EUCOM Engr Div Constr Br, 25 Oct 51. RESTRICTED.

[32] (1) The Christian Science Monitor, May 13, 1949, p. 2. (2) For a summary of general conclusions, particularly regarding training, see The Berlin Air Lift - 1948, par. 36. SECRET. (3) For conclusions of specific interest to the Air Force see USAFE monograph, USAFE and the Berlin Airlift 1948, especially pp. 232 - 237, (SECRET); USAFE monograph, USAFE and the Berlin Airlift 1949, pp. 353 - 380, (SECRET); and Berlin Airlift, A USAFE Summary, (RESTRICTED); containing conclusions and recommendations throughout the test. BAFO, Report on Operation Plainfare, pp. 75 - 87 (RESTRICTED), contains recommendations under the headings organization, operations, airfields, freight handling, signals, technical, equipment, and personnel.

a. Outstanding Developments. A number of developments of
general value, in addition to developments in ground support to
be discussed in the course of this study, are cited here. Specifically, these included development of a four-layer paper sack
suitable for air shipment of coal,[33] (see paragraph 58) better
control of loading (with emphasis on less mixing of commodities
and more straight cargoes) to simplify unloading procedures at
the receiving airport[34] (see paragraphs 47 through 54), construction of a new railhead and an adjacent truck dispatch area at
Rhein/Main Air Base (see paragraph 43),[35] expansion of runway
facilities at Tegel and Tempelhof (see paragraphs 40 and 42),[36]
use of British tanker aircraft to carry gasoline and oil to Berlin
(replacing the use of 55-gallon drums which had required steaming
after each trip, see paragraph 59),[37] and the establishment of the
United States Army Airlift Support Command to give unified direction to ground elements engaged in supporting the lift at
Rhein/Main and Wiesbaden Air Force Bases (see paragraph 14). The
support afforded by this command, under which coordinated agencies were functioning, enabled the U.S. Air Force to attain the
highest daily tonnage lift.

b. Cost and Value. The total cost of the Berlin air lift,
from 26 June 1948 to 30 September 1949, has been estimated at
$405,950,000. The Army phase of the lift has been estimated as
costing $11,000,000.[38] The Army cost figure does not include the

---

[33]Interv, E. S. Lay, EUCOM Hist Div, with Mr. David Tatum,
Office of General C. L. Adcock, BICO, 10 Aug 49. CONFIDENTIAL.

[34]Interv, E. S. Lay, EUCOM Hist Div, with Lt Col J. F.
Phillips, BMP Trans Off, 23 June 1950. RESTRICTED.

[35]Interv, E. S. Lay, EUCOM Hist Div, with Lt Col J. B.
Andrews, USAASC, 2 Aug 1949. UNCLASSIFIED.

[36]Interv, E. S. Lay, EUCOM Hist Div, with Mr. Nelson G.
Greene, BMP Engr Br, 22 Jun 50.

[37]Interv, E. S. Lay, EUCOM Hist Div, with Lt Col F. B. L.
Myer, BMP QM, 16 Feb 49. RESTRICTED.

[38](1) Figure of $405,950,000 used by BMP briefing officer.
Interv, E. S. Lay, EUCOM Hist Div, with Capt J. T. Babbitt, C/BMP
Compt Br Stat Sec, Jun 50. (2) Cable WCL - 49375, COFSA to
CINCEUR, 20 Oct 49, cites an Associated Press release quoting
a USAF announcement that the cost was $252,540,000. According
to Captain Babbitt, BMP, the Army phase of the lift cost $11,000,000.

depreciation or replacement of trucks, tractors, trailers, and other shop type equipment. Regarding costs, General Clay declared: "We were gaining invaluable experience in the use of air transport to support military operations and for civil use. The cost of the airlift could well be justified in its contribution to national defense."[39]

---

[39]Lucius D. Clay, Decision in Germany, p. 386.

CHAPTER II

Ground Support Organization and Personnel

Section I: Evolution of Organization

11. Command of Ground Support Units, 1 January 1949

As a result of a conference at European Command headquarters, 27 July 1948, the Army was assigned certain responsibilities in connection with motor transportation, traffic control, and cargo handling.[1] To implement these and related responsibilities, EUCOM designated an officer to provide liaison with USAFE and BICO,[2] and assigned cargo-hauling and loading responsibilities to the chief of transportation. In practice the chief of transportation controlled operations only at Wiesbaden and Rhein/Main. Ground support functions in the British Zone remained a British responsibility and were performed under command of the British Army Air Transport Organization (AATO).[3] All Army participation in the lift at Berlin was controlled by Berlin Military Post.[4] By the beginning of 1949 the lack of a unified command for Army support units in the

---

[1]Ltr, Brig Gen W. B. Palmer, Dir EUCOM Log Div, to Maj Gen C. L. Adcock, U.S. Chm BICO, 28 Jul 49, cited in The Berlin Air Lift - 1948, par. 11. SECRET.

[2]Col Hall S. Crain of Logistics Division served as EUCOM Liaison Officer on the staff of Maj Gen W. H. M. Tunner, CG FALTF, from 28 July 1948 until the summer of 1949.

[3](1) The British ground organization for Operation PLAINFARE is described in Department of the Army, Observers' Report, Washington, 16 Feb 49, Annex 4, Appendix E. RESTRICTED. (2) See also mimeographed paper, The Rear Airfield Supply Organization at Celle, in EUCOM Trans Div USAASC File No. 3, British Fields. UNCLASSIFIED.

[4]See The Berlin Air Lift - 1948, pars. 10, 17. SECRET.

Frankfurt-Wiesbaden area was causing concern at EUCOM headquarters. The Transportation Corps Airlift Field Operations Officer, responsible for "traffic control point" operations at Rhein/Main and Wiesbaden airfields, had to depend on coordination and tact alone in dealing with the Air Force, with BICO, and even with labor and transportation support units, then controlled by Frankfurt Military Post and the 24th Transportation Truck (TT) Battalion respectively. (See Chart 2.)

12. Recommendation for Unified Ground Command

The Chief, Transportation Division, EUCOM headquarters, submitted to the Director, Logistics Division, on 4 January 1949, recommendations regarding the creation of a unified ground command for Operation VITTLES. He pointed out that the various ground elements of the operation had been committed piecemeal since the inception of the operation, without regard to unified control or responsibility. At the same time increasing complexities of the system and a lack of clearcut authority and responsibility indicated the need for improvement in the organizational structure. No one agency had both responsibility and necessary authority to insure the success of the ground force mission. Various elements handling specific matters relative to the operation were responsible to their military posts (Berlin and Frankfurt); to their chiefs of services, such as Transportation and Ordnance; to the Air Forces, through air installation officers; and to general staff divisions of EUCOM headquarters, for instance, Logistics. Services had been forced to send various representatives into the operation for specific duties, often without time to become thoroughly familiar with the problems of the operation. The various other civil and military agencies were at a loss to know with whom to conduct business. The lack of unified control over the ground operation was resulting in lack of emphasis on this part of the total operation and failure to secure the facilities and service indicated by the importance of the operation. The lack of a responsible headquarters was reflected in absence of long-range planning. The chief of transportation recommended creation of a unified VITTLES ground command, with full operational control of the various units and individuals of the U.S. Army engaged in the operation, after the pattern of the Air Forces' Air Lift Task Force and the British Coordination Traffic Office. Sufficient separate units and personnel to perform the required VITTLES tasks should be assigned directly to the VITTLES Ground Command as a primary mission. All ground units presently assigned from technical service organizations, military posts, and separate units should be assigned directly to the command. It should be constituted as a separate major command under EUCOM headquarters, to be supplied with logistical support from the military post or air installation on which situated. The command would have a staff of 46 enlisted men, 3 warrant officers, and 28 commissioned

Chart 2

TRANSPORTATION TRAFFIC CONTROL POINT,

VITTLES AIR LIFT

COORDINATION RESPONSIBILITIES

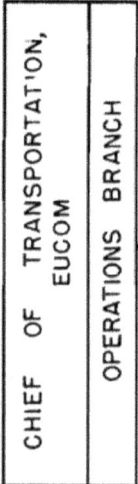

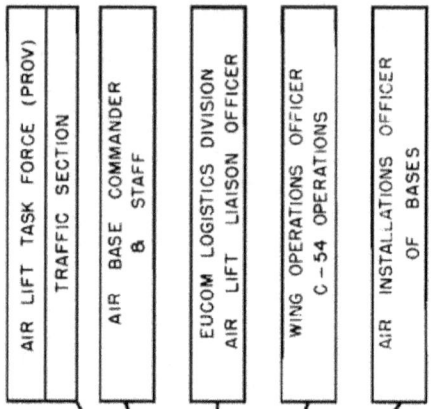

CHIEF OF TRANSPORTATION, EUCOM

OPERATIONS BRANCH

TRANSPORTATION CORPS AIRCRAFT FIELD OPERATIONS OFFICER

COORDINATION RESPONSIBILITIES

- AIR LIFT TASK FORCE (PROV) TRAFFIC SECTION
- AIR BASE COMMANDER & STAFF
- EUCOM LOGISTICS DIVISION AIR LIFT LIAISON OFFICER
- WING OPERATIONS OFFICER C-54 OPERATIONS
- AIR INSTALLATIONS OFFICER OF BASES

COORDINATION RESPONSIBILITIES

- 24th TRANS TRUCK BN (Hvy)
- FRANKFURT MILITARY POST LABOR SUPERVISION OFFICERS
- AREA TRANSPORTATION OFFICE BAD NAUHEIM
- BICO TRANSPORT GROUP MOVEMENTS BRANCH
- 7795 TRANS TRAFFIC REGULATION DETACHMENT

OPERATIONAL CONTROL

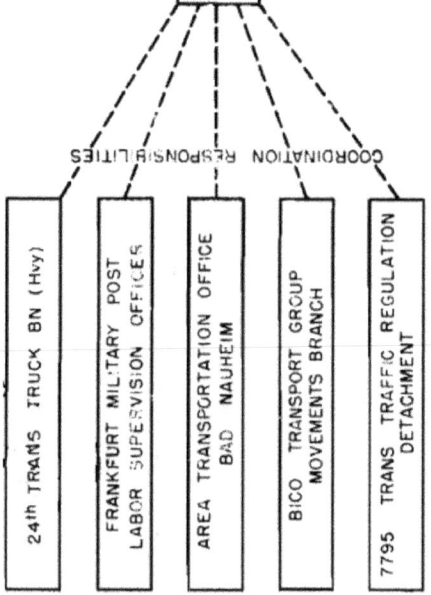

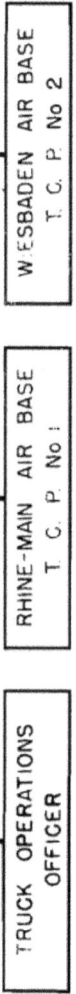

TRUCK OPERATIONS OFFICER

RHINE-MAIN AIR BASE T. C. P. No 1

WIESBADEN AIR BASE T. C. P. No 2

Source Hq EUCOM, Transportation Division, Operations Manual for Transportation Officers on Vittles Airlift, 1 Feb 49, Appendix A, Section II, Chart 1

AGU U 50 23401

VITTLES GROUND COMMAND
COMMANDING GENERAL
DEPUTY

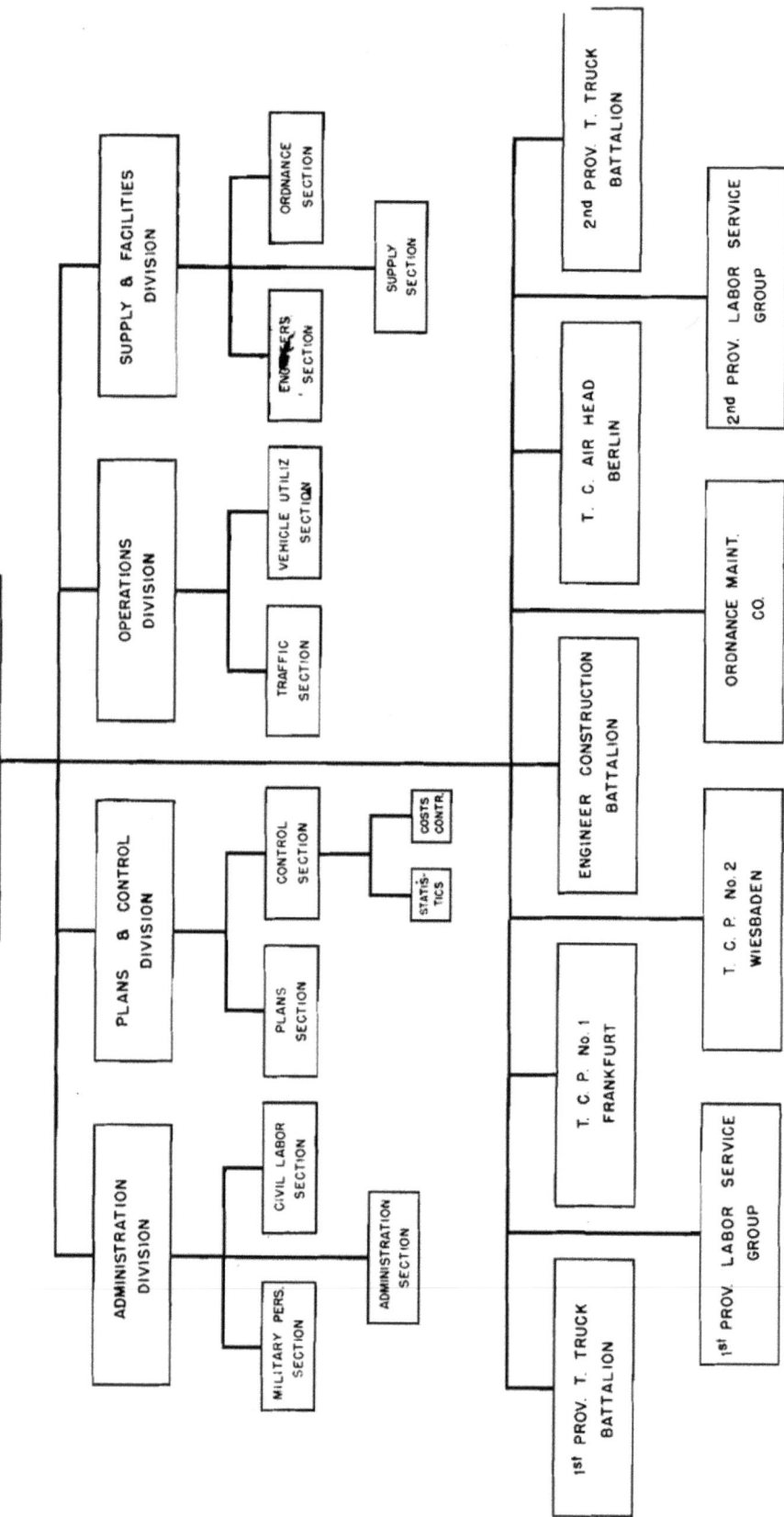

ADMINISTRATION DIVISION
- MILITARY PERS. SECTION
- CIVIL LABOR SECTION
- ADMINISTRATION SECTION

PLANS & CONTROL DIVISION
- PLANS SECTION
- CONTROL SECTION
  - STATISTICS
  - COSTS CONTR.

OPERATIONS DIVISION
- TRAFFIC SECTION
- VEHICLE UTILIZ SECTION

SUPPLY & FACILITIES DIVISION
- ENGINEERS' SECTION
- ORDNANCE SECTION
- SUPPLY SECTION

- 1st PROV. T. TRUCK BATTALION
- T. C. P. No. 1 FRANKFURT
- ENGINEER CONSTRUCTION BATTALION
- T. C. AIR HEAD BERLIN
- 2nd PROV. T. TRUCK BATTALION

- 1st PROV. LABOR SERVICE GROUP
- T. C. P. No 2 WIESBADEN
- ORDNANCE MAINT. CO.
- 2nd PROV. LABOR SERVICE GROUP

Source: Department of the Army, Observers' Report, Operation VITTLES, 16 Feb 49

AGL (1) 10-51- 50-23505

officers, headed by a brigadier general. (Chart 3.)[5]

13. Interim Developments

The Logistics Division agreed in general with these recommendations but questioned the practicability of certain aspects of the proposal. Commenting that such an organization "should encompass the operation at Berlin and in the British Zone," Logistics Division cited the following objections in a reply dated 27 January:

In the first place, it is not believed possible to place the tight little operation of Berlin under the control of a general officer at Frankfurt. The operation in the British Zone also presents difficulty. All that is left is the operation at Wiesbaden and Rhein/Main. But these operations are not clear cut. Frankfurt Military Post is assisting to the limit of its ability in certain phases of this work. It would be difficult to determine who should command who in such an assignment. Too many agencies and activities are contributing part time. The transfer of these agencies in whole or in part to a new major command would present major difficulties.

Organization of a VITTLES ground command was therefore not immediately approved.[6] Late in January an Army observer group of five officers arrived in Germany to study the airlift. The group's report contained the following comment on the responsibilities of Army service units in the airlift: "The most outstanding characteristic of the participating Army Service Units in this operation is the apparent lack of unilateral control or unified command over the U.S. Army units. In spite of this situation, the various components functioning entirely on a cooperative and coordinating basis, have been capable of producing unbelievable results."[7] The observer group recommended that in any such mission planned for the future there

---

[5]EUCOM COT to Dir EUCOM Log Div, sub: Establishment of a VITTLES Ground Command, 4 Jan 49. In DA Observers' Rept, Annex 4, App D, and in EUCOM Trans Div 580 (1949). UNCLASSIFIED.

[6](1) C/N 2, EUCOM Log Div to C/EUCOM Trans Div, 27 Jan 49, sub: Establishment of a VITTLES Ground Command. (2) USAASC, History of the United States Army Airlift Support Command, 6 April 1949 - 15 October 1949 (Frankfurt, 1949), Appendix A. UNCLASSIFIED.

[7]DA Observers' Rept, Annex 5, Appendix B. RESTRICTED.

should be created for Army service units a task force headquarters, to be responsible for organizing all ground units participating in the operation, and for developing and executing a plan of operation.[8] On 25 March Brig. Gen. W. B. Palmer, Director, Logistics Division, inspected Army support activities at the two U.S. Zone air bases. Two days later, in following discussions with Maj. Gen. W. H. M. Tunner, Commanding General, CALTF, and others, General Palmer recommended to Lt. Gen. C. R. Huebner, Deputy Commander in Chief, EUCOM, that all Army support activities at Rhein/Main and Wiesbaden Air Force Bases be placed at once under a single commander.[9] Formal recommendations to this effect were submitted and approved on 28 March.[10]

14. Mission and Organization of USAASC

On 30 March Brig. Gen. Philip E. Gallagher, then EUCOM Director of Posts, was directed to organize and assume command of the U.S. Army Airlift Support Command (see Appendix B).[11] The new agency, as a subordinate command of U.S. Army, Europe, was made responsible for "all operations in direct support of the Air Lift Task Force at Rhein/Main Air Force Base and Wiesbaden Air Force Base."[12] USAASC opened a temporary headquarters in the Operations Building, Rhein/Main Air Base, on 6 April and on the following day the permanent headquarters was opened in the Allianz Building in Frankfurt.[13] It moved to 30 Wiesenhuettenplatz, Frankfurt, on 5 August, and to Rhein/Main airfield on 22 September. The 7933 Headquarters, U.S. Army Airlift Support Command, was organized effective 13 April with an authorized strength of 16 officers,

---

[8]Ibid., p. 33. RESTRICTED.

[9]IRS, Brig Gen W. B. Palmer, Dir EUCOM Div, to EUCOM DCOFS, 28 Mar 49, sub: U.S. Army Airlift Support Command. UNCLASSIFIED. In EUCOM AG Decimal File 381, Vol. I (1949), Item 1.

[10]Ibid., and C/N 2, EUCOM DCOFS to EUCOM AG Div, 28 Mar 49. UNCLASSIFIED. In ibid.

[11]Ltr, Hq EUCOM to Brig Gen Philip E. Gallagher, EUCOM 30 Mar 49, sub: U.S. Army Airlift Support Command. AG 381 GSP - AGO. UNCLASSIFIED. Included as Appendix B. A similar letter dated 4 April 1949 substituted Frankfurt for Wiesbaden as location for the headquarters.

[12]EUCOM GO 28, 5 Apr 49, sub: Establishment of U.S. Army Airlift Support Command. UNCLASSIFIED.

[13](1) USAASC GO 1, 6 Apr 49, sub: Establishment of Headquarters, U.S. Army Airlift Support Command. (2) USAASC GO 2, 6 Apr 49, sub: Location of Headquarters, U.S. Army Airlift Support Command. UNCLASSIFIED.

Chart 4

ORGANIZATION CHART

TRANSPORTATION TRAFFIC CONTROL POINT, VITTLES AIR LIFT
RHINE-MAIN AIR BASE

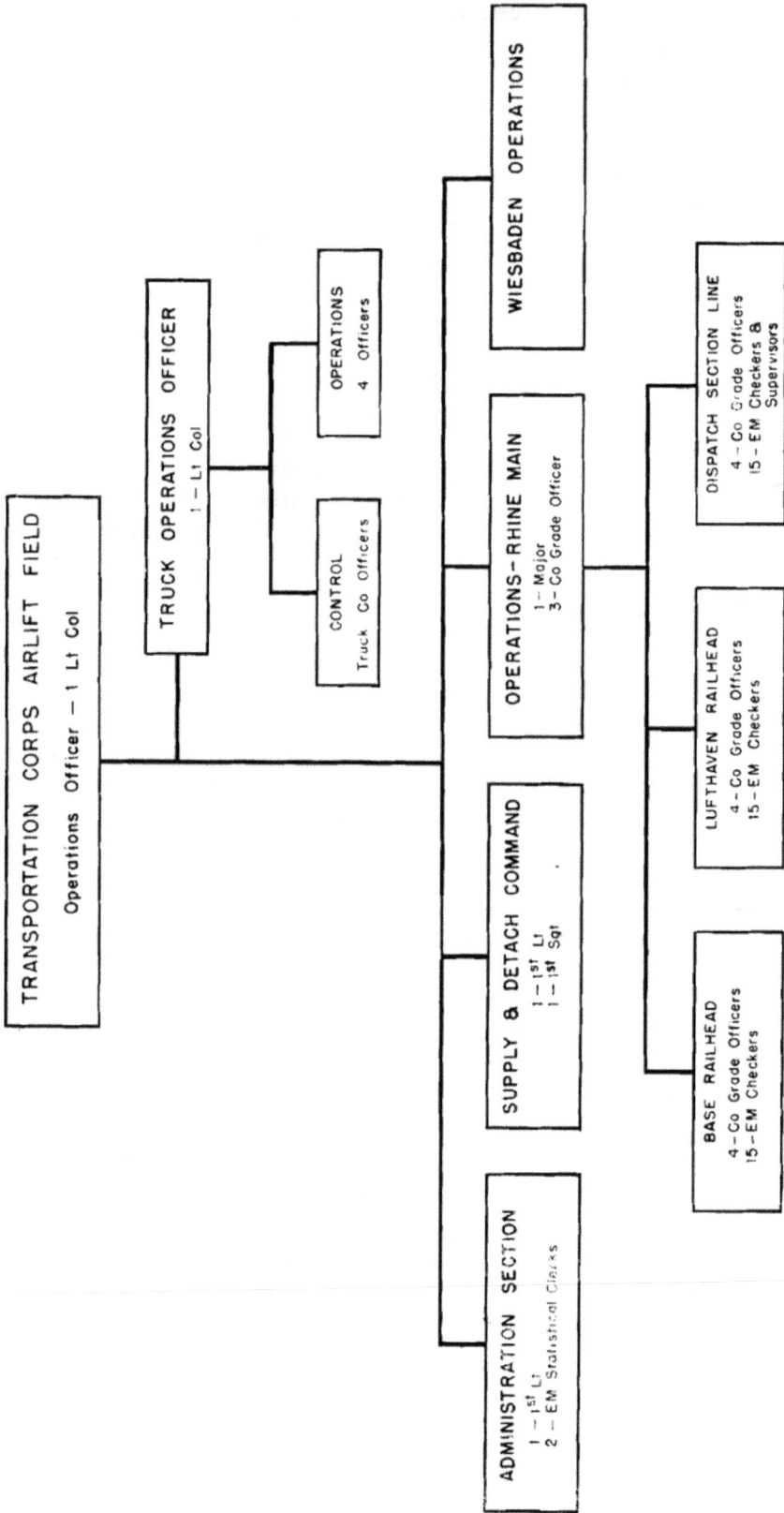

TRANSPORTATION CORPS AIRLIFT FIELD
Operations Officer — 1 Lt Col

TRUCK OPERATIONS OFFICER
1 — Lt Col

CONTROL
Truck Co Officers

OPERATIONS
4 Officers

WIESBADEN OPERATIONS

OPERATIONS—RHINE MAIN
1 — Major
3 — Co Grade Officer

SUPPLY & DETACH COMMAND
1 — 1st Lt
1 — 1st Sgt

ADMINISTRATION SECTION
1 — 1st Lt
2 — EM Statistical Clerks

BASE RAILHEAD
4 — Co Grade Officers
15 — EM Checkers

LUFTHAVEN RAILHEAD
4 — Co Grade Officers
15 — EM Checkers

DISPATCH SECTION LINE
4 — Co Grade Officers
15 — EM Checkers &
Supervisors

Source Hq EUCOM, Transportation Division, Operations Manual for Transportation Officers on Vittles Airlift, 1 Feb 49, Appendix A, Section II, Chart II

AGL(1) 11 51 50 23401

Chart 5

ORGANIZATION CHART

TRANSPORTATION TRAFFIC CONTROL POINT, WIESBADEN AIR BASE

(AS OF 1 FEBRUARY 1949)

TRAFFIC CONTROL POINT № 2
WIESBADEN A.B.
OFFICER IN CHARGE

RECEIVING & ASSEMBLY POINT

1 – Officer in Charge
1 – EM Clerk

DISPATCH SECTION

3 – Officers
3 – NCO Dispatchers
8 – EM Supervisors

ADMINISTRATION, REQUISITION &
PRIORITIES SECTION

1 – Officer
1 – EM Clerk

ERBENHEIM RAIL HEAD

3 – Officers
3 – EM Clerks

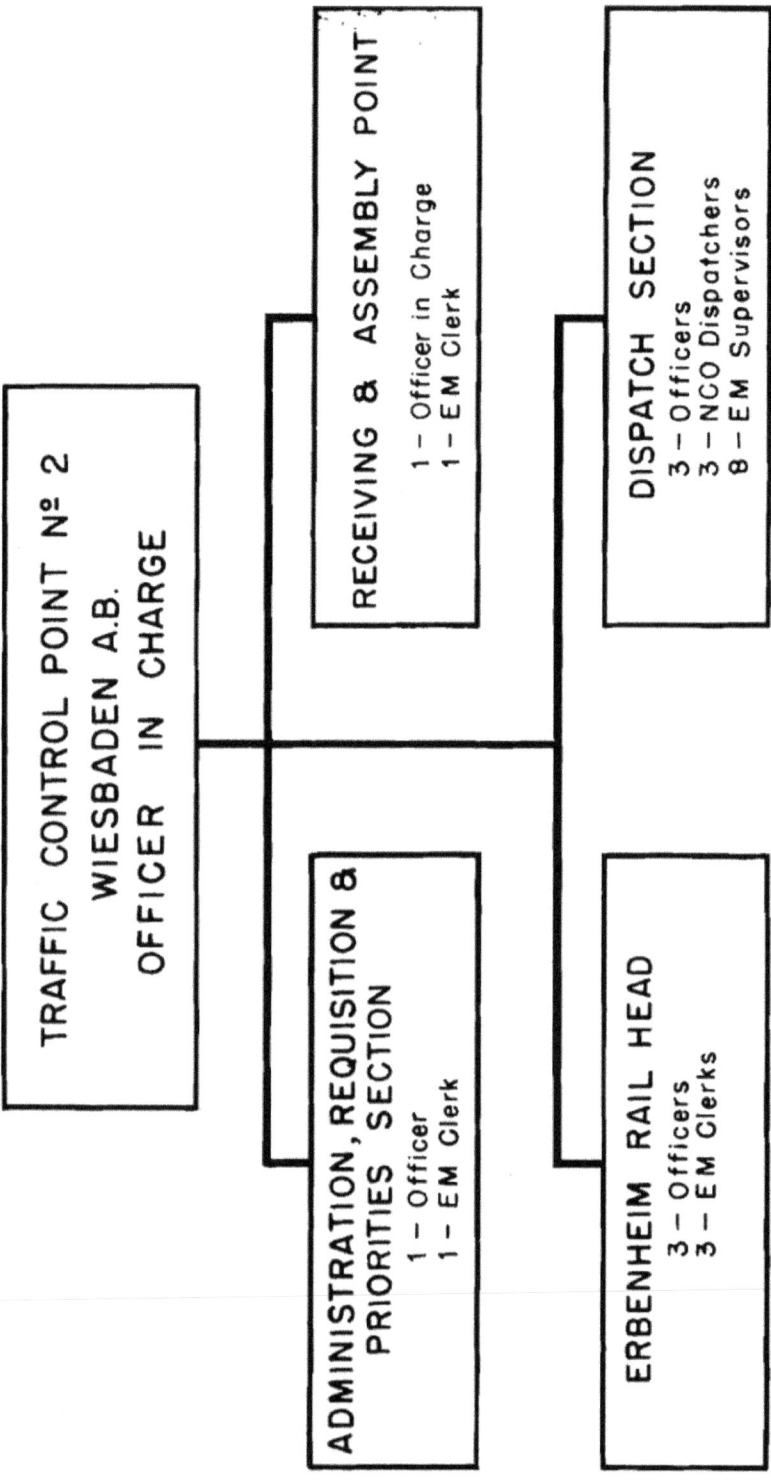

Source: Hq EUCOM, Transportation Division, Operations Manual for Transportation Officers on VITTLES
Air Lift, App A, Sec II, Chart 3, 1 Feb 49

AGL (1) 11-51 50 2340

Chart 6

AGL (1) 11-51

USAASC

CO
DEPUTY COMDR

- ADJUTANT DIVISION
- MOVEMENTS & PLANNING DIV
- OPERATIONS DIVISION
- SUPPLY & MAINT DIVISION

R/M Det, USAASC
Has optnl control of elements of 24th Bn, 559 Ord & labor personnel while on base.

- SUPPLY & ADMIN
  - LUFTHAVEN RAILHEAD
- LABOR SUPV BRANCH
  - BASE RAILHEAD
- TRAFFIC CONTROL POINT #1
  - DISPATCH POINT
- MAINT BRANCH
  - ORG. MAINT 24th BN 559 ORD

559 Ord MAM Co
T/O & E 2-197

24th TT Bn
- 67 T Trk Co
- 69 T Trk Co
- 70 T Trk Co
- 76 T Trk Co
- 83 T Trk Co
- 89 T Trk Co
- 543 T Trk Co

110 Lab Sv Cen
- 2958 & 503 LS Co
- 4543 & 36 LS Co
- 8957 & 501 LS Co
- 8958 & 523 LS Co
- 405 & 38 LS Co
- 8512 & 54 LS Co
- 2905 & 7880 LS Co
- 7441 & 7881 LS Co
- 4060 & 506 LS Co

Wbdn Det, USAASC
Has optnl control of elements of 24th Bn, 559 Ord & labor personnel while on base

- MAINT BRANCH
  - ORG. MAINT MAINZ KASTEL
- TRAFFIC CONTROL POINT #2
  - DISPATCH POINT
- LABOR SUPV BRANCH
  - TRUCK TRANSFER POINT
- SUPPLY & ADMIN
  - ERBENHEIM RAILHEAD

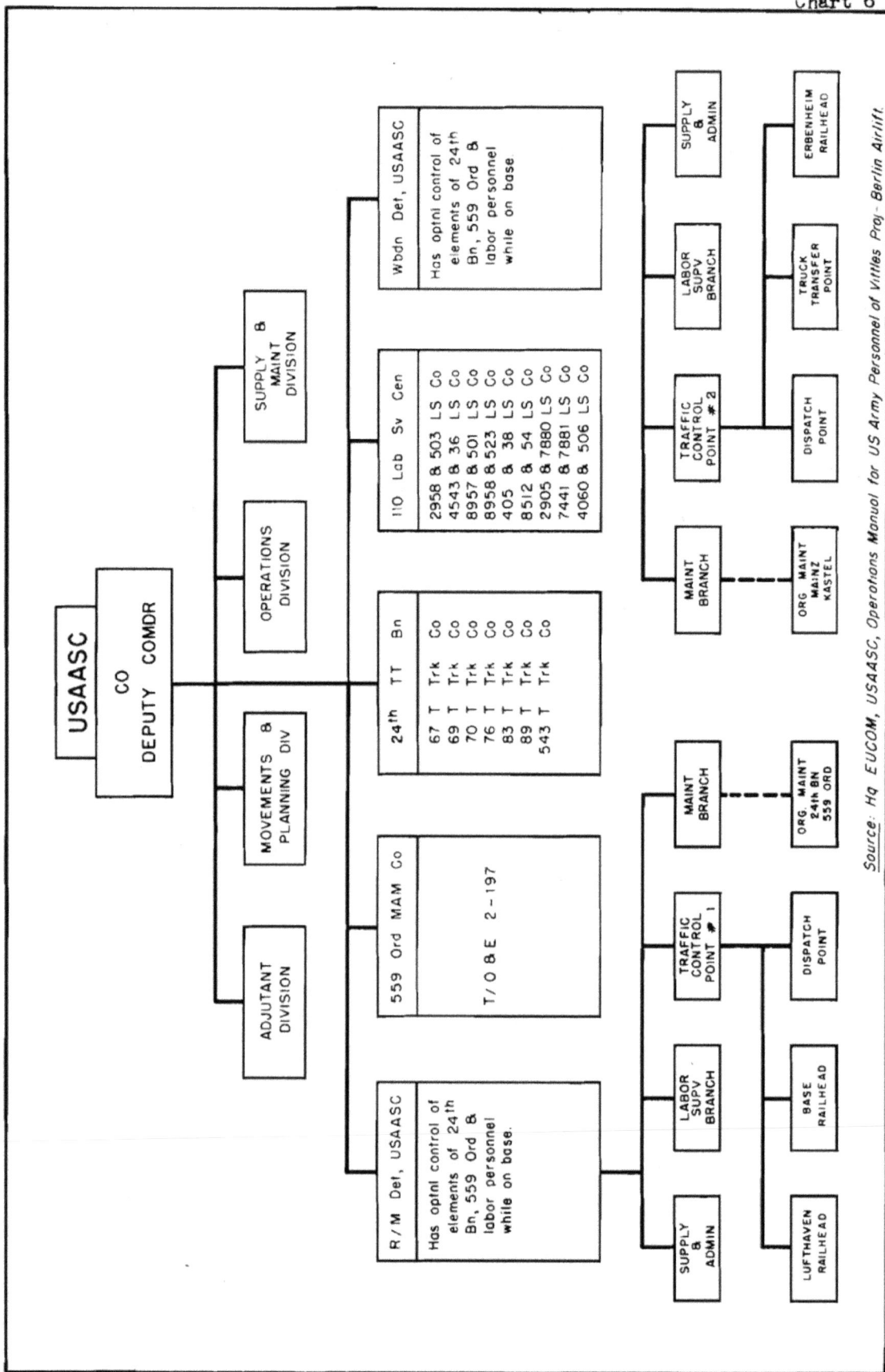

Source: Hq EUCOM, USAASC, Operations Manual for US Army Personnel of Vittles Proj – Berlin Airlift.

2 warrant officers, and 13 enlisted men.[14] The following units
were assigned to USAASC and attached for administration to Frankfurt
Military Post (except as noted):[15] two Airlift Detachments from
the 7795 Traffic Regulating Detachment (assigned to Transportation
Division, United States Army, Europe (USAREUR), and attached to
USAASC), the 24th Transportation Truck Battalion including six
heavy truck companies, the 559th Ordnance Medium Automotive Maintenance (MAM) Company, and the 7934 Labor Supervision Center, Headquarters, with nine labor service and nine labor supervision companies. (See Appendix C). Charts 4 and 5 show the organization
of the traffic control points at Rhein/Main and Wiesbaden, respectively, prior to the establishment of the USAASC. Chart 6 shows
the organization of USAASC. The 7934 Labor Supervision Center,
Headquarters, was discontinued and replaced by the 110 Labor Supervision Center, Headquarters, effective 10 May 1949.[16] The total
strength of the U.S. Army Airlift Support Command immediately prior
to the phase-out period was 4,075, including 1,393 military personnel and 2,682 civilians, distributed as follows:[17]

Unit	Military		Civilian		Total
	Officers	EM	US	Other	
USAASC	18	13	2	8	41
7795 TRD	25	61	–	–	86
559 Ord	4	116	–	–	120
110 LS Center	21	64	–	2,525	2,610
24 TT Bn	64	1,007	1	146	1,218

Key personnel are listed in Appendix D.[18]

15. Organizational Role of USAASC

The new headquarters supplied the element of management needed
to analyze procedures, determine requirements, and take effective

---

[14]USAASC GO 3, 13 Apr 49, sub: Organization of the 7933 Headquarters, U.S. Army Airlift Support Command. UNCLASSIFIED.

[15]EUCOM Trp Assign No. 8, 5 Apr 49. UNCLASSIFIED. Included
as Appendix C.

[16]7933 USAASC GO 5, 8 May 49.

[17]Strength Table, 1 August 1949. UNCLASSIFIED. In EUCOM Trans
Div file 29, USAASC Personnel Roster.

[18]USAASC Roster of Key Personnel, 12 Oct 49 UNCLASSIFIED.

action to have requirements met. Many of the facilities needed to make the work move more smoothly, especially at Rhein/Main, had been planned for in 1948 and had been provided, or were in process of being provided, by April of 1949. USAASC expedited solution of remaining problems.[19] Upon its establishment it took over from the Transportation Corps (TC) Airlift Field Operations Officer at Rhein/Main responsibility for dealing with BICO, USAFE, CALTF, EUCOM, the Rhein/Main and Wiesbaden Air Base headquarters, and Berlin. Command channels replaced the uncertainties of coordination, so far as transportation, ordnance, and labor units were concerned. (See Chart 7.)

Section II: Personnel

16. Manpower for the Lift

The steady expansion of the air lift during the first half of 1949 placed increasing demands on military personnel and continued to require the employment of thousands of civilian laborers. Comprehensive figures on manpower involved, as well as on other phases of airlift operations, are difficult to obtain, since no agency was charged with current analysis and reporting of all airlift activities. Certain aspects concerning the Combined Air Lift Task Force are given in Annex A.

a. Assignment of Military Personnel. At military posts and at EUCOM headquarters, airlift responsibilities were ordinarily handled as additional duties. Very few officers at EUCOM headquarters were assigned full-time to the lift, but for many it occasioned a heavier workload.

b. Army Personnel Assigned to Airlift Support. Apart from Air Force crews and technicians brought to Germany for the big air operation, most of the military units needed to support the lift were shifted from less urgent assignments within the command. Direct assignment of military personnel in support of the operation proved to be desirable. It was found that assignment of men on

---

[19]Interv, E. S. Lay, EUCOM Hist Div, with Lt Col W. E. Schoenfeld, CO USAASC, 13 Oct 49. RESTRICTED.

Chart 7

ORGANIZATION CHART
USAASC
RHEIN/MAIN DETACHMENT

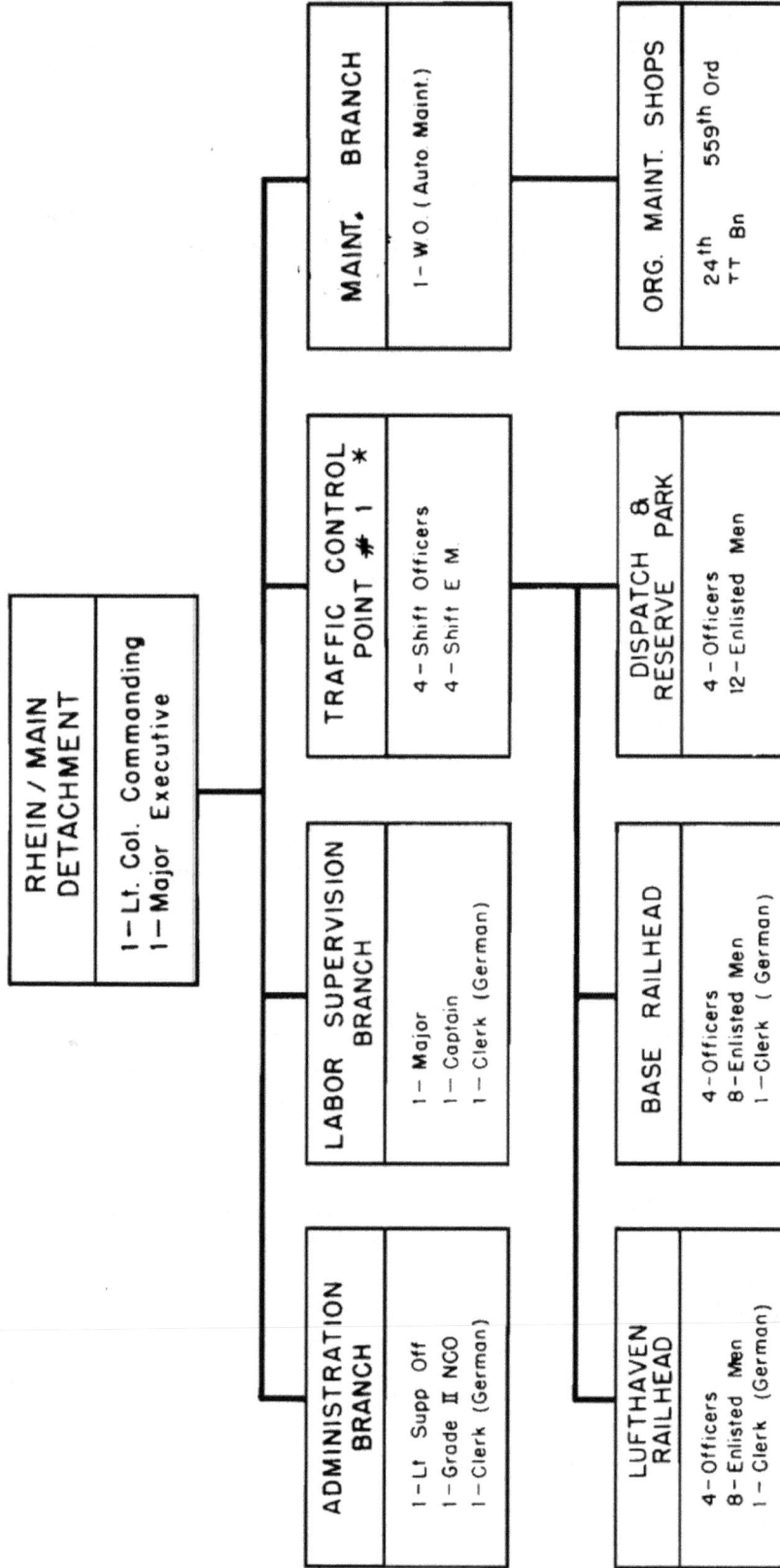

RHEIN/MAIN DETACHMENT

1 – Lt. Col. Commanding
1 – Major Executive

ADMINISTRATION BRANCH

1 – Lt Supp Off
1 – Grade II NCO
1 – Clerk (German)

LABOR SUPERVISION BRANCH

1 – Major
1 – Captain
1 – Clerk (German)

TRAFFIC CONTROL POINT # 1 *

4 – Shift Officers
4 – Shift E M

MAINT. BRANCH

1 – W O. (Auto Maint.)

LUFTHAVEN RAILHEAD

4 – Officers
8 – Enlisted Men
1 – Clerk (German)

BASE RAILHEAD

4 – Officers
8 – Enlisted Men
1 – Clerk (German)

DISPATCH & RESERVE PARK

4 – Officers
12 – Enlisted Men

ORG. MAINT. SHOPS

24th TT Bn   559th Ord

---

* Operates on a 24 hour, seven day basis (4 shifts)   Augmented by labor crews from 110 Labor Superv. Center

Source: <u>Hq EUCOM, USAASC, Operations Manual for US Army Personnel of Vittles Proj – Berlin Airlift.</u>

temporary duty (TDY) for short periods hindered the development of a highly trained staff and esprit de corps.[20] As of 1 January 1949 Army support was estimated by the EUCOM Logistics Division to have included the following occupation personnel:[21]

		QM	Engr	Trans	Sig	Med	Ord
Grand Total	1,204						
Total		44	216	354	263	120	207
Officer	123	3	18	58[22]	11	26	7
EM	1,009	24	185	290[22]	235	90	185
Civilian (US)	62	14	13	6	10	4	15
Allied/neutral	10	3	0	0	7	0	0

Approximately 700 officers and enlisted men were assigned to the six truck companies not included above,[23] making a total of 1,904 U.S. and Allied personnel engaged in airlift support. At the end of the blockade, EUCOM estimated that the number of Army personnel had reached a peak in support of the airlift during March, when the total comprised 149 officers, 12 warrant officers, 1,789 enlisted men, and 11 Department of the Army civilians.[24]

c. Labor Service Units. Only in the Frankfurt area did the Army use organized labor service units in direct support of the lift. There, throughout the entire operation, organized displaced persons and Germans provided the manpower for all hand-labor loading and unloading of airlift cargo. The nine companies which had served in the fall of 1948 continued to work at Wiesbaden and Rhein/Main, and at the nearby railheads where Army trucks were loaded, until the phase-out of the operation. During the first six months of 1949, displaced persons in the labor service units were replaced

[20]Interv, B. V. Hall, EUCOM Hist Div, with Lt Col K. A. Darragh, Asst C/EUCOM Trans Div Opns Br, 8 Jun 49.

[21]Ltr, EUCOM to CG FALTF, 10 Feb 49, sub: Department of the Army Personnel Engaged in Operation(s) VITTLES. AG 230 GSP. CONFIDENTIAL. In EUCOM AG 230 Gen Vol. I Civilian Personnel (1949), Item 10.

[22]Six truck companies not included.

[23]Interv, E. S. Lay, EUCOM Hist Div, with Lt Col H. Y. Chase, CO 24th TT Bn, 21 Jan 49.

[24]Cable S - 2697, EUCOM to COFSA, 12 May 49. SECRET. In EUCOM SGS 094 (1949), Item 48.

by Germans at the rate of about one company per month. There were also some organizational changes. The United States Army Airlift Support Command took over the labor units from Frankfurt Military Post on 6 April, the 7934 Labor Supervision Center was established (and subsequently replaced by the 110th),[25] and two of the supervision companies were redesignated. Details concerning the labor service companies which supported the lift during 1949 are shown in the following tabulation:[26]

Labor Svc Co	Type	Personnel 1 Jan 49	Changes in Personnel	Labor Supv Co 1 Jan 49	Labor Supv Co 6 Apr-Sep
2958	QM Lbr	Polish	German (Jan)	503	503
4543	QM Lbr	Polish	German (Feb)	36	36
4052	QM Lbr	Polish	German (Mar)	38	38
8512	QM Lbr	Pol/Estonian	German (Apr(	54	54
4060	QM Lbr	Lithuanian	German (May)	506	506
8958	Ord Dep	Polish	German (Jul)	523	523
8957	Ord Dep	Polish	Absorbed DP's from other units	501	501
7441	QM Lbr	German		7,880	509
2905	QM Lbr	German		7,881	97

Up to 30 June 1949 company strength was 300 men, with two companies allowed to increase their actual strength to 350 men in order to take care of short-term requirements. Later, as commitments were reduced, company strength was cut to 250.[27]

d. German and Displaced Persons Labor. Resident manpower for the lift fell into several categories, according to the hiring authority and the source of funds used for payment. Most of the labor

---

[25](1) FMP GO 12, 4 Apr 49. (2) EUCOM Trp Assign No. 8, 5 Apr 49. UNCLASSIFIED. In Appendix C. (3) USAASC GO 4, 8 May 49. (4) EUCOM Troop Assignment No. 13, 25 May 49. UNCLASSIFIED.

[26](1) Interv, E. S. Lay, EUCOM Hist Div, with Lt Col Edward T. Whiting, C/FMP LS Sec, 24 Jan 49. (2) Interv, E. S. Lay, EUCOM Hist Div, with Capt Herman W. Stevens, Exec Off 110th LS Ctr, Eschborn, 29 Jul 49. (3) EUCOM CSD Mthly Status Repts. In files of EUCOM LSD. RESTRICTED. (4) See also The Berlin Air Lift - 1948, p. 30. SECRET.

[27](1) Interv, E. S. Lay, EUCOM Hist Div, with Capt Herman W. Stevens, Exec Off 110th LS Ctr, 29 Jul 49. (2) Interv, E. S. Lay, EUCOM Hist Div, with Mr. C. A. Carleson, EUCOM Bud Div Manpower Ctl Br, 9 Aug 51. RESTRICTED.

required by the occupation forces in support of Operation VITTLES, including labor service units, was charged to the German economy as a "non-occupation cost."[28] Persons in this category were hired directly by the military but their use in Operation VITTLES was regarded as being for the benefit of the German population rather than in support of the occupation forces. Personnel employed in Operation VITTLES on this basis on 1 January 1949 numbered as follows:[29]

Headquarters	Number Employed
Total	7,494
U.S. Air Forces in Europe	4,833
Frankfurt Military Post	2,515
Heidelberg Military Post	40
Berlin Military Post	56
Bremerhaven Port of Embarkation	50

By 1 February this total had increased to 9,430.[30] Subsequent totals were 10,465 on 31 March, 8,190 on 30 April, and 8,011 as of 31 May.[31] Germans and displaced persons paid from occupation cost funds numbered 3,062 in March 1949. In addition the air lift had the services, at Berlin, of a number of German laborers provided and administered by the West Berlin city government (Magistrat).[32]

---

[28]Nonoccupation costs are defined as follows in the EUCOM, Comptroller Division, Report of Operations, 1 Jan - 31 Dec 1949, p. 17: "Definition of Mandatory Expenditures (Formerly Non-Occupation Costs). Mandatory expenditures are those expenditures, other than for the maintenance of the Allied Forces, which are incurred in German currency under the direct financial and administrative control of the Occupation Forces and Authorities." UNCLASSIFIED.

[29](1) The Berlin Air Lift - 1948, par. 14d, for 1948 figures. SECRET. (2) EUCOM DCINC's Wkly Staff Conf Notes, No. 4, 25 Jan 49, par. 15. UNCLASSIFIED.

[30]Ibid., No. 8, 21 Feb 49, par. 14. UNCLASSIFIED.

[31]Figures obtained by E. S. Lay, EUCOM Hist Div, from Mr. J. J. Hackett, EUCOM Off of the Compt Program Review and Analysis Br, 22 Aug 51. UNCLASSIFIED.

[32]The Magistrat was the supreme executive organ of the West Berlin city government; it was headed by the Oberbuergermeister or chief mayor.

17. Personnel for Transportation Corps Support at Berlin

The TC airhead organization at BMP employed six officers, comprising one for each eight-hour shift, one administrative officer, and one field officer-in-charge. The 7784th Motor Transport Battalion provided passenger car service for direct and indirect support of VITTLES activities and the 7807th Motor Transport Battalion (Cargo) furnished trucking service.[33] Personnel of the 7798th Traffic Regulating Detachment and the BMP Transportation Branch were used in the TC airhead organization. Germans were employed as truck drivers, loaders and unloaders, dispatchers, in clerical work, and to perform approximately 90 percent of ground-vehicle maintenance.[34] Some fifteen German cargo checkers were assigned to each shift, making it possible for enlisted crew supervisors to spend their time watching the entire crew, preventing pilferage, and keeping the operation in hand.[35] The average daily tonnage moved per man rose from 3.08 short tons in December 1948 to 4.4 tons in March. The average number of Germans employed on each shift at Tempelhof fell from 478 in December to 388 in March.[36] Officers and enlisted men, including those borrowed from local security troops, were assigned to four eight-hour shifts or teams, each working 8 hours on and 24 hours off. German laborers were also organized in four shifts, including a swing shift. Germans for loading and unloading were provided by the Berlin city government.[37] The following figures show the reduction in transportation personnel which began at Tempelhof in December 1948 and continued through the first six months of 1949 despite substantial increases in cargo.[38]

---

[33]Interv, E. S. Lay, EUCOM Hist Div, with Lt Col J. F. Phillips, BMP Trans Off, 21 Jun 50.

[34]Cable V - 39847, OMGUS to DA for PID, 12 May 49. UNCLASSIFIED.

[35]BMP Rept of Opns, 1 Jan - 31 Mar 49, p. 140. RESTRICTED.

[36]Ibid., p. 141.

[37]Interv, E. S. Lay, EUCOM Hist Div, with Lt Col J. F. Phillips, C/BMP Trans Br, 23 Jun 50.

[38]Mimeographed pamphlet, "Operation VITTLES" - Tempelhof, a Transportation Corps Milestone, by Colonel Donald C. Foote, BMP Trans Off, Sep 49. UNCLASSIFIED.

	Incoming Cargo	Outgoing Cargo	Trucks Utilized	Total Personnel Per Shift
1948 Total	340,339	13,681		
Jul	38,713	1,311	108	344
Aug	63,515	1,754	108	537
Sep	61,688	2,090	106	593
Oct	61,158	2,552	104	641
Nov	48,521	1,924	101	679
Dec	66,744	4,050	79	608
1949 Total	469,861	19,309		
Jan	68,282	3,383	74	548
Feb	59,395	2,352	66	545
Mar	76,347	3,251	61	516
Apr	95,066	4,193	61	516
May	88,432	3,566	59	512
Jun	82,339	2,564	59	464

18. Personnel for Engineer Support at Berlin

The extensive construction program scheduled for Berlin Military Post during 1949 forced the Engineer Section to seek an aug-
mentation of its technically-skilled personnel. For airport work
in 1948 the Engineer Section had utilized 107 operators and mechanics
from Berlin and 150 from the U.S. Zone. Early 1949 found the section
staffed with 42 assigned officers, 2 warrant officers, and 323 enlisted men, including a total of 68 operators and mechanics.[39] To
provide manpower for a construction program that was expected to
place a heavy burden on BMP Engineers from March until the end of
November, EUCOM requested the Department of the Army on 15 January
to dispatch a composite engineer group of 182 technicians for arrival by 1 March.[40] On 18 January, EUCOM cancelled the request,
after authorizing the use of technicians of combat units for airlift duty. Nevertheless, a total of 65 white and 15 Negro enlisted
technicians were shipped. Shipments ceased when EUCOM cabled on

---

[39]Memo for rcd, sgd Brig Gen D. C. Shingler, C/EUCOM Engr,
14 Jan 49, sub: Additional Engineer Operators Requested at Berlin.
In EUCOM Engr Div file "Berlin VITTLES." No classification indicated.

[40]Cable SC - 11063, EUCOM to COFSA, 15 Jan 49. UNCLASSIFIED.
In EUCOM SGS 094 (1949), Item 5.

15 March that the number shipped was sufficient in view of a reduction in VITTLES projects.[41] As a result of this reduction the Chief Engineer, EUCOM, concluded that the revised BMP requirements could be met by formation of an Engineer Light Equipment Company from the Hanau Engineer Base Depot, augmented by thirty-three of the specialists sent from the zone of the interior. The revised Berlin requirements were as follows:[42]

SSN	Type	Number
359	Dozer Operator	15
359	Grader Operator	6
081	Air Compressor Operator	10
359	Rock Crusher Operator	6
063	Crane Shovel Operator	4
319	Construction Equipment Mechanic	24
356	Foreman Labor	20
227	Surveyor	1

Early in March the heaviest snowstorm of the year forced BMP to request a delay in the arrival of the light equipment company until about 21 March.[43] The unit, later designated the 503d Engineer Light Equipment Company, moved to Berlin on 20 March. It returned to the U.S. Zone at the end of July.[44]

---

[41](1) Cable SC - 11308, EUCOM to COFSA, 18 Jan 49. UNCLASSIFIED. In EUCOM SGS 094 (1949). (2) Memo for rcd, sgd Lt Col Geo. H. Walker, C/EUCOM Engr Div Mil Br, 20 Jan 49, sub: Airport Construction Specialists Required for Berlin. In EUCOM Engr Div file "Berlin VITTLES." UNCLASSIFIED. (3) Cable WCL — 45080, TAG DA to EUCOM, 16 Feb 49. UNCLASSIFIED. In EUCOM SGS 094 (1949), Item 21. (4) Cable SC - 14148, EUCOM to COFENGRS, 10 Mar 49. UNCLASSIFIED. In ibid., Item 23.

[42]IRS, EUCOM Engr Div to EUCOM Log Div, sub: Requirements for Berlin VITTLES Construction, 1 Mar 49. UNCLASSIFIED. In EUCOM Engr Div file "Berlin VITTLES."

[43]Memo, Lt Col G. H. Walker, C/EUCOM Engr Div Mil Br, to Brig Gen D. G. Shingler, EUCOM C/Engr, sub: Specialists for Berlin VITTLES Construction. UNCLASSIFIED. In EUCOM Engr Div file "Berlin VITTLES."

[44](1) EUCOM DCINC's Wkly Staff Conf Notes No. 12, 22 Mar 49, par. 14. UNCLASSIFIED. (2) The Stars and Stripes, Eur. ed., July 24, 1949. The 683d Engr Lt Equip Co, inactivated effective 14 Jan 46, was redesignated the 503d Engr Lt Equip Co and was activated and organized effective 25 June 1949 at Gross Auheim, Germany, per EUCOM GO 11, 15 Jun 49.

19. Personnel for Transportation Corps Support at Frankfurt Military Post

In its dual role of supporting the airlift and providing transportation for Frankfurt Military Post (FMP) the 24th Transportation Truck (TT) Battalion had a peak strength of 1,300 officers, warrant officers, and enlisted men.[45] Although truck companies were over-strength in the spring of 1949 there was a shortage of trained heavy truck drivers and qualified automotive mechanics.[46] Replacements received in the command were of good caliber although lacking training and experience. They were unqualified as drivers, mechanics, welders, tire repairmen, carpenters, and other type skills required. This necessitated immediate on-the-job training. Due to shortage of personnel, very few replacements were trained in the existing technical service schools, the men being required to follow the system of on-the-job training. In the first three months of 1949, approximately two hundred enlisted men were trained as heavy truck drivers at Giessen and transferred to VITTLES truck companies at Frankfurt.[47] In May and June a command-wide cut of 21 percent in Negro personnel threatened to hamper airlift support operations, since the 24th TT Battalion was a Negro unit. Units of the 24th TT Battalion averaged only a 5 percent reduction, however, and airlift activities were not seriously affected.[48] As of 29 August the eight units under the 24th TT Battalion were assigned 54 officers, 408 drivers, and 98 mechanics.[49] Because of their heavy workload, personnel of the 24th TT Battalion were not given the usual military training while on airlift support duty. Beginning in July, however, a three-fold program of military training, on-the-job instruction, and training to bring all personnel up to high school level was established by battalion headquarters.[50]

---

[45]24th TT Bn Rept of Opns, 1949, p. 3. RESTRICTED.

[46]5th Ind, USAASC to CINCEUR through OCOT, to basic ltr, 11 Aug 49, sub: Separation of Undesirable Enlisted Personnel from Transportation Corps Truck Companies. AG 220.801 (23 Jul 49) GPA. UNCLASSIFIED. In EUCOM Trans Div file 19, USAASC.

[47]EUCOM OCOT Rept of Opns, 1 Jan - 31 Mar 49, p. 32. CONFIDENTIAL.

[48]Interv, E. S. Lay, EUCOM Hist Div, with Lt Frederick P. Ross, Adj 24th TT Bn, 12 Oct 49. RESTRICTED.

[49]Rept, 24th TT Bn, FMP, to CO USAASC, sub: Status of Personnel. UNCLASSIFIED. In EUCOM Trans Div file 24, USAASC.

[50]24th TT Bn Rept of Opns, 1949, p. 3. RESTRICTED.

20. Supervision and Orientation of Military Personnel

Adequate control of ground-support operations required close supervision. Given a shortage of maintenance personnel, close operational supervision was necessary to insure proper preventive maintenance of vehicles engaged in airlift support.[51] Organization to allow maximum supervision by a limited number of personnel was found essential at Tempelhof to achieve efficiency and to curb pilferage. Airlift experience also underlined the importance of giving special attention to the welfare and recreation of troops required to work unusually long hours. Orientation of participating military personnel with regard to the issues at stake was found to be highly desirable. Such training helped to overcome ignorance and carelessness and to lessen the losses in food cargo resulting from failure to understand the seriousness of the airlift mission.[52]

21. Driver Responsibilities

Members of truck companies carried heavy responsibilities. The conditions under which they worked were difficult and exacting. Trucks were parked in open, unpaved areas which resulted in drivers having to perform first echelon maintenance, and mechanics to make minor repairs in the open, exposed to all elements of the weather. Their equipment had already seen hard service and repair parts were in short supply. Day and night they had to maneuver their vehicles into position for loading operations at planeside and at the side of rail cars. They were under constant pressure to drive in such a manner as to avoid loss of cargo, damage to plane doors and rail cars, and excessive wear on their own vehicles. Early in April, with all heavy truck companies overstrength in personnel, an additional enlisted man was placed on each tractor used on the air bases, to serve as assistant driver.[53] His duties included guiding the driver in coupling and uncoupling tractors and when backing into position

51 24th TT Bn, FMP Hist Rept for 1949, p. 4. RESTRICTED.

52(1) Interv, E. S. Lay, EUCOM Hist Div, with Mr. C. A. Dix (formerly OMGBS Transport Advisor) HICOG BE Transport Advisor, 23 Jun 50. CONFIDENTIAL. (2) Interv, E. S. Lay, EUCOM Hist Div, with Mr. Leon J. Steck, C/HICOG BE Trade and Program Br, 20 Jun 50. CONFIDENTIAL.

53 24th TT Bn, FMP, Opns Air Lift Memo No. 7, sub: Organizational Commitments for Month of April, 5 Apr 49. In EUCOM Trans Div file 19, USAASC. UNCLASSIFIED.

at planeside, placing chock blocks in proper position, assuring that landing gears of trailers were raised or lowered correctly, and making certain that trailer tarpaulins were properly tied in place.[54] On the establishment of USAASC a standing operating procedure for drivers was published and drivers were required to carry copies (pasted on boards or stiff cardboard) in the cabs of all tractors used at Rhein/Main and Wiesbaden air fields. (For text, see Appendix E.)[55]

22. Requirements for Loading Personnel

Both at zonal airfields and at Berlin enough laborers had to be on hand to take care of peak periods of loading and unloading. Twelve-man teams were found most satisfactory for unloading at Rhein/Main. Time required for loading a single C-54 with coal varied ordinarily from 12 to 18 minutes, although on 12 August a group at Rhein/Main loaded three planes at five minutes each. Although the group had an average loading time of 5.62 minutes on that date, it loaded a total of only eight planes.[56] The average amount loaded per man was five tons at Wiesbaden and six tons at Rhein/Main. At Rhein/Main the average number of planes loaded was six per group because of the different type of cargo, and at Wiesbaden, it was four.[57] One ton per man per hour was the standard rate of work for laborers working at railheads.[58]

23. Control of Non-Military Labor

At Berlin where there was plenty of German labor available, unsatisfactory labor could be readily replaced.[59] Experience with organized labor units at Rhein/Main and Wiesbaden was satisfactory on the whole, but occasional incidents in the summer of 1949 indicated potential difficulties in utilizing organized German personnel.

---

[54]Ibid.

[55]Memo, USAASC to CO 24th TT Bn, 11 May 1949, sub: Standing Operation Procedure for Drivers, Incl. I. UNCLASSIFIED.

[56]Records on loading times. UNCLASSIFIED. In EUCOM Trans Div file 52, USAASC.

[57]Interv, Miss E. S. Lay, EUCOM Hist Div, with Capt Herman W. Stevens, Exec Off 110th LS Ctr, 29 Jul 49.

[58]Interv, E. S. Lay, EUCOM Hist Div, with Lt Col Edward T. Whiting, C/FMP LS Sec, 24 Jan 49.

[59]24th TT Bn, FMP Hist Rept, 1949, p. 4. RESTRICTED.

The labor supervision log book for Rhein/Main recorded instances in which German group leaders argued with American supervisors, laborers stated that they did not take orders from Americans but only from their group leaders, and a few other laborers refused to work, kicked coal sacks from the trailers, or showed signs of laziness. Only a few of these problems, however, went beyond the officer in immediate charge.[60] Displaced persons and German laborers worked best on loading operations when permanently organized into teams and encouraged by material and other incentives. When German and displaced persons were used as truck drivers in the absence of sufficient enlisted personnel, careful and detailed scheduling of operations was required.[61]

24. Incentives to Increase Efficiency of German Labor at BMP

Beginning 1 April the Transportation Corps Airhead at Tempelhof put into effect a system to increase the efficiency of German labor crews. The performance of each shift was measured under a point system and scores were displayed on a master chart at TC Airhead Tempelhof. At the end of the month all members of the winning shift received individual prizes at a ceremony of recognition. The outstanding crew was further rewarded. Points were earned or deducted separately for (1) absenteeism, (2) accidents and pilferage, and (3) operational delays. Care was taken to explain the system to German supervisors, crew leaders, and laborers, and to impress upon them the intent of the transportation officer to have the rules applied with absolute fairness despite unavoidable variations in unloading conditions. Points were figured only for the unloading of coal and German food. This system worked successfully throughout the remainder of the air lift and was adopted as standard procedure for future use.[62]

25. Absenteeism at BMP

Absenteeism of German laborers at Tempelhof was regarded by

---

[60]Labor Supervision Log Book, 30 Jun - 30 Sep 49. UNCLASSIFIED. In EUCOM Trans Div USAASC files.

[61]24th TT Bn, FMP Hist Rept, 1949, p. 4. RESTRICTED.

[62]BMP Trans Br, TC Shift Performance Chart "Operation VITTLES," 8 May 49. Text included in USAASC Manual for U.S. Army Personnel of VITTLES Project, Berlin Airlift. UNCLASSIFIED. As Annex B, this document accompanies the first six copies of this monograph, including copies distributed to the Chief, Military History, Special Staff, United States Army, the Adjutant General, European Command, and the Documents Branch, Historical Division, EUCOM.

TC officials as closely connected with pilferage. Having acquired
a sack of sugar or other items by theft, laborers were likely to
spend a few days disposing of these items on the black market.[63]
During 1948 no Army figures on absenteeism were maintained. In
January the average number of German laborers absent per shift was
38. From 9 to 19 January, the daily average of absences per shift
was 55.2. On 20 January the German foremen were told to cut down
on absenteeism; for the following ten days the average was 16. By
the end of March this average had fallen to less than 10 men per
shift per day.[64]

26. Improvements in Living and Working Conditions at FMP

USAASC added to the efficiency of ground support operations
at FMP by improving the living and working conditions of its German
and displaced person laborers. The labor service camps at Eschborn
and Zeilsheim, west of Frankfurt, were inspected by the Commanding
General and Deputy Commanding General, USAASC, and FMP Engineers,
and orders were issued to improve sanitary conditions, to build security fences, and to make other improvements. At the Rhein/Main
dispatch area and the Zeppelinheim, tents were being used as shelters
for laborers between loading operations. Lighting in these tents
was poor, the tents were generally dirty, and "latrine and sanitary
conditions were abominable."[65] Tents and trailers were being used
for operations personnel on duty at the traffic control point. Inspections in April led to a decision by USAASC to construct a proper
building for the dispatch office and operations staff, and waiting
rooms and a messhall for the laborers. In his 12 April summary of
action to be taken, the Commanding General, USAASC, directed that
canteens for laborers be opened in the messhall and in the new standby rooms, when finished, and that provision be made for clothing for
cooks, a radio for use during meals, a washroom or a washstand outside, walks, flowers around the building, paint, a separate dishwashing room, dishwashing equipment, etc. In addition, he directed
that the question of pay and clothing for the German labor companies
be looked into, and that both laborers and supervisory personnel be
"cleaned up." The fact that coal was being handled should not be

---

[63]Interv, E. S. Lay, EUCOM Hist Div, with Lt Col John U. Schiess,
BMP Trans Br Opns Off, 14 Feb 49.

[64](1) Ibid. (2) BMP Rept of Opns, 1 Jan - 31 Mar 49, p. 142.
RESTRICTED.

[65]Interv, B. V. Hall, EUCOM Hist Div, with Lt R. A. Little, Asst
Adj USAASC, 17 May 49. RESTRICTED.

made an excuse for sloppiness.[66]

27. Other Steps to Improve Labor Motivation at FMP

Laborers were encouraged to do better work by a system of competition and rewards. Loading teams were permanently organized, under their own leaders, and recognition was given to better production through material rewards (chocolate and cigarettes), the granting of free time, and an improved promotion system.[67]

28. Working Hours and Shifts at FMP

Up to the end of 1948 the transportation units in airlift support worked in shifts of 12 hours on and 12 hours off, seven days a week. Under a system of "rotational rehabilitation," each company was given 10 days in the company area after each 30-day period at the airfield.[68] To ease this schedule, the commanding officer of the 24th TT Battalion put into operation at the end of December a plan for using three full truck companies and two companies committed by platoon, at Rhein/Main. The new plan called for three 12-hour shifts, with one company and one platoon on each shift, each group working one 12-hour shift, followed by two 12-hour shifts off duty.[69] Responsibilities of company commanders and platoon leaders in making this plan effective are described in Appendix F. Eight-hour shifts for military personnel in truck units replaced the 12-hour tours of duty at the end of June.[70] Under the new system an 8-hour shift was followed by 16 hours off duty. Companies at Rhein/Main worked a block of six consecutive tours of duty followed by 24, 48, or 72 hours of free time so alternated as to require duty on day, evening, and night shifts by all companies in turn. Laborers preferred the 12-hour shifts

---

[66]USAASC Memo, To Whom It May Concern, sgd, Brig Gen P. E. Gallagher, 12 Apr 49. UNCLASSIFIED. In EUCOM Trans Div file 6, USAASC Construction.

[67]Ibid. Development of team competition had been stressed by General Gallagher in his memo of 12 April 1949.

[68]See The Berlin Air Lift - 1949, par. 18f. SECRET.

[69]24th TT Bn, FMP, Opn Air Lift Memo No. 11, 29 Dec 48, sub: Organizational Commitments for Air Lift Operations. UNCLASSIFIED. Included as Appendix F.

[70]24th TT Bn, USAASC, Opn Air Lift Memo No. 12, 27 Jun 49. UNCLASSIFIED. In EUCOM Trans Div file 19, USAASC.

and were permitted to retain them.[71]   On 1 August the air lift changed from a 24-hour to a daylight or 8-hour operation,[72] and by the middle of August the air lift was reduced to a 5-day week.

29. Safety

To prevent accidents, laborers had to be strictly supervised. The injury rate dropped when such practices as jumping from moving trucks, standing in moving trucks, riding on top of loads, and lifting cargo incorrectly were prohibited.[73]

[71]Interv, E. S. Lay, EUCOM Hist Div, with Lt Col J. B. Andrews, C/USAASC Opns Br, 2 Aug 49. RESTRICTED.

[72]Interv, E. S. Lay, EUCOM Hist Div, with 1st Lt Frederick F. Ross, 24th TT Bn Adj, 12 Oct 49. UNCLASSIFIED.

[73]Interv, B. V. Hall, EUCOM Hist Div, with Lt Col M. A. Darragh, Asst C/EUCOM Trans Div Opns Br, 8 Jun 49.

CHAPTER III

Facilities and Procedures

30. Appointment of Board to Study Ground Support

The Deputy Commander in Chief, European Command, directed late in January 1949 that a board of officers be appointed to examine the manner of performance of the ground forces mission in the Berlin airlift to determine if economies of manpower and equipment could be effected. Nine officers and one U.S. civilian, representing Logistics, Ordnance, Quartermaster, and Transportation Divisions of Headquarters, EUCOM, were named to this board on 31 January.[1] The VITTLES Board, as the new agency was called, was directed to make such studies and experiments as might be necessary to accomplish the following:

(1) Develop faster and more efficient methods of loading and unloading aircraft.

(2) Determine more economical and efficient methods of transportation of supplies from railhead to field to aircraft.

(3) Determine the need for new types of equipment which would be more economical, considering procurement, operational expense, and efficiency.

----

[1] EUCOM SO 23, 31 Jan 49, par. 21. UNCLASSIFIED.

(4) Make recommendations to the chief of Transportation Division as to the erection of warehousing facilities at Rhein/ Main and Wiesbaden airfields.[2]

Findings of the board were to be reported by the Chief, Transportation Division, to the Director, Logistics Division, by 15 February.

31. VITTLES Board Reports

The VITTLES Board held frequent meetings during February. In his report of 15 February the Chief, Transportation Division, informed the Director, Logistics Division, that CALTF had changed the proposed method of operation at Rhein/Main Air Base three times within the past three weeks, making it impossible for the VITTLES Board to reach final findings on all of the matters assigned to it for study.[3] The board continued its work into early March, in order to conduct certain practical experiments in the use of trucks and loading equipment. In a final memorandum on the results of these experiments, the president of the board, Lt. Col. W. B. Bunker of Transportation Division, stated that it was impossible to arrive at definite conclusions as to types of materials and the handling of equipment and vehicles best suited for the VITTLES operation because no information had been received from the Air Force as to the type of operation which it contemplated.[4] Nevertheless the board reported that it had made a number of findings which, if in conformity with the preferred operational methods of the Air Force would permit greater efficiency in cargo-loading operations. The main recommendations and findings of the board were as follows:[5]

---

[2]IRS, Dir EUCOM Log Div to EUCOM Trans Div, 27 Jan 49, sub: Materials Handling Methods, Operation VITTLES. UNCLASSIFIED. In EUCOM Trans Div, Notes of Meeting of VITTLES Board of 2 Feb 49, Incl 2.

[3]IRS, C/EUCOM Trans Div to Dir EUCOM Log Div, sub: Materials Handling Methods, Operation VITTLES, 15 Feb 49. UNCLASSIFIED. In EUCOM Trans Div 580, Item 4.

[4]Memo, Lt Col W. B. Bunker, C/EUCOM Trans Div Opns Br, for Col A. V. Winton, EUCOM Log Div, 18 Mar 49. UNCLASSIFIED. In ibid., Item 1.

[5]In general these findings did not warrant any changes in operating methods already being used.

a. In-Transit Warehousing Facilities at Rhein/Main. On 15 February the chief of Transportation Division transmitted to Logistics Division the following recommendation by the board: "It is very desirable to erect 'in transit' warehousing or shed facilities at Rhein/Main. Facilities available in Hanger 27, at Wiesbaden, appear to be adequate. A shed approximately 1,700 x 14' high with open sides and with a 20' wide covered apron on the truck side and 10' wide covered apron on the rear side is desirable."[6] It was agreed by Maj. Gen. William H. Tunner, Commanding General, CALTF, that the warehouse would be constructed on the north side of the railroad, with a paved area 200 feet wide between the warehouse platform and the runway.[7]

b. Use of Forklift Tractor. An experiment conducted at Wiesbaden indicated that under ideal conditions a forklift tractor (one American operator plus five laborers) could compete satisfactorily with hand labor (10 laborers) in loading palletized coal and other sacked commodities. Such loading would eliminate the backing of a semitrailer to the plane door, saving time and lessening the possibility of damage to the plane. On the other hand, the board also noted that from a cost standpoint there would be little or no saving, since the American forklift operator would cost the Army appropriated dollars, while the laborers he would replace were paid in marks chargeable to German sources.

c. Use of 2½-ton 6-by-6 Trucks to Haul Trailers. Board members also found it practical, under ideal conditions, to use a 2½-ton 6-by-6 truck to haul a 10-ton semitrailer, using a dolly converter. Further experimentation under actual operating conditions was regarded as necessary before this method could be fully recommended.

d. Palletized Loads. A series of experiments with palletized loads led to the following conclusions: (1) Twenty-four sacks or approximately 2,600 pounds of coal or other commodities were a practical load, per pallet; (2) Palletized loads could be

---

6C/N 2, C/EUCOM Trans Div to Dir EUCOM Log Div, sub: Materials Handling Methods, Operation VITTLES, 15 Feb 49. UNCLASSIFIED. In EUCOM Trans Div 580, Item 4.

7EUCOM Trans Div, Notes of VITTLES Board Mtg of 14 Feb 49. UNCLASSIFIED. Addition of two feet to the height of the warehouse would increase its capacity an estimated 50 percent, as recommended by the VITTLES Board.

stacked either three, six, or nine feet high without injury to
cargo containers; (3) Commodities could be palletized and stored
either on the ground, on an apron, or in warehouses; (4) Palletized loads were practical in either warehouse-to-plane or rail-
head-to-plane operations.[8]

32. Ground Transport and Loading Equipment

At the beginning of 1949 U.S. Army, Europe (USAREUR) was
supplying all common user items of equipment to both Air Force
and Army elements engaged in supporting Operation VITTLES.[9]

33. Vehicles

Over 1,000 vehicles were needed by the Air Force for airlift
operations. Army support required 336 truck tractors and 672
trailers.[10] Of these, 238 tractors and 476 10-ton trailers were
in use by Transportation Corps units at Rhein/Main and Wiesbaden
airfields.[11] At Tempelhof, BLF had begun with 108 trucks in July
1948. This number had been reduced to 79 in December 1948. In
1949 it was further reduced to 74 in January, 66 in February, 61
in March, and 59 in May.[12] Both $2\frac{1}{2}$-ton cargo trucks and 10-ton
semitrailers were used in lift operations at Tempelhof. Additional vehicles were used by the British at Gatow and at the six
airfields in the British Zone, and by the French at Tegel.

34. Trucks and Trailers used by 24th TT Battalion

The 24th TT Battalion utilized 308 4-5 ton tractors and 576
10-ton trailers in airlift support during the period 1 July 1948 -

---

8Memo, Lt Col W. B. Bunker, C/EUCOM Trans Div Opns Br, for
Col A. V. Winton, EUCOM Log Div, 18 Mar 49, UNCLASSIFIED. In
EUCOM Trans Div 580, Item 1. It should be noted that palletizing
of loads for air transport would have resulted in the loss of
approximately 20 percent of aircraft cargo space.

9EUCOM Log Div Rept of Opns, 1 Jan - 31 Dec 49, p. 8.
SECRET. In EUCOM Hist Div Docs Br.

10EUCOM Ord Div Ann Nar Rept, 1949, p. 46. RESTRICTED. In
EUCOM Hist Div Docs Br.

11Interv, E. S. Lay, EUCOM Hist Div, with Lt Col H. Y. Chase,
CO 24th TT Bn, FMF, 21 Jan 49.

12Figures given to E. S. Lay, EUCOM Hist Div, by BLF Trans
Br, 21 Jun 50.

31 July 1949.[13] Each of the heavy truck companies was equipped with 48 tractors and 96 trailers.[14] Effective 1 January each shift at Rhein/Main (comprising one company and one platoon) was responsible for using 56 tractors and 96 semitrailers. This equipment was supplemented, during part of the air lift, by 2½-ton cargo trucks of the 543d Transportation Truck Company (Troop).[15]

35. Utilization of Vehicles (Rhein/Main Airfield)

Planes loaded, tractors and trailers in support (during a 24-hour period), and trailers in maintenance at Rhein/Main Airfield, for the first day of each month of 1949, and the last day of the lift, were as follows:[16]

1949	Planes Loaded	Tractors	Trailers	Trailers in Maintenance Shop
1 January[17]	175	50	282	19
1 February	193	108	306	14
1 March	166	104	319	22
1 April[18]	261	111	319	55
1 May	301	100	315	28
1 June	166	100	315	38
1 July	263	96	242	28
1 August	143	96	159	16
1 September	108	51	95	6
30 September	37	24	58	0

---

[13]24th TT Bn USAASC Memo, sub: Statistical Report on Airlift Operations from 1 July 1948 to 31 July 1949, 11 Aug 49. UNCLASSIFIED. In EUCOM Trans Div file 91, USAASC. Tractors included 254 Internationals, 45 Auto-Cars, 8 Whites, and 1 Federal.

[14]EUCOM Log Div Rept of Opns, 1 Jan – 31 Mar 49, p. 6. SECRET.

[15]24th TT Bn, FLF, Opn Air Lift Memo No. 7, 5 Apr 49, sub: Organizational Commitments for Month of April. UNCLASSIFIED. In EUCOM Trans Div file 19, USAASC. See also Memoranda No. 8, No. 10, and No. 12, in the same series.

[16]USAASC Rhein/Main Det, Sum Rept Tonnage Movements. UNCLASSIFIED. In EUCOM Trans Div USAASC file.

[17]2 January 1949: 102 Tractors employed on lift.

[18]16 April 1949: 405 planes loaded.

36. Suitability of Tractor-Trailer Combination

Experience at Rhein/Main led transportation officers to conclude that the 4-5 ton tractor and 10-ton semitrailer were unsuitable for aircraft loading operations, even with the modifications made on these vehicles during the lift. (See Appendix G.) Standard commercial 10-ton trucks were considered preferable to the tractors and trailers actually used at Rhein/Main and Wiesbaden airfields.[19]

37. Utilization of Vehicles (Berlin)

By the spring of 1949 the Transportation Corps Airhead Tempelhof (TCAHT) was using 35 tractors, 52 10-ton trailers, 22 2½-ton cargo trucks, three 1/4-ton jeeps, 1 wrecker, and 1 weapons carrier. Cargo trucks were used for **hauling** military cargo to warehouses. Tractors with semitrailers were standard equipment for hauling cargo to and from the planes.[20] The average number of tons moved per vehicle per month increased from 905.2 in December to 1225.5 in March.[21] Factors **contributing to more efficient** use of trucks included construction of better roads to the land pier, use of a single ready line, and use of warehouse space at Tempelhof instead of trucks for temporary storage of incoming military and German industrial cargo. Earlier in the lift, military supplies were delivered directly to the depots.[22]

38. Maintenance

Throughout the period vehicles at Rhein/Main were given production line maintenance by Polish mechanics under military supervision and field maintenance by the 559 MAM Company, at shops located on the air base.[23] In March Frankfurt Military

---

[19](1) Interv, B. V. Hall, EUCOM Hist Div, with Lt Col M. A. Darragh, Asst C/EUCOM Trans Div Opns Br, 8 Jun 49. (2) 24th TT Bn, USAASC Memo, 11 Aug 49, sub: Statistical Report on Airlift Operations from 1 July 1948 to 31 July 1949; UNCLASSIFIED. In EUCOM Trans Div file 91, USAASC. Included as Appendix G.

[20](1) Ibid. (2) BMP Trans Br, Supply and Operational SOP for TC Airhead Tempelhof, 4 Apr 49.

[21]BMP Rept of Opns, 1 Jan - 31 Mar 49, p. 141. RESTRICTED.

[22]Interv, E. S. Lay, EUCOM Hist Div, with Lt Col J. F. Phillips, BMP Trans Off, 21 Jun 50.

[23]EUCOM CCLT Rept of Opns, 1 Jan - 31 Mar 49, pp. 23 - 24. CONFIDENTIAL.

Post received 65 extra vehicles so that the field maintenance shop at Rhein/Main could furnish a ready-for-issue vehicle to replace any vehicle requiring more than seven days' work.[24] The gradual upward trend in tractor maintenance in 1949 is shown by the following figures:[25]

	Assigned	Available	PM[26]	2d Ech[27]	Ordnance	Other
January						
1st week	356	211	47	30	61	7
3rd week	308	184	43	22	53	6
February						
1st week	308	186	40	30	45	7
March						
1st week	308	167	38	43	59	1
April						
1st week	308	210	48	31	14	5
May						
1st week	308	215	51	27	13	2
June						
1st week	308	205	51	28	19	5
July						
1st week	260	184	40	18	13	5
3rd week	308	213	47	21	24	3

---

[24](1) Ibid., p. 33. CONFIDENTIAL. (2) Ltr, EUCOM to CG FMP, 16 Mar 49, and Memo for Rcd, sgd Lt Col John J. Petro, Jr., EUCOM Log Div Equip Maint Br, 16 Mar 49. In EUCOM AG 451 General, Vol. II (1949), Vehicles, Items 47 & 38. (3) Interv, E. S. Lay, EUCOM Hist Div, with Lt Col A. B. Evans, C/EUCOM Trans Div Plans and Intel Br, 29 Nov 51.

[25]24th TT Bn USAASC Memo, sub: Stat Rept on Airlift Opns from 1 July 1948 to 31 July 1949, 11 Aug 49. UNCLASSIFIED. In EUCOM Trans Div file 91, USAASC. See Appendix G.

[26]Production line maintenance

[27]Second echelon or organizational maintenance

The number of trailers requiring repairs decreased as follows:[28]

	Trailers in Shop (average per day)	Number repaired (average per day)
April	32	10
May	33	9
June	18	8
July	10	6

Items causing the most serious problems in maintaining tractors for airlift support service were axles, clutches, fifth wheels, engine replacements, and (in cold weather) batteries. Trailers required frequent maintenance or special modifications of landing gears, side panels, reflectors, and safety chains. Maintenance problems were noticeably reduced by the assignment of an additional truck company to the operation in January and the inauguration of the new schedule (paragraph 28, above) placing less arduous demands upon truck transportation personnel.[29]

39. Vehicle Maintenance

Better organizational maintenance was achieved by USAASC through expert supervision and through increased success in obtaining second echelon repair parts.[30] These factors, together with improvement in driving conditions, resulted in a striking reduction in the number of vehicles requiring repairs. In January an average of sixty tractors and seventy trailers were being sent to ordnance daily. These numbers were reduced to twenty tractors and thirty trailers, in April, and to

---

[28]Ibid.

[29]The importance of the new schedule for both maintenance and morale is stressed in 24th TT Bn Rept of Opns, 1 Jan – 31 Mar 49. UNCLASSIFIED. For directives showing efforts of the battalion headquarters to keep maintenance at a high level, see 24th TT Bn, Opn Air Lift Memo No. 2, 2 Feb 49, sub: Organizational Maintenance; Ibid., Memo No. 4, 10 Mar 49, sub: Drivers' Daily Preventive Maintenance Service; Ibid., Memo No. 5, 17 Mar 49, sub: Care and Security of Automotive Equipment; and Ibid., Memo No. 6, 28 Mar 49, sub: 24th Transportation Truck Battalion Installations. In 24th TT Bn Rept of Opns, 1 Jan – 31 Mar 49. UNCLASSIFIED. In EUCO Hist Div Docs Br.

[30]Interv, E. S. Lay, ASCOM Hist Div, with Lt Col W. E. Schoenfeld, CO USAASC, RLAFB, 13 Oct 49. RESTRICTED.

TEGEL AIRBASE

SCALE 1:4000

British Air Control

GCA
Land

OVERRUN

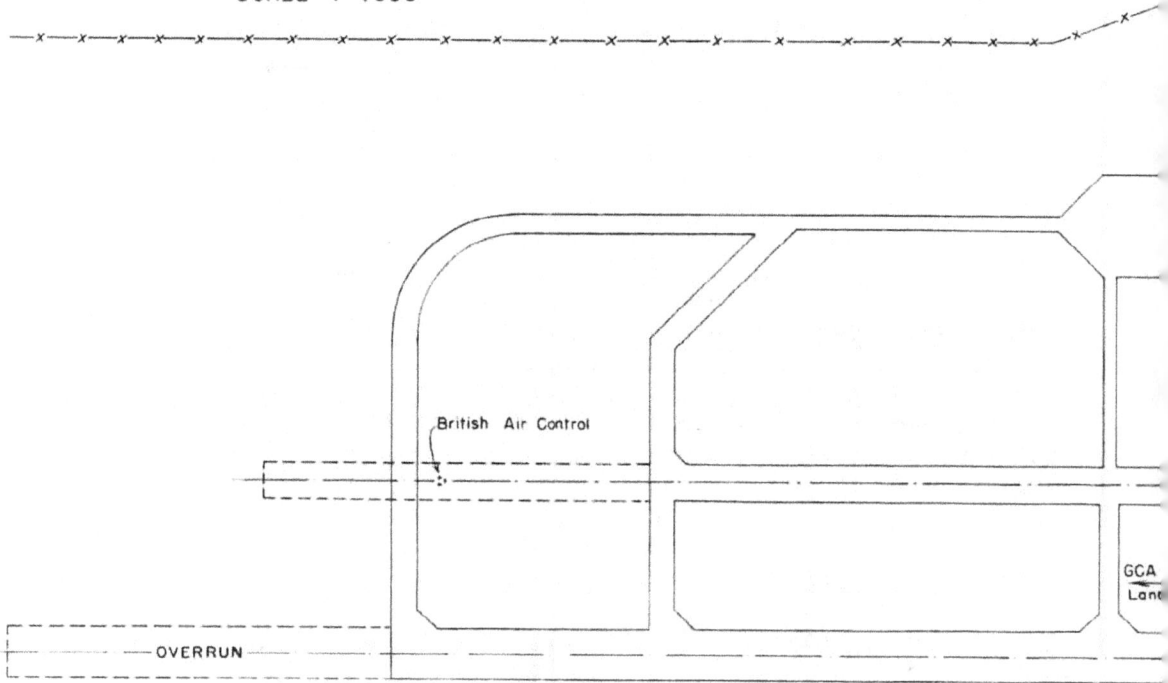

Drawn by Hist Div, EUCO

APRON

Taxiway

as Tanks

GCA Control Apron
Landing Direction →

WARM UP

(BABS)
British Air Control

— EXISTING RUNWAY —

— NEW RUNWAY — — — — — OVERRUN — — —

I 50
Glide Angle

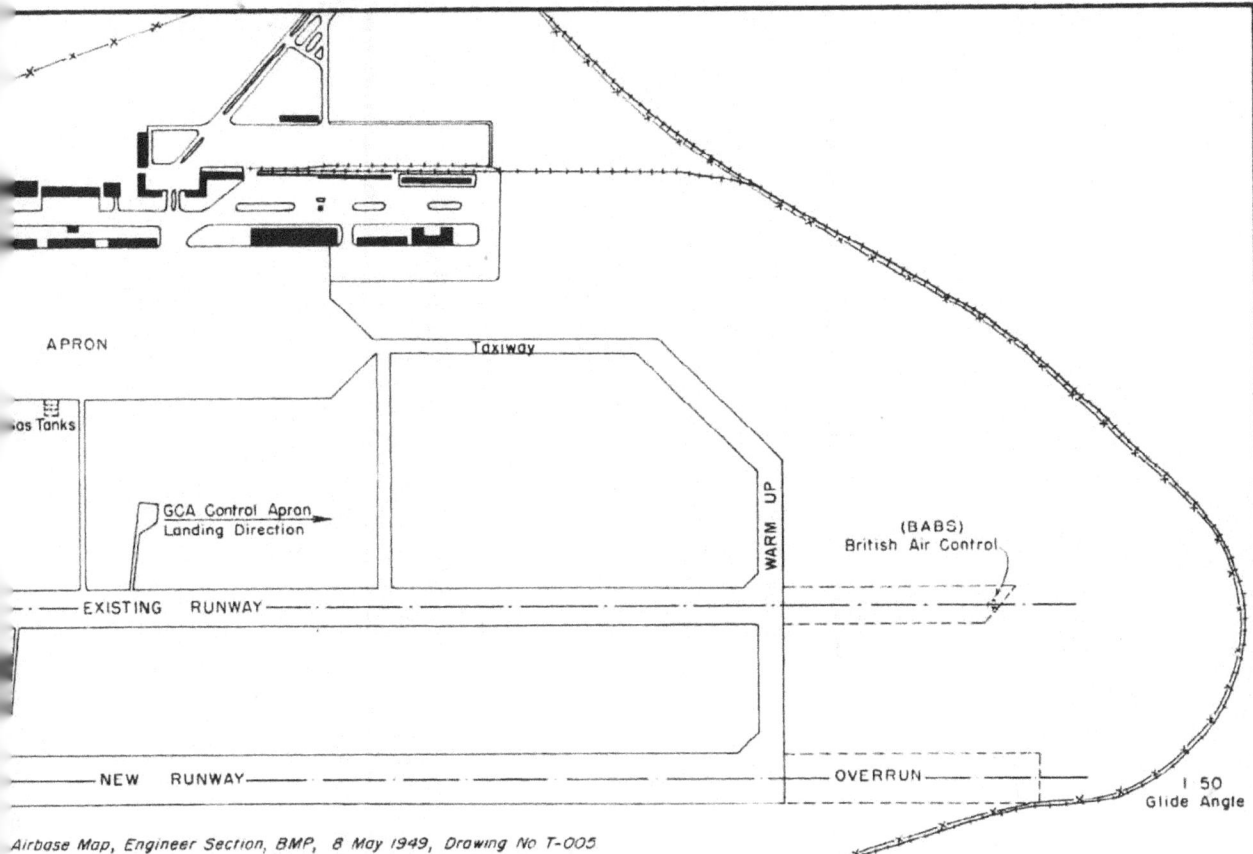

Airbase Map, Engineer Section, BMP, 8 May 1949, Drawing No T-005

approximately six tractors and five trailers, in June.[31] In general, lift experience showed that vehicles subjected to around-the-clock usage under adverse weather and road conditions could be used indefinitely if maintenance practices were strictly observed, rebuilt engines were available, and far above normal supplies of tires and spare parts were obtainable. As tractors and trailers were old and parts not readily available, a great deal of difficulty was experienced due to vehicles being dead-lined.

40. Construction at Tegel Airfield

The biggest job of BMP Engineers in 1949 was the building of a second runway at Tegel Airfield. This runway was started on 14 March 1949 and made operational on 4 August. (See Plan 1.)

a. Dimensions. The new runway at Tegel measured 6,500 x 200 feet. To this was added 1,500 feet of 24-inch base which could be surfaced (with six inches of asphaltic macadam) on short notice should characteristics of new planes demand an 8,000-foot runway. The completed runway contained 145,000 square yards of paving; the taxiways and warm-up pads, 50,000; the overrun, 56,000; and new roads, 1,530 square yards.[32]

b. Materials. BMP engineers used crushed brick, with old street car rails for ballast. By arrangement with the city government, whole bricks were salvaged by local labor from bombed-out buildings (those over 60 percent destroyed could be razed by the city) within a radius of five miles, shoveled into trucks by engineer equipment, and crushed at the airfield site. Despite some initial skepticism the resulting construction proved highly successful. California bearing ratios (CBR's)[33] of from 72 to 80 were attained in the compaction of the base, which was laid over a sub-base of sand and silt with a CBR of not more than 30.[34] In building the second runway the engineers moved 600,000 cubic yards of earth and used 350,000 cubic yards of brick rubble,

---

[31]Interv, E. S. Lay, Hist Div, with Lt Col J. B. Andrews, C/USAASC Opn Br, 2 Aug 49. RESTRICTED.

[32]Off of BMP Engr Br C/Opns file, Statistics on building and construction at airfields.

[33]Unit of compaction employed in engineering.

[34]Interv, E. S. Lay, EUCOM Hist Div, with Mr. Nelson G. Greene, C/BMP Engr Br C/Opns, 22 Jun 50. CONFIDENTIAL.

36,000 cubic yards of crushed rock, and 570,000 gallons of asphalt. All of the asphalt was shipped from the United States and flown from the U.S. Zone to Berlin.35

c. Manpower. Only 300 German laborers, engaged by French authorities at the airfield, 60 German mechanics and 10 German supervisors hired by the U.S. Army, and 110 U.S. military personnel were needed in building the second runway at Tegel. Where thousands had supplied hand labor to build the first runway, machines airlifted from the U.S. Zone were used in grading the second. Military manhours totaled 111,467, German manhours 357,406.

d. Costs in Deutsche Marks. Total Deutsche Mark (DM) costs of the second runway, including expenditures for German employees and brick, rubble, and stone, amounted to DM 2,634,353.60,36 charged to the non-occupation cost German budget.

41. Study of Airfield Construction, Berlin

By the beginning of 1949 valuable experience in new construction techniques had been gained. To this progress the EUCOM Chief Engineer contributed by sponsoring a visit to Germany by Mr. Charles R. Foster, an expert in soil mechanics and flexible pavements from the Flexible Pavements Laboratory, Waterways Experiment Station, Vicksburg, Mississippi. His mission was to survey airfield sites, to see whether construction methods could be modified to reduce the use of critical supplies and equipment, and to develop design factors of prepared surface based upon determined load-bearing qualities of subsurface and base course material. With Mr. F. G. Scherrer, Construction Branch, EUCOM Engineer Division, Mr. Foster made soil surveys of Tempelhof and Tegel airfields on 16 September 1949. Resulting recommendations were referred to USAFE for use in subsequent planning.37

42. Resurfacing of South Runway at Tempelhof

A secondary project completed by BMP Engineers in 1949 was the resurfacing of the south runway at Templehof Air Force Base.

35Ibid.

36(1) Ibid. (2) Interv, E. S. Lay, EUCOM Hist Div, with Mr. Nelson G. Greene, BMP Engr Br, C/Opns, 22 Jun 50. RESTRICTED.

37Interv, E. S. Lay, EUCOM Hist Div, with Mr. Fred G. Scherrer, EUCOM Engr Div Constr Br, 29 May 51. RESTRICTED.

54. Handling of Food at Airfields

It was the experience of BICO that loading, unloading and storage of food should be done under supervision of personnel competent to judge whether the handling was being properly done and having sufficient authority over personnel doing the work to take immediate corrective action. (Appendix A.)

55. Packaging of Foods

In packaging foods for air transport it was found desirable to keep tare weights low and at the same time to use packages that would protect the food from pilferage, weather, etc., and be of a size to be easily moved by hand. Types and weights of food packages were standardized as much as possible in the Berlin Air Lift, to facilitate aircraft loading, although many German firms were reluctant to make any changes in their packaging and labeling practices. (Appendix A.)

56. Pilferage

Pilferage of cargo was a more serious problem at Tempelhof, where laborers were supplied mainly by the city government, than at Rhein/Main and Wiesbaden, where they were members of organized units under Army supervision. At Berlin much of the pilferage consisted of removal of sugar and flour, by countless ingenious methods, during cargo unloading and hauling. Sugar, flour, butter and other food items were removed from containers and concealed on the person of the pilferer or hidden on the air base, where many small packages were found by Transportation personnel. Such pilferage presented a double problem of loss to the proper recipient and added sales on the black market. During the entire lift about one hundred laborers were released from employment at Tempelhof on account of pilferage. Opportunities for large-scale thefts were reduced by placing the unloading of planes and the delivery of goods off the air base under separate systems of control.[60]

57. Packaging of Commercial Goods

Packaging of commercial goods required attention to the problem of pilferage, as well as to correct marking and ease of handling. Files of the U.S. Army Airlift Support Command contain

---

[60]Interv, E. S. Lay, EUCOM Hist Div, with Lt Col J. F. Phillips, BAP Trans Off, 23 Jun 50. RESTRICTED.

complaints from a representative of a German firm, stating that shoes had been removed both from pasteboard containers and from wooden boxes fastened with iron bands.[61] Pilferage of shoes practically ceased when, on recommendation of CMGLS, shoes for only the left or the right foot were forwarded to Berlin over a period of several days.

58. Packaging of Coal

Since coal was the principal item of cargo lifted to Berlin it was urgent to find the most economical method of shipping it. Experiments with a direct drop, which would have avoided the delay of landing at Berlin, proved unsuccessful; coal dropped directly from the airplane became pulverized on hitting the ground. Airlift agencies therefore continued to face the problem of finding sacks in which to send coal to Berlin.

a. Experience with Jute and Canvas. Early in the lift the Quartermaster Corps supplied nearly 500,000 duffel bags for use as coal sacks. Later a type of jute bag was procured by the United Kingdom and heavy jute bags were obtained from Switzerland. On 27 January BEALCON reported that a UK-procured jute bag could be counted on for three trips to Berlin and a Swiss bag for five trips, while a U.S. Army duffel bag would make 20 or 21 trips successfully. It was agreed that BEALCON should recommend to BICO that all future purchases of coal sacks be of the duffel bag type.[62]

b. Requirements for Sacks. On the basis of a daily average lift of 5,000 gross short tons and a 10-day turnaround the lift was estimated to require 1,000,000 coal sacks. An additional 300,000 sacks were required to provide a 15,000-ton reserve stock at the various air shipping points.[63] In January the BICO Coal Branch representative estimated that the lift would require approximately 850,000 sacks per month. Approximately 1,716,800 serviceable or recoverable sacks were available at the end of January, and 883,000 new sacks were due in. The total was

---

61Ltr, German Civ to CALTF, 8 Jun 49. In EUCOM Trans Div file 28, USAASC Pilfered Cargo.

62BEALCON Mins, Decisions Reached 27 Jan 1949. UNCLASSIFIED. In EUCOM Trans Div file 1, USAASC.

63Ibid.

regarded as sufficient to meet requirements up to 15 March.[64] On
21 April a review of the sack situation showed that 100,000 cotton
sacks had been received from the U.S. on an order for 370,000;
Commerce and Industry Group of BICO had approved purchase of
450,000 jute sacks from Switzerland, using Joint Export-Import
Agency funds; 400,000 jute sacks were being delivered monthly
from Germany; and 2,000,000 sacks had been ordered for June and
July.[65]

c. Control of Supply of Sacks. Airlift experience showed
that procedures must be worked out for inspection and prompt return of coal sacks to coal-loading areas after use, and that controls must be established to avoid their loss. Early in 1949 it
was arranged to have bags sorted at Berlin and returned in lots of
ten. Nine serviceable bags were placed in a serviceable bag of
the same type (either jute or canvas) while unserviceable jute
bags were put in a canvas bag and vice versa.[66] Over $3,000,000
worth of sacks were found to have been wrongfully disposed of by
German coal firms during the build-up period. Of these, approximately 330,000 duffel bags, worth around $1,000,000 were located
by BICO in the Frankfurt area and recovered by direct action.[67]
Controls on the return of sacks were then set up at the south end
of the lift and losses through theft dropped to 1 or 2 percent.
About 15 February a sack sorting and storage point was organized
in Sachsenhausen (in Frankfurt) and sack control and distribution
responsibilities were assigned by BICO to a German contractor.[68]

d. Development of Paper Sacks. The most useful lesson concerning air shipment of coal was that it could be accomplished
in specially-manufactured but inexpensive paper bags. Development of multiwalled paper sacks for shipping coal began in the
early spring of 1949. A representative of BICO worked with
Transportation Corps officers to make a sack with the right dimensions and wearing characteristics. Experimental sacks were

---

[64]BEALCOM Mins, Decisions Reached 12 Jan 1949, and Decisions
Reached 27 January 1949. UNCLASSIFIED. In EUCOM Trans Div file
1, USAASC.

[65]BICO, Agreed US/UK Conclusions, sub: Decisions taken by
BEALCOM, 21 Apr 49. UNCLASSIFIED. In EUCOM Trans Div File 1,
USA SC.

[66]EM Rept of Opns, 1 Jan - 31 Mar 49, p. 140. RESTRICTED.

[67]Interv, E. S. Lay, EUCOM Hist Div, with Mr. David Tatum,
Office of Gen C. L. Adcock, BICO Chairman, 10 Aug 49. CONFIDEN-
TIAL.

[68]Ibid

tested successfully from the end of March until May. Each sack had four layers of paper, the inside one being waterproof. Filled sacks were fastened at the top with wire. Repairing of jute sacks stopped in April and paper sacks were used extensively in May. Produced in Germany at a cost of less than one cent each, paper sacks reduced the cost of coal sacks for the lift from $250,000 to $12,000 per month. In August the sack control point at Sachsenhausen was employing a staff of 150, including Germans sorting and counting sacks at the control point and bookkeepers located at the plants of 21 local sacking firms.[69]

59. Air Transport of Gasoline

Shipment of gasoline in 55-gallon drums proved unsatisfactory for several reasons. The metal drums were difficult to handle, they had to be steamed when emptied, and backloading them to the western zones was awkward and time-consuming. These problems were solved by resort to bulk shipment of gasoline and oil in British tanker aircraft.[70]

[69](1) Ibid. (2) Stars and Stripes, Eur. ed., March 27, 1949, "Lift Testing Paper Bags."

[70]According to report on the Army Air Transport Organization distributed 29 September 1949, a report covering details of the technical arrangements for the handling of liquid fuel at rear and forward airfields was then being prepared by Headquarters British Army of the Rhine (Supply and Transport Directorate). Ltr, Brigadier J. A. Dawson, AATO, to BAOR, 29 Sep 49, sub: Organization, responsibilities and duties of the Army Air Transport Organization. In EUCOM Trans Div, USAMSC unnumbered file.

CHAPTER IV

Supply Levels, Priorities, and Tonnages

60. Cargo Requirements During 1949

From 1 January 1949 throughout the remainder of the blockade the air lift more than met the minimum requirements of West Berlin. General Clay states in his book, Decision in Germany, "We could sustain a minimum economy with an average daily air lift of 4,000 tons for the German population and 500 tons for the Allied occupation forces."[1] A detailed study by the Office of Military Government, U.S. (OMGUS) concluded that minimum daily requirements for Berlin for the period 1 April 1949 to 30 March 1950 would be 7,250 tons,[2] comprising 6,586 tons German civil cargo, 284 tons U.S. military cargo, 249 tons British military cargo, 91 tons French military cargo, and 40 tons in passengers. Essential minimum daily requirements for the summer months were estimated at only 4,500 tons daily. Normal Berlin requirements were placed at 12,000 tons daily.[3] By comparison with the foregoing estimates, airlift cargoes for Berlin actually averaged 4,490.9 short tons daily in January 1949, [4]

---

[1]Lucius D. Clay, Decision in Germany (New York, 1950), p. 365.

[2]Type of ton not specified. OMGUS ordinarily used net or gross metric tons in reporting airlift shipments. A metric ton is 2,204.6 pounds.

[3]Cable SX - 3059, CINCEUR to USMA, Paris for Dorr and Magruder, 11 Jun 49. SECRET. In EUCOM SGS 094 Berlin, Item 58.

[4]Based on January total of 139,218.8 given in USAFE, History of Headquarters, United States Air Forces in Europe, February 1949, p. 14. SECRET.

7,825 in April,[5] 8,011 in June,[6] and 7,953.1 in July.[7]

61. Supply Levels at Berlin Military Post

Faced with having to depend solely on air transport for its maintenance, Berlin Military Post had contracted its installations and reduced consumption of many items soon after the start of the blockade.[8] Post exchange daily consumption rates, for example, were cut from a pre-blockade average of 18 tons to 3 tons.[9] Despite the continuing expansion of the lift into the late spring of 1949, incoming shipments of military supplies were carefully controlled at all times to avoid their encroaching on tonnages needed for civil supplies. Supplies held by the technical services at Berlin as of 1 January 1949 are shown in Table 1.

62. Requirements for Military Cargo

First estimates of the requirements of BMP for air lift had been stated on 1 April 1948, in terms of monthly tonnages and cubic measurements.[10] This early plan called for a maximum of fifty C-47 plane trips per day. A later computation revised the estimate (at 2½ tons per plane) to ninety-nine and one-half C-47's (at 2½ tons per plane), exclusive of the lift which might be needed for coal, petroleum products, and engineer construction materials.[11] During January 1949, military cargo received at Tempelhof Air Base included 2,517.82 tons of quartermaster supplies, 177.1 tons of Air Corps materiel, 670.82 tons of supplies for other services and of miscellaneous cargo such as household goods, baggage and mail, 6,711 tons

---

[5]Ltr, W. A. Fagan, BEALCON Chm to CO USAASC, 13 May 49, sub: Operational Report for April 1949. In EUCOM Trans Div file No. 18, USAASC.

[6](1) USAFE, History of Headquarters, United States Air Forces in Europe, June 1949, p. 50. SECRET. (2) OMGUS Air Lift Report (ALREP) No. 305, Pt. 2 gives a figure of 7,622.2 short tons and OMGUS Mthly Rept of the Mil Gov No. 49, July 1949, p. 7, UNCLASSIFIED, gives a daily average of 6,914.8 gross metric tons.

[7](1) OMGUS Mthly Rept of the Mil Gov No. 49, Jul 49, p. 7. UNCLASSIFIED. (2) OMGUS ALREP No. 310, 5 Aug 49. CONFIDENTIAL. In Office BMP C/Trans Br.

[8]See the Berlin Air Lift - 1948, par. 32. SECRET.

[9]Interv, E. S. Lay, EUCOM Hist Div, with Lt Col Kenneth G. Haymaker, BMP S4, 21 Jun 50. CONFIDENTIAL.

[10]The Berlin Air Lift - 1948, App. I. SECRET.

[11]Interv, E. S. Lay, EUCOM Hist Div, with Lt Col Kenneth G. Haymaker, BMP S4, 21 Jun 50. CONFIDENTIAL.

Table I -- Berlin Military Post Supplies, 1 January 1949

Service	Days of Supply On Hand
Quartermaster	
Individual clothing and equipment	20
Organizational equipment	20
Office supplies	27
Packing and crating supplies	30
Cleaning and preserving materials	40
Class "X" clothing	22
Non-standard and miscellaneous items	5
Class I - Subsistence:	
(a) Perishables ("A" ration and commissary sales)	20-40
(b) Non-perishables	25-50
Class III - POL:	
(a) Gasoline	32
(b) Kerosene	88
(c) Diesel fuel	28
(d) Lubricating oils	27
(e) Greases	22
Ordnance	
60 percent of line items	180
2 percent of line items	150
3½ percent of line items	120
3 percent of line items	90
11 percent of line items	60
4 percent of line items	45
2 percent of line items	25
½ percent of line items	10
14 percent of line items	0*
Engineer	
Class II (general supplies)	115
Class III (solid fuels) including coal in bins under control of consumer:	

---

*Items which were not required or were on order and immediately available on call at Ordnance depots.

of engineer coal, and 819 tons of supplies for the French authorities in Berlin. Eleven tons of U.S. supplies were landed at Gatow and one third of a ton of Air Corps materiel was received at Tegel. Outbound military cargo processed at Tempelhof totaled 1,124.64 tons.[12]

63. Military Coal Requirements and Supply

From 1 July through 30 September 1948 no coal had been added to BMP stocks. On 30 September these stocks contained 10,017 metric tons. On 31 December they amounted to 6,485 metric tons.[13] Between 1 October 1948 and 1 February 1949 the Solid Fuels Division of the Hanau Engineer Depot was responsible for preparing military coal for shipment to Berlin. Coal sacked for BMP at Rheinau (the engineer coal supply point) totaled 5,838 metric tons in October, 4,718 in November, 3,679 in December, and 7,507 in January.[14] On 12 January it was agreed at a meeting of BEALCOM that U.S. military coal requirements should be met from the over-all tonnage dispatched to Berlin.[15] On 27 January BEALCOM provided that during the period 1 - 28 February the Rhein/Main civil economy daily coal allocation should include 280 tons of U.S. military coke, the Celle allocation should include 101 tons of British military coal, and the Fassberg allocation should include 94 tons of military coal for the French. This made a total of 475 tons of coke and coal to be shipped daily in addition to 3,632 tons for the German economy.[16] Throughout the spring and most of the summer of 1949 BMP retained its daily lift allocation of 182 tons of coal.[17] But in practice, after 1 February, engineer coal for BMP was obtained at Berlin, through purchase from civil economy stocks. On 30 September 1949, the final day of the air lift, BMP had solid fuel supplies amounting to 28,533 metric tons.[18]

---

[12]Figures supplied to E. S. Lay, EUCOM Hist Div, by BMP Trans Br, 17 Feb 49. UNCLASSIFIED.

[13]EUCOM Off of the Compt, Mthly Rept to the DCINC, 31 Dec 48. SECRET. In EUCOM Hist Div Docs Br.

[14]Interv, E. S. Lay, EUCOM Hist Div, with Mr. J. L. Collins, EUCOM Engr Div Opns Br, 29 May 51. UNCLASSIFIED.

[15]BICO, Decisions reached by BEALCOM at Mtg of 12 Jan 49. UNCLASSIFIED. In EUCOM Trans Div file No. 1, USAASC.

[16]Ibid., Mtg of 27 Jan 49. UNCLASSIFIED. In EUCOM Trans Div file No. 1, USAASC.

[17]This allocation was listed as "Engineer Class III solid fuels, 182 tons." See allocations given in EUCOM Trans Div file No. 33, USAASC, U.S. Military Tonnages Allocations. UNCLASSIFIED.

[18]EUCOM Log Div Rept of Opns, 1 Jan - 31 Dec 49, p. 20. SECRET. In EUCOM Hist Div Docs Br files.

64. Miscellaneous Military Shipments

In addition to cargo for the normal support of the military community, BMP was concerned with the air shipment of certain specialized items. These additional types of cargo included baggage, household goods, privately-owned vehicles, and sacks. By 1 January 1949 some 6,564,879 pounds of household goods had been flown from Berlin to Rhein/Main.[19] Air transport of baggage and household goods into and out of Berlin during the first three months of 1949 was as follows:[20]

Month (1949)	Baggage (pieces) In	Out	Household goods (pounds) In	Out
January	190	127	11,715	174,518
February	246	118	13,854	96,017
March	264	130	43,568	140,923

Between 21 July 1948 and 31 March 1949, 336 privately-owned automobiles were delivered to Gatow and Tempelhof for out-shipment by air.[21] So long as military coal was distinguished from civilian coal en route to Berlin, there were "military" coal sacks to be shipped back to the western zones. Outbound engineer coal sacks totaled 295.5 short tons during January 1949.[22]

65. Tonnage Allocations for Military Cargo for BMP

Maximum daily airlift tonnages allocated for main categories of military requirements for BMP during 1949 are shown in Table 2. In practice these allocations were flexibly utilized by BMP in calling cargo forward from zonal supply points. Requisitions were screened by the S4 to keep them within military tonnage limits but extra tonnages for one service were brought in on the allocation of some other service, when necessary.[23]

---

[19]EUCOM OCOT Rept of Opns, 4th qtr 1948, p. 38. CONFIDENTIAL. In EUCOM Hist Div Docs Br files.

[20]BMP Rept of Opns, 1st qtr 1949, p. 142. RESTRICTED. In EUCOM Hist Div Docs Br files.

[21]Ibid., p. 138.

[22]From figures supplied to E. S. Lay, EUCOM Hist Div, by BMP Trans Br, 17 Feb 49. UNCLASSIFIED.

[23]Interv, E. S. Lay, EUCOM Hist Div, with Lt Col Kenneth G. Haymaker, BMP S4, 21 Jun 50. CONFIDENTIAL.

66. Supply Levels of Civil Stocks at Berlin

By the beginning of 1949 it was plain that the blockade could not force West Berlin to go hungry or to shut down its public utilities and its growing industries. Stock levels of food and coal, and requirements for air transport of consumer and industrial products, were closely watched by military government and civil authorities in West Berlin. Representatives of the U.S., British, and French commandants met in the Air Lift Staff Committee, and this agency in turn advised BEALCOM of changing requirements for the delivery of food, coal, and other types of civil cargo. The problems faced by BICO with regard to the procurement and shipment of food for West Berlin are described in Appendix A.

a. Civil Food Stocks. By 5 January 1949, food stocks at Berlin had risen to a 41-day level of supply, based on an estimated requirement of 1,435,02 short tons per day.[24] During the first ten days of 1949 the daily lift of food to Berlin exceeded the BEALCOM target by 41.5 percent, supplying an average of 1,640.4 gross tons per day instead of the indicated 1,159. (See Table 3, BEALCOM Performance Index, 1 – 10 January 1949.) On 12 January BEALCOM emphasized instructions that any available airlift capacity beyond the approved daily targets should be used to carry coal rather than food or miscellaneous cargo, in order to build up Berlin coal stocks.[25] From a 41-day level on 5 January food stocks fell to a 37-day level on 17 January.[26] Food stocks reflected over-all averages of 30 days on 1 February, 28 days on 8 February, and 26 days on 20 February. On 1 March they stood at a 25-day level, from which they increased to a 32-day level on 7 March, a 33-day level on 29 March, and a 34-day level on 19 April.[27] After the lifting of the blockade on 12 May 1949 the proportion of airlift tonnage allocated to food for West Berlin was gradually reduced despite the interruptions which took place in rail service to Berlin during the late spring and early summer. At the end of June it was announced by BICO that

---

[24] USAFE Monograph, USAFE and the Berlin Airlift 1949 (Wiesbaden 1950), p. 352. SECRET.

[25] (1) BICO, Agreed US/UK Conclusions, sub: Decisions Taken by BEALCOM Mtg of 12 Jan 49. UNCLASSIFIED. In EUCOM Trans Div file 1, USAASC. (2) OMGUS Mthly Rept of the Mil Gov, Jan 49, p.7, states that "the daily average was deliberately reduced in January to 953 net metric tons from 1,363 tons in December because the stocks of food already in Berlin were higher than necessary." UNCLASSIFIED.

[26] BICO, Agreed US/UK Conclusions, sub: Decisions Taken by BEALCOM Mtg of 27 Jan 49. UNCLASSIFIED. In EUCOM Trans Div file 1, USAASC.

[27] Ibid., Mtgs of 23 Feb, 10 Mar, and 21 Apr 49. UNCLASSIFIED.

Table 2 -- Maximum Daily Airlift Allocations for Berlin Military Post, 1949

Type of Cargo	Gross Short Tons
Total	423.0
Subtotal	68.0
Quartermaster	
Class I	55.0
Class II and IV	5.0
Class III (oils and greases)	3.0
Subtotal	36.0
Engineer	
Class II and IV	15.0
Ordnance	
Class II, IV and V	5.0
Medical	
Class II and IV	0.1
Signal	
Class II and IV	0.3
EES (including Coca-Cola)	10.5
Special Service	0.1
Miscellaneous (including mail)	5.0
Subtotal	58.0
Quartermaster	
Class III	
Gasoline 32	
AF Construction 8	40.0
Diesel 10	
AF Construction 8	18.0
Engineer	
AF Construction and maintenance (equipment and supplies	84.0
Solid Fuels	182.0

Source: Figures supplied to F.S. Lay, EUCOM Hist Div, by BMP S4, 21 Jun 50. UNCLASSIFIED.

Table 3 — BEALCOM Performance Index

Daily Averages

(All Figures in Gross Short Tons)

Period 1 – 10 Jan (Incl) Airport	Food Target	Food Perform.	Coal Target	Coal Perform.	Misc. Target	Misc. Perform.	Totals Target	Totals Perform.	Perform Index
Totals	1159	1640.4	3328	3283.1	796	675.6	5283	5599.1	105.9%
Celle	220	255.3	738	615.4	0	.2	958	870.9	90.9%
Fassberg	0	0	1500	1488.6	0	0	1500	1488.6	99.2%
Hamburg	56	87.1	0	0	40	6.7	96	93.8	97.7%
Lubeck	0	0	100	137.4	82	46.8	182	184.2	101.2%
Rhein/Main	298	642.1	890	937.2	312	273.8	1500	1853.1	123.6%
Schleswigland	0	0	100	76.6	52	25.1	152	101.7	66.9%
Wiesbaden	102	210.6	0	24.1	193	205.2	295	439.9	149.1%
Wunstorf	483	445.3	0	3.8	117	117.8	600	566.9	94.5%
Performance Index		141.5%		98.7%		84.9%		105.9%	

Source: BICO, Agreed US/UK Conclusions, sub: Decisions Taken by BEALCOM, 7th Mtg, 12 Jan 49. UNCLASSIFIED.

- 63 -

the food lift from Wiesbaden and Rhein/Main would be discontinued as soon after 1 July as the rail pipeline supporting these airfields had been emptied.[28]

 b. Civil Coal Stocks. The normal coal consumption of West Berlin in winter was 520,000 tons per quarter[29] or about 5,700 tons per day. On 5 January 1949 Berlin had a 22-day supply of coal for utilities (based on a daily requirement of 1,917.48 short tons) and a 21-day supply of coal for other purposes (daily requirement 1,212.2 tons).[30] Air deliveries of coal to Berlin averaged 3,233.1 gross short tons in the first ten days of 1949, just short of the 3,328-ton daily target. (See Table 3.) Civil coal consumption, as of 12 January 1949, was approximately 3,195 short tons daily.[31] For the following ten days, revised allocations were set up by BEALCOM to insure an increased coal lift. The urgency of shipping not only large quantities of coal, but specific amounts of special kinds of coal, was indicated at the eighth meeting of BEALCOM, on 27 January.[32] For the period 1 - 25 January the coal lift rose to 116 percent of target, while the food lift averaged 96 percent.[33] In February Berlin was getting about one half the coal needed for utilities and one-fourth the amount needed for other consumption. To the Air Lift Staff Committee, coal was "the practical problem of the air lift,"[34] and it formed the bulk of the cargo lifted during 1949. By 10 March daily civilian coal consumption in Berlin was averaging 3,100 short tons (1,665 metric tons of utilities coal and 1,150 metric tons of other coal) compared with 3,195 short tons two months earlier, and by 21 April daily consumption was down to 2,808 short tons.[35] During April the coal lift averaged

---

 [28]Ltr, BICO Food, Agriculture, and Forestry Gp to distribution, 27 Jun 49, sub: Deliveries of Food to Airfields for Berlin. BIPFA III B/7. UNCLASSIFIED. In EUCOM Trans Div file 10, USAASC.

 [29]Interv, E. S. Lay, EUCOM Hist Div, with Mr. V. R. Shrigley, BICO Fuel and Power Br Coal Sec, 11 Aug 49. UNCLASSIFIED.

 [30]USAFE, USAFE and the Berlin Airlift 1949, p. 352. SECRET.

 [31]BICO, Decisions Taken by BEALCOM, 7th Mtg, 12 Jan 49. UNCLASSIFIED. In EUCOM Trans Div file 1, USAASC.

 [32]Ibid., 8th Mtg, 27 Jan 49, App D to Mins. UNCLASSIFIED. In ibid.

 [33]Ibid.

 [34]Interv, E. S. Lay, EUCOM Hist Div, with A. W. Moran, Dep Dir OMGBS, 12 Feb 49. UNCLASSIFIED.

 [35]BICO, Decisions Taken by BEALCOM, Mtg of 21 Apr 49. UNCLASSIFIED. In EUCOM Trans Div file 1, USAASC.

5,242 gross short tons daily.[36] The consumer coal target was set at 4,006 gross short tons per day for May.[37] At the end of May Berlin had an 87-day reserve of coal for public utilities and an 86-day reserve for all other purposes.[38] The public utilities reserve rose to a 131-day supply by 30 June and to a 230-day supply by 31 July. Reserves of coal for other purposes were estimated at 50 days' supply on 30 June and 95 days' supply on 31 July, at current rates of consumption.[39] By early August, coal shipments to Berlin were beginning to cause storage problems. Nevertheless, coal was the main item carried by the air lift throughout August and September.

67. Movement of German Industrial and Commercial Cargo

Berlin required not only food and coal but the economic stimulus of commercial exports and imports. Allocation of airlift space for industrial and consumer goods was controlled by the Air Lift Staff Committee at Berlin, while details of scheduling shipments to Berlin and arranging for the receipt and transfer of shipments received at U.S. Zone airfields were coordinated by the Commerce and Industry Group of BICO.[40]

a. Types of Cargo. Industrial and consumer goods shipped from Berlin to the U.S. Zone consisted mainly of electrical equipment. Other items included machine tools, pharmaceuticals, medical instruments, and small mine locomotives. Steel, iron, plastics, vehicle spare parts, chemicals, textiles, shoes, medical supplies, and raw materials were shipped from the bizonal area to Berlin.[41]

b. Industrial Cargo Lifted from Berlin. Tonnages figures for industrial cargo lifted out of Berlin in U.S. and British aircraft are shown in Table 4.

---

[36]Ltr, W. A. Fagan, BEALCON Chm, to CO USAASC, 13 May 49, sub: Operational Report for April 1949. UNCLASSIFIED. In ibid., No. 18, USAASC.

[37]Cable ALX - 564, Allied Kommandatura to BICO for W. A. Fagan, 22 Apr 49. SECRET. In EUCOM SGS 094 (1949), Item 34.

[38]OMGUS Mthly Rept of the Mil Gov, No. 47, May 49, p. 7. UNCLASSIFIED. In EUCOM Hist Div Docs Br.

[39](1) Ibid., No. 48, Jun 49, p. 6. UNCLASSIFIED. (2) Ibid., No. 49, Jul 49, p. 7, UNCLASSIFIED. In ibid.

[40]Interv, E. S. Lay, EUCOM Hist Div, with Mr. R. N. Armstrong, BICO Trans Gp, 3 Feb 49. UNCLASSIFIED.

[41](1) Cable V - 39847, OMGUS to DA for PID, 12 May 49. UNCLASSIFIED. (2) OMGUS Mthly Rept of the Mil Gov, No. 43, Jan 49, p. 61. UNCLASSIFIED. In EUCOM Hist Div Docs Br.

Table 4 -- Industrial Cargo Airlifted from Berlin

Period a/	Net Metric Tons
Total (26 June 48 - 31 July 49)	21,185.0
(Total, 26 June 48 - 11 May 49) b/	(18,050.8)

1948

July c/	930.7
August	985.4
September	1,152.5
October	1,320.7
November	949.3
December	2,712.7

1949

January	1,921.0	
February	2,065.4	
March	2,627.0	
April	2,359.8	
(May 1 - 11)		(1,026.3)
May	2,382.9	
June	1,163.0	
July	614.6	

a/ Accurate figures for the period from July 1949 until the end of the airlift are not available.

b/ Period of the actual blockade.

c/ Includes 26 June - 31 July 1948.

Source: OMGUS Mthly Rept of the Mil Gov, No. 46, Apr 49, p. 6; Ibid., No. 47, May 49, p. 8; Ibid, No. 48, Jun 49, p.6; Ibid., No. 49, Jul 49, p. 6. UNCLASSIFIED.

c. _Industrial and Consumer Cargo Transported into Berlin_. In January 1949 United States planes lifted 479 net metric tons of industrial goods and 296 tons of consumer goods into Berlin.[42] Combined industrial and consumer lift tonnages to Berlin from February through July 1949 were as follows:[43]

Month	Net Metric Tons
February	3,823.0
March	4,526.0
April	7,088.0
May	7,520.3
June	2,692.0

d. _Estimated Value of Industrial Cargo Lifted_. The value of Berlin industrial products airlifted to western Germany during the blockade (to 12 May 1949) averaged DM 17,400,000 ($4,151,200) per month.[44]

68. Additional Types of Cargo Lifted for the Civilian Economy

Other important types of cargo carried to Berlin by air, for the civilian economy, were liquid fuel, newsprint, and medical supplies. During the blockade 17,724.8 metric tons of German mail were airlifted from Berlin to the west. In addition, approximately 15,000 children were sent by air to the three western zones for better food and care.[45] Up to 12 May 1949 combined outgoing cargoes from Berlin included 18,470.4 gross metric tons of miscellaneous German cargo, consisting mainly of sacks and containers.[46]

69. Cargo Priorities for Zonal Airfields

In addition to setting tonnage targets for major types of cargo the Allied Kommandatura (through the Air Lift Staff Committee) assigned priorities to the kinds of cargo to be shipped from each of the airfields in the U.S. and British Zones. For May 1949 such priorities were assigned as follows:[47]

---

[42]Ibid., No. 43, Jan 49, p. 7. UNCLASSIFIED. In ibid.

[43]Ibid., No. 45, Mar 49, p. 7; Ibid., No. 46, Apr 49, p. 7; Ibid., No. 47, May 49, p. 8; Ibid., No. 48, Jun 49, p. 6. All UNCLASSIFIED. In ibid.

[44]HICOG Info Bul, Dec 49, p. 57. UNCLASSIFIED.

[45](1) The Stars and Stripes, Eur. ed., August 8, 1949. (2) Cable V - 39847, OMGUS to DA for PID, 12 May 49. UNCLASSIFIED.

[46]OMGUS ALREP No. 289, Pt. III, 12 May 49. CONFIDENTIAL. In BMP Trans Br files.

[47](1) Ibid. (2) Cable ALX - 564, Allied Kommandatura to BICO, 22 Apr 49. SECRET.

Airport	First	Second	Third	Fourth	Fifth	Sixth
Celle	Food	Coal				
Fassberg	Coal					
Fuhlsbuettel	Food					
Lueback	Newsprint	C & I[48] Supplies	Coal			
Rhein/Main	Perishable foods	Coal	Other foods			
Schleswigland	C & I[48] Supplies	Coal				
Wiesbaden	Newsprint	Airfield construction	U.S. & French maintenance	C & I[48] Supplies	Food	Coal
Wunstorf	British Maintenance	Food	Airfield construction	Coal		

70. Reporting of Tonnages Shipped

The tonnages carried to Berlin by planes of the Combined Air
Lift Task Force were reported in varying ways by the different
agencies concerned. Over-all figures are extremely hard to obtain. Figures giving total combined tonnages and tonnages by
major commodities carried were included by CALTF in its monthly
statistical reports. (See Annex A.) But CALTF phased out before
the end of the lift,[49] leaving no successor at combined level.
The OMGBS Air Lift Reports (ALRFP's), published daily until 20 May
1949, and thereafter weekly until September 1949, reported totals
for German, military and miscellaneous (including liquid fuel)

---

[48]Consumer and industrial.

[49]CALTF was deactivated as of 0001 hours, 1 September 1949.
(see paragraph 102c below.) However, as explained in this paragraph, CALTF figures do not agree with other figures on the lift,
since they were reported on a different tonnage basis.

supplies, in gross and metric tons.[50] Statistical tables on the entire operation are contained in the "Statistical Summary of Operation 'Plainfare,'" compiled by the Command Statistical Officer of British Air Forces of Occupation (BAFO) in October 1949, and in the supplement published in January 1950. Most of the other agencies connected with the air lift were responsible for only a limited part of the operation. Figures and summaries provided by them are of value, however, in showing how they carried out their special responsibilities. The following variations in reporting methods should be noted when comparing the airlift figures compiled by different agencies and headquarters.

a. <u>Units of Measurement</u>. There was no common unit for measuring tonnages. Military government offices at Berlin referred to cumulative cargoes in terms of metric tons, the unit in which German firms measured their shipments. The British lift was reported in long tons, while the U.S. lift was usually reported in short tons.[51] Some figures show net and others show gross tonnages.

b. <u>Lack of Standard Reporting Periods</u>. There was also a lack of uniformity, especially at the beginning of the lift, in regard to daily and weekly reporting periods. The Air Force preferred a reporting period from 1200 to 1200 hours. The Transportation Corps agreed to follow this practice for airlift reporting purposes.[52] OMGBS used the 7-day period from Friday noon to Friday noon in its weekly ALREP's but on 22 August, for its last few reports, changed to a week beginning at 0800.[53]

c. <u>Inclusion of Passengers</u>. BICO, OMGBS, and the Transportation Corps included only supplies and materiel in their cargo and

---

[50]OMGBS ALREP No. 316, issued on 17 September 1949, was the latest of these reports noted by the author in the files of BMP Trans Br, Jun 50.

[51](1) See the Berlin Air Lift - 1948, par. 15<u>b</u>. SECRET. There were some U.S. figures in long tons, as illustrated in <u>Tables 4 and 5</u>. (2) BALCOM Mins, in EUCOM Trans Div file 1, USAMSC. On 1 December 1948 it was agreed that the UK element would continue to report to CALTF in long tons. (3) BAFO, Report on Operation Plainfare, used the short ton, however, in all figures on air freight.

[52]See the Berlin Air Lift - 1948, par. 15<u>b</u>. SECRET.

[53](1) See OMGBS ALREP No. 310, 5 Aug 49, and ALREP No. 316, 17 Sep 49. CONFIDENTIAL. In files of C/BMP Trans Br. Photostated copies of these reports through Jul 49 only, are in EUCOM Hist Div Docs Br. (2) Tonnage reports in EUCOM Trans Div file 54, USAMSC, Cumulative Tonnage Monthly (August and September), contain a statement that the period for reporting tonnage was changed from 1200 to 0800 hours on 22 August.

tonnage reports. USAFE, on the other hand, counted passengers as "tons lifted."

71. Total Combined Tonnages Shipped

Total cargo brought to Berlin in British and U.S. planes between 26 June 1948 and 30 September 1949 amounted to approximately 2,343,301 tons.[54]

72. Supplementary Tonnage Totals

Statistical information on significant aspects of airlift tonnages is presented in Tables 5 - 9.

a. The Combined Lift, 26 June 1948 - 26 June 1949. Figures compiled by BMP show a total of 1,961,621.6 tons brought to Berlin by British and U.S. aircraft during the first year of Operation VITTLES. These figures, showing percentages received in U.S. and British planes at each of the three airfields in Berlin, as well as U.S. and British percentages of the combined lift, are given in Table 5.[55]

---

[54](1) Stars and Stripes, Eur. ed., October 1, 1949, p. 16. (2) Lowell Bennett, C/HICOG - BF Pub Rel Br, "Memorial to Airlift Dead," in HICOG Info Bul, Aug 51, p. 13. (3) OMGBS records (ALRTP) No. 316, 17 Sep 49, states that 2,045,512.5 gross metric tons (1,818,179.7 net metric tons) had reached Berlin by combined lift as of 0800 hours 17 September 1949, while the OMGUS Mthly Rept of the Mil Gov, No. 50, 1 Aug - 20 Sep 49, p. 9, states that combined airlift cargo for civilian consumption, for the entire period, amounted to 1,823,073.7 net metric tons. The HICOG Info Bul for Aug 51, indicates 2,343,301 tons as the short tonnage figure for the total combined lift. Berlin Airlift, A USAFE Summary, p. 12, gives 2,325,509.6 as the total inbound tonnage (RESTRICTED). Statistical Summary of Operation 'Plainfare,' 28 June - 30 September 1949, compiled by Command Statistical Officer, BAFO, Germany, October 1949 (RESTRICTED), gives the total from June 1948 to September 1949 as 2,325,808.7 short tons, including 1,783,572.7 in U.S. planes and 542,236.0 in British planes.

[55]The USAFE History of Headquarters, United States Air Forces in Europe, for June 1949, SECRET, page 51, cites a Stars and Stripes figure of 1,935,155.9 tons carried by combined airlift planes between 26 June 1948 and 25 June 1949.

Table 5 — First Year Record for Combined Berlin Airlift (26 June 1948 to 26 June 1949)

Tonnages and Planes

	Planes	Tonnages	
Combined Figures			
For 3 Airbases		1,961,621.6	
Total British Tonnage			
For 2 Airbases		486,708.5	25% of Combined Total
Total U.S. Figures			
For 3 Airbases	211,421	1,474,913.1	75% of Combined Total
U.S. Figures			
Tempelhof Airbase	115,103	829,500.7	56.2% of U.S. Total — 42.2% of Combined Total
Gatow Airbase	59,861	383,894.6	25.9% of U.S. Total — 19.5% of Combined Total
Tegel Airbase	36,457	261,517.8	17.9% of U.S. Total — 13.3% of Combined Total

Source: BMP Trans Br. UNCLASSIFIED.

Table 6 -- Tonnages Lifted Monthly to Berlin in U.S. Aircraft Between 1 January and 30 September 1949 and Cumulative Totals, 21 June 1948 - 30 September 1949

(Figures from January through July in long tons; August and September figures in short tons; totals in right-hand column in short tons, except as indicated.)

Inbound Cargo	January[1]	February[2]	March[3]	April[4]	May[5]	June[6]	July[7]	August[8]	September[9]	Total Short[9] Tons 21 Jun 48 - 20 Sep 49
Totals	133,870.2	114,171.0	148,799.0	180,327.1	182,064.5	172,901.2	185,051.1	52,186.9	11,004.8	1,700,563.9
Quartermaster Class I	946.0	487.1	1,186.7	2,507.6	701.7	760.0	-739.5	---	---	17,314.7
Quartermaster Class I(r)	422.3	669.1	336.7	174.8	56.4	67.3	39.1	---	---	6,179.8
Quartermaster Class III	1,075.1	83.9	41.1							
Quartermaster Class II and IV	76.9	78.8	143.9	197.5	62.2	125.5	8.5	0.1	---	1,678.0
Engineer II & IV	165.3	233.4	420.5	218.1	52.4	144.5	121.6	---	---	2,980.7
Engineer Air Force	52.1	38.5	1.2	1,792.9	1,502.4	54.7	16.6	---	---	13,239.0
Ordnance II & IV	29.6	116.2	256.9	203.6	29.0	78.6	56.6	---	---	1,250.0
Ordnance V	43.3	---	12.5	0.3	20.0	4.8	---	---	0.8	81.7
Medical	4.2	3.5	6.7	7.7	2.4	5.2	2.8	---	---	96.9
Signal	15.9	3.6	8.0	24.8	2.0	7.6	2.1	---	---	142.2
Engineer Coal	6,711.0					---	---	---	---	19,676.7
EUCOM Exchange Service	341.6	105.2	93.0	258.3	151.1	567.6	62.7	---	0.2	2,159.4
Special Services	15.7	1.2	5.2	3.1	3.1	2.8	---	---	---	36.7
U.S. Mail	115.2	189.1	214.7	186.0	123.5	162.2	68.4	0.9	0.5	1,856.4
Air Force Supply	111.8	61.4	48.9	100.3	20.7	5.5	31.8	---	---	225.0
Air Force Miscellaneous	---	---	29.8	---	---	---	---	0.5	0.1	483.5
Air Force Maintenance	102.2	59.2	72.0	98.0	66.1	136.3	77.3	38.7	78.8	89.0
Miscellaneous	14,192.9	17,722.1	120.0	27,372.1	28,810.9	10,201.2	105.1		10,923.3	1,310.1
CA Food	15.7	28.5	14,131.1			45.1	110.6	42.3	1.1	284,430.1
CA Mail	85.1	71.3	100.3	86.2	94.2	64.0	11.4	8.6		261.5
CA Medical	1,743.5	2,726.8	4,024.9	5,016.3	5,913.3	2,314.3	228.1	46.3		781.9
CA Miscellaneous	103,773.5	88,092.8	114,174.2	138,650.8	141,166.0	155,443.7	186,913.6	55,049.5		25,266.4
CA Coal	137.0									1,292,153.0
British Coal	2,904.9	2,623.3	2,906.9	2,813.0	2,871.5	2,338.2	271.0			137.0
French Coal	805.0	704.0	535.8	615.7	415.9	322.1	184.3			21,613.9
French Miscellaneous										7,571.3

a/ Category not listed.
b/ Long tons.
c/ Air Force maintenance discontinued as a separate listing. Cumulative totals (89.0 tons) included in Engineer Air Force figures.

Source: (1) EUCOM CINC's Wkly Staff Conf Notes, No. 12, 22 Mar 49, par. 22. (2) Ibid. (3) Ibid., No. 16, 19 Apr 49, par. 23. (4) EUCOM Actg CINC's Wkly Staff Conf Notes, No. 20, 17 May 49, par. 15. (5) Ibid., No. 24, 14 Jun 49, par. 10. (6) Ibid., No. 28, 12 Jul 49, par. 15. (7) Ibid., No. 33, 16 Aug 49, par. 13. (8) EUCOM CINC's Wkly Staff Conf Notes, No. 37, 13 Sep 49, par. 15. (9) Ibid., No. 41, 11 Oct 49, par. 16. All RESTRICTED.

Table 7 -- Tonnages Lifted Monthly From Berlin in U.S. Aircraft Between 1 January and 30 September 1949 and Cumulative Totals, 21 June 1948 – 30 September 1949

(Figures from January through July in long tons; August and September figures and totals in right-hand column in short tons)

Cargo	Jan[1]	Feb[2]	Mar[3]	Apr[4]	May[5]	Jun[6]	Jul[7]	Aug[8]	Sep[9]	Total Short Tons[9] 21 Jun 48–30 Sep 49
Totals	1,844.7	1,383.7	1,955.2	2,702.2	2,221.0	979.6	597.2	304.2	62.6	23,538.0
Quartermaster II and IV	55.3	42.4	51.8	52.4	34.3	75.2	51.8	1.2	--	1,301.6
Quartermaster III	160.6	84.5	6.7	--	--	--	--	--	--	542.6
Medical	3.0	--	--	--	--	--	6.0	--	--	10.0
Engineer II and IV	13.2	13.0	43.3	37.8	35.2	38.8	32.3	--	--	482.7
Household Goods	92.5	52.5	67.1	70.8	47.4	91.5	84.2	--	--	2,600.2
Ordnance II and IV	236.1	103.1	149.7	122.5	126.6	98.6	102.9	1.4	--	1,160.2
Ordnance V	a/	a/	9.8	--	--	1.8	16.6	6.0	--	34.2
Signal	9.0	3.5	--	22.6	1.6	18.2	--	--	--	152.9
Air Force Supply	20.6	28.3	21.2	34.2	21.1	26.8	8.0	--	--	216.8
Documents	72.1	3.5	3.1	--	--	--	--	--	--	471.0
Miscellaneous Freight	46.0	17.8	50.1	61.6	66.6	78.7	76.9	53.7	50.4	901.3
Miscellaneous (Airhead)	51.9	71.8	19.4	16.0	20.6	7.6	7.8	3.5	--	531.2
U.S. Mail	26.7	27.9	28.1	41.9	19.4	36.6	16.7	2.2	1.6	578.4
Private Vehicles	30.0	31.1	45.0	36.4	9.5	--	--	--	--	739.4

- 73 -

Table 7 -- Tonnages Lifted Monthly From Berlin in U.S. Aircraft Between 1 January and 30 September 1949 and Cumulative Totals, 21 June 1948 - 30 September 1949 (contd)

Cargo	Jan[1]	Feb[2]	Mar[3]	Apr[4]	May[5]	Jun[6]	Jul[7]	Aug[8]	Sep[9]	Total Short Tons[9] 21 Jun 48-30 Sep 49
Ordnance Vehicles	12.9	--	24.9	--	52.4	68.3	--	--	--	178.5
War Dead	1.6	--	--	--	--	--	--	--	--	2.6
French Miscellaneous	54.8	73.0	60.5	39.2	23.9	--	--	--	--	491.8
CA Industry	853.1	810.5	1,171.5	1,140.0	1,204.4	437.0	191.4	231.2	10.3	9,357.8
CA Mail	30.5	--	202.5	940.4	557.4	--	--	--	--	3,455.1
CA Newsprint	0.3	0.4	0.5	0.4	0.6	0.5	2.6	5.0	0.3	12.6
CA Baggage	--	--	--	--	--	--	--	--	--	120.2
CA Miscellaneous	74.5	20.4	--	86.0	--	--	--	--	--	196.9

a/ Not listed.

Source: (1) EUCOM DCINC's Wkly Staff Conf Notes No. 12, 22 Mar 49, par. 22. (2) Ibid.
(3) Ibid., No. 16,19 Apr 49, par. 13. (4) EUCOM Actg CINC Wkly Staff Conf Notes,
No. 20, 17 May 49, par. 15. (5) Ibid., No. 24, 14 Jun 49, par. 10. (6) Ibid.;
No. 28, 12 Jul 49, par. 15. (7) Ibid., No. 33, 16 Aug 49, par. 13. (8) EUCOM
CINC's Wkly Staff Conf Notes, No. 37, 13 Sep 49, par. 15. (9) Ibid., No. 41,
11 Oct 49, par. 16. ALL RESTRICTED.

Table 8 -- Supplies Lifted into Berlin for German Civilian Economy by US/UK Air Forces
26 June 1948 - 11 May 1949

Thousand Net Metric Tons

Period	Total Tons	Coal Tons	Coal Percent of Total	Food Tons	Food Percent of Total	Liquid Fuels Tons	Liquid Fuels Percent of Total	Newsprint Tons	Newsprint Percent of Total	Miscellaneous Tons	Miscellaneous Percent of Total
Totals	1,217.9	782.8	64.3	374.7	30.8	27.5	2.2	8.3	0.7	24.6	2.0
1948											
July[a]	53.0	15.6	29.5	37.3	70.3	0.0	0.08	0.0	0.0	0.1	0.1
August	93.7	63.3[b]	67.6	29.7	31.7	0.4	0.4	0.2	0.2	0.1	0.1
September	112.5	73.1[b]	64.9	38.4	34.2	0.0	0.0	0.9	0.8	0.1	0.06
October	114.9	76.3	66.4	36.5	31.7	0.7	0.6	0.9	0.8	0.5	0.5
November	84.6	48.1	56.8	33.8	40.0	0.9	1.1	0.7	0.8	1.1	1.3
December	107.8	59.1	54.8	45.3	42.0	0.6	0.5	1.1	1.0	1.8	1.7
1949											
January	131.8	97.9	74.3	28.0	21.3	2.5	1.9	1.3	0.9	2.1	1.6
February	113.8	77.4	68.0	29.1	25.6	2.6	2.3	0.8	0.7	3.9	3.4
March	149.6	99.3	66.4	37.5	25.0	7.2	4.8	1.0	0.7	4.6	3.1
April	180.8	123.7	68.4	41.4	22.9	7.5	4.1	1.1	0.6	7.2	4.0
May 1 - 11	75.4	49.0	65.0	17.6	23.3	5.3	7.0	0.4	0.5	3.1	4.2

[a] Includes 26 June - 31 July.

[b] Includes 4,236.6 metric tons coal flown in on 18 September for distribution to Western Sector Berlin families having two or more children 10 years old or younger.

Source: OMGUS Mthly Rept of the Mil Gov, No. 46, 19 Apr 49, p. 6. UNCLASSIFIED.

Table 9 -- Cargo Lifted Out of Berlin by US/UK Air Forces for
German Civilian Economy, 26 June 1948-11 May 1949

| | Total | Industrial Materials | | Mail | Gross Metric Tons |
Period	Tons	Tons	Percent of Total	Tons	Percent of Total
Total	35,775.6	18,050.8	50.5	17,724.8	49.5
1948					
July[a]	2,063.3	930.7	45.1	1,132.6	54.9
August	2,164.8	985.4	45.5	1,179.4	54.5
September	2,291.2	1,152.5	50.3	1,138.7	49.7
October	2,826.9	1,320.7	46.7	1,506.2	53.3
November	3,015.7	949.3	31.5	2,066.4	68.5
December	5,264.0	2,712.7	51.5	2,551.3	48.5
1949					
January	3,261.0	1,921.0	58.9	1,340.0	41.1
February	3,492.0	2,065.4	59.1	1,426.6	40.9
March	4,502.9	2,627.0	58.3	1,875.9	41.7
April	4,971.0	2,359.8	47.5	2,611.2	52.5
May 1 - 11	1,922.8	1,026.3	53.4	896.5	46.6

[a] Includes 26 June 1948 - 31 July 1948.

Source: OMGUS Mthly Rept of the Mil Gov, No. 46, Apr 49, p. 6.
UNCLASSIFIED.

b. Total Tonnages in U.S. Planes. From 21 June 1948 to 30 September 1949 a total of 1,700,563.9 short tons were carried to Berlin in U.S. aircraft. Types of cargo included, and monthly totals for shipments made during 1949, are listed in Table 6. Tonnages lifted out of Berlin in U.S. aircraft, over the same period, totaled 23,538.0 short tons (see Table 7).

c. Total Civilian Lift During the Blockade. Supplies lifted into Berlin for the German economy during the period 26 June 1948 to 11 May 1949 totaled 1,217,900 net metric tons (Table 8). Civilian economy cargo lifted out of Berlin for the same period totaled 35,775 gross metric tons (Table 9).

d. Tonnages from Rhein/Main and Wiesbaden. The United States Army Airlift Support Command was concerned with cargo operations at Rhein/Main and Wiesbaden airfields only. USAASC records indicate that 976,789.1 short tons were lifted from these two fields during the entire operation. Monthly totals of planes loaded and tons lifted are shown below:[56]

Month	Planes	Tonnages
Total	111,279	976,789.1
1948		
June	610	1,576.28
July	7,601	40,340.91
August	8,903	65,231.10
September	8,742	61,186.22
October	6,512	61,061.67
November	4,341	41,541.17
December	5,888	58,726.30
1949		
January	8,708	66,731.26
February	4,231	62,492.57
March	7,989	80,947.15
April	13,351	102,647.16
May	9,845	97,782.76
June	8,995	89,002.35
July	10,192	100,677.15
August	3,953	34,692.20
September	1,381	11,846.39
October	37	306.46

[56]USAASC, Cumulative Tonnage Records, Total Airlift (Rhein/Main and Wiesbaden to Berlin). UNCLASSIFIED. In EUCOM Trans Div file 12, USAASC.

Movement of outbound tonnage at Rhein/Main and Wiesbaden, during the lift is pictured in Graph 1.

73. Over-all Daily Tonnage Forecast for May 1949

May was the last month in which the air lift operated under blockade conditions. Tonnage forecasts for May are therefore the last ones to be based on the necessity of supplying West Berlin exclusively by air. While allocations of airlift tonnage for military cargo varied from time to time in accordance with special supply and shipping needs, the tonnages approved by the Allied Kommandatura for May 1949 may be regarded as typical of the final months of the blockade period. The over-all tonnage forecast for May called for an average of 7,370 gross short tons per day, to include 6,818 tons in freighter and 552 tons in tanker aircraft. These tonnages were assigned as shown in Table 10.

74. Adequacy of Air Support for Western Berlin

The question of whether a military lift could meet the long-term requirements of a large city is answered to some extent by the experience of Berlin. In April 1948 freight from the bizonal area for Berlin included approximately 12,000 tons daily by rail and 300 tons per day by water. These rates may be considered as representing a fair average for the preceding six months.[57] On 11 April 1949 the lift set a record by bringing 8,246 tons to Berlin. In the "Easter Parade" of 16 April 12,940.9 tons reached Berlin in 1,398 flights.[58] But 8,000 tons per day was the top capacity of the lift under average conditions. By 11 June, when rail transport was suspended by the rail strike at Berlin, the city was receiving daily average shipments of 2,625 tons by road, 1,000 tons by barge, and 7,000 tons by air, totaling 10,625.[59] Figures for July 1949, one of the biggest months of the air lift, show how additional supplies poured into the city when supplementary transport became available.[60]

---

[57] Interv, E. S. Lay, EUCOM Hist Div, with Mr. W. J. Burns, EICO Trans Gp Mvmts Br, 8 Feb 49. RESTRICTED.

[58] (1) Stars and Stripes, Eur. ed., September 27, 1949. (2) The figure for 11 April is from USAFE, History of Headquarters USAFE, Apr 49. SECRET. This gives a newspaper headline as its source.

[59] Cable SX - 3059, CINCEUR to USMA, Paris, 11 Jun 49. SECRET. In EUCOM SGS 094 Berlin (1949), Item 58.

[60] OMGUS, Mthly Rept of the Mil Gov, No. 49, Jul 49, pp. 7 - 8. UNCLASSIFIED.

Graph 1

RHEIN / MAIN — WIESBADEN

Total Airlift Tonnage

Tons

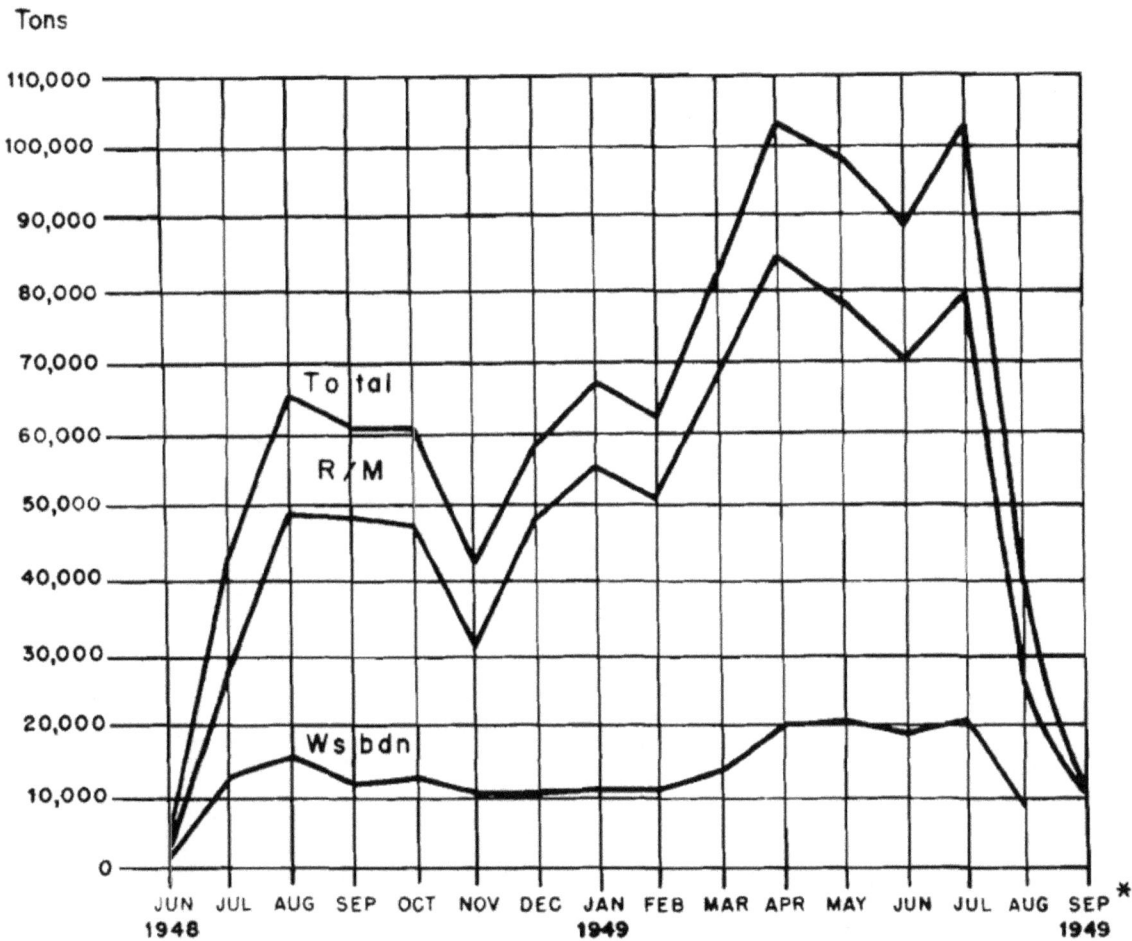

*Wiesbaden Shipments Ceased At 0800, 2 September 1949

Source: USAASC Rhein-Main Detachment, "Summary Report
Tonnage Movements"

Table 10 -- Daily Tonnage Forecast for May 1949 in Gross Short Tons

Grand Total	7,370
Freighter Aircraft Total	*6,818
Military	
British Maintenance	271
Solid Fuel	65
Miscellaneous Supplies	206
U.S. Maintenance	281
Solid Fuel	182
Class I	55
Class II, IV, V	41
Special Oil and Grease	3
French Maintenance	98
Solid Fuel	62
Miscellaneous Supplies	36
Airfield Construction and Maintenance	109
U.S. Account	84
British Account	25
German Civilian	6,124
Food	1,800
Newsprint	38
Industrial and Medical Supplies	280
Coal	4,006
Tanker Aircraft Total	552
Gasoline	76
British Account	25
U.S. Account (including 8 for airfield construction)	40
French Account	8
German Economy	3

Table 10 — Daily Tonnage Forecast for May 1949
in Gross Short Tons (Cont'd)

Diesel	<u>423</u>
British Account	19
U.S. Account (including 8 for airfield construction)	18
French Account	2
German Economy	384
Kerosene	<u>53</u>
British Account	1
German Economy	52

*Although the cable stated that 6,818 gross short tons would be the daily average by freighter aircraft for the month of May, the itemized tonnages listed in the cable actually totaled 6,883 short tons by freighter aircraft.

Source: Cable AIX - 564, Allied Kommandatura to BICO, 22 Apr 49. SECRET.

Category	Total	Rail	Road	Inland Waterway	Combined Airlift[61]
				(In thousands of gross metric tons)	
Total	740.3	303.0	[62]94.6	113.7	229.0
Coal	N.A.[63]	237.8	N.A.	68.2	202.5
Food	N.A.	1.1	N.A.	32.0	14.1
Other	N.A.	64.1	N.A.	13.5	12.4

The air lift carried just enough industrial export cargo from Berlin to keep the city industrially alive. Monthly tonnages of industrial freight leaving the western sectors of Berlin for West Germany were as follows, from May through December 1949:[64]

1949	Rail, waterway and road (permits) (Net Metric Tons)	Air (Net Metric Tons)
May	15,460	1,721
June	48,422	1,060
July	94,200	307
August	90,847	406
September	72,990	40
October	85,648	0
November	68,284	0
December	67,914	0

---

[61]As reported by the Bipartite Transportation Group.
[62]Estimated at a daily average of 3,050 tons per day.
[63]N.A. - Not available.
[64](1) Figures for shipment by railway, road, and waterways show total of net tons approved by the Magistrat, Economic Department, for movement to Western Germany. Goods covered by the bills of lading submitted for approval usually left Berlin two to three weeks after approval had been granted by the Magistrat. Ltr, Treuhandstelle fuer den Interzonenhandel beim Deutschen Industrie-U. Handelstag, Berlin, to Mr. Zane, HICOG, Office of Economic Affairs, Repts and Statistical Analysis Sec, Industry Br, 170 Clay Allee, Berlin-Zehlendorf, 16 Mar 50. (2) Interv, E. S. Lay, EUCOM Hist Div, with Mr. E. C. C. Springer, HICOG - BE Repts and Stats Br, 23 Jun 50.

CHAPTER V

Support by Technical Services

75. Support at EUCOM Level

Support of Operation VITTLES was a major logistic problem
for EUCOM technical services on 1 January 1949.[1] Supplies and
equipment, housing, and transportation had to be furnished for
USAFE in far more than normal amounts, in addition to the operational support provided by the EUCOM Chief of Transportation.
The burden of meeting these additional requirements rested primarily on the Logistics Division, while the EUCOM Liaison Officer at CALTF headquarters served as an expediter and coordinator
for special requests by the Air Force.[2] At the beginning of 1949
EUCOM, through U.S. Army, Europe, was supplying all common-user
items of equipment, including such items as heavy Engineer construction equipment and Ordnance tractors and trailers, to Air
Force as well as Army elements supporting the lift. Because of
the emergency nature of the operation, many items were supplied
over and above normal authorizations, on a loan basis.[3] The burden
of providing housing for an additional 4,000 men rested mainly on
Frankfurt Military Post, subject to inspection and guidance by
EUCOM headquarters. Housing at Bremen and Kassel was made available by EUCOM for dependents of Air Force personnel stationed at

---

[1] DCINC's Wkly Staff Conf Notes, No. 1, 4 Jan 49, p. 8. RE-
STRICTED.

[2] (1) Cf. par. 11, above. (2) Interv, E. S. Lay, EUCOM Hist
Div, with Col Hall S. Crain, EUCOM Ln Officer CALTF, Wiesbaden,
22 Dec 48. RESTRICTED.

[3] EUCOM Log Div Rept of Opns, 1 Jan - 31 Dec 49, par. 10.
SECRET.

Celle and Fassberg, and over fifty hotel spaces were supplied by
.etzlar Military Post.[4] In addition to the direct support furnished by the technical services, both at EUCOM and at post headquarters levels, as described in this chapter, the air lift also
required much indirect support from EUCOM organizations and agencies, as a result of the influx of military personnel and the
heavy demands of the lift for facilities, equipment, and maintenance.

76. Transportation Support at EUCOM Level

Transportation support for the air lift followed substan-
tially the same pattern in 1949 as in 1948[5] although command
channels for certain units were modified in the Frankfurt area
and operating methods continued to undergo improvement at all
U.S.-supported airfields. The Berlin air lift gave the Chief of
Transportation, EUCOM, an added mission of operating railheads,
providing transportation to and from railheads, and loading and
unloading aircraft at Rhein/Main, Wiesbaden, and Tempelhof airfields.[6] Transportation Division was also concerned with the
assignment of units for airlift support, the provision of personnel, the training of drivers, the provision of trains to meet
travel and transport needs arising from the air lift, the maintenance of airlift vehicles, the standardization of operating
procedures, and, after the ending of the blockade, the sending
of truck convoys to Berlin. These responsibilities were in
addition to the support required in actual cargo-hauling operations.

77. Units

Although only six heavy truck companies were employed in
airlift support, at Rhein/Main and Wiesbaden airfields at any one
time, the 66th, 67th, 68th, 69th, 70th, 76th, 83d and 84th Transportation Truck Companies (Heavy) were all used at least part of

---

[4]Interv, E. S. Lay, EUCOM Hist Div, with Col Hall S. Crain,
EUCOM Log Div, 16 Aug 49.

[5](1) The Berlin Air Lift - 1948, par. 17. SECRET. (2) Report on Operation Plainfare, p. 68 and pp. 553 - 596, Appendix
"T," Report by the Army Air Transport Organization, a valuable
analysis of ground transport operations under British control.

[6]EUCOM Trans Div Rept of Opns, Vol. XXVII, Oct - Dec 48,
p. 24. UNCLASSIFIED.

the time between 27 December 1948 and 1 February 1949.[7] The 70th
Transportation Truck Company (Heavy), the 524th Transportation Car
Company, and the 543d Transportation Truck Company (Troop) were
attached to the 24th Transportation Truck Battalion for operational
control.[8] During the first quarter of 1949, while operating as a
reserve company for airlift support, the 70th was responsible for
carrying labor service personnel to and from their work at Rhein/
Main and Wiesbaden airfields. Units not engaged in airlift support
were used by the battalion to provide transportation for Frankfurt
Military Post. Effective 10 March, five of these companies, the
67th, and 83d (assigned to Wetzlar Military Post), the 68th and 76th
(assigned to Heidelberg Military Post), and the 69th (assigned to
Munich Military Post), were assigned to Frankfurt Military Post,
remaining attached to the office of the Chief of Transportation,
EUCOM, for operations.[9] At the same time, the 66th Transportation
Truck Company (Heavy) was relieved from assignment to Munich Military Post and assigned to Frankfurt Military Post, remaining attached to Wuerzburg Military Post.[10] All of these companies continued to support the air lift under command of the 24th Transportation Truck Battalion. Effective 1 April the 68th and 84th
were assigned to Wetzlar and Heidelberg Military Posts, respectively,
while the 89th was assigned to FMP.[11] Truck companies assigned to
the Airlift Support Command upon its establishment are listed in

---

[7]24th TT Bn, FMP, Opn Air Lift, Memo No. 11, sub: Organizational Commitments for Air Lift Operations, 29 Dec 49, Annex.
Most reports say that only six companies were engaged in airlift
support, whereas the Commanding Officer of the 24th Transportation
Truck Battalion, thinking in terms of the 27 December - 28 February
schedule, issued 29 December, stated on 21 January 1949 that eight
heavy companies were being utilized. See monograph, The Berlin Air
Lift - 1948, par. 18a. SECRET. As originally published in the
spring of 1949, paragraph 18a listed eight heavy truck companies
assigned to Operation VITTLES at the end of 1948. This was modified in the monograph as republished in 1951 (Special Studies
Series) to list the six companies actually on airfield support duty
in the closing week of 1948, with a note stating that the 69th and
83d Transportation Truck Companies replaced the 66th and 84th on
airfield duty during January.

[8]24th TT Bn Rept of Opns, 1 Jan - 31 Mar 49, p. 7. UNCLASSIFIED.

[9]EUCOM OCOT Rept of Opns, 1 Jan - 31 Mar 49, p. 31. CONFIDENTIAL.

[10]Ibid.

[11]EUCOM Trp Assign No. 7, 1 Apr 49. UNCLASSIFIED.

Appendix C.[12] During July 1949 the Airlift Support Command had seven truck companies in active support of the lift and two in reserve.[13]

78. Transportation for Rhein/Main and Wiesbaden Airfields

The 24th Transportation Truck Battalion continued to support airlift operations at Rhein/Main and Wiesbaden airfields until the close of the airlift operation.[14] Prior to 6 April 1949 this battalion was assigned to Frankfurt Military Post. Effective 6 April the Battalion and its subordinate units were assigned to the U.S. Army Airlift Support Command and attached to FMP for administration.[15]

79. Transportation Support at Berlin

Next to its role in construction of airfields the main function of Berlin Military Post in support of Operation VITTLES was the unloading of cargo and its transfer to appropriate military and civilian agencies. This function was the immediate responsibility of the Transportation Corps Airhead Tempelhof (TCAHT). Early in 1949 further progress was made in the streamlining begun by the Transportation Corps at Tempelhof in 1948.[16] The Transportation Corps Standing Operating Procedure (SOP) for Tempelhof, included as Appendix H, outlines the essential aspects of the ground-support operation.[17]

---

[12]EUCOM Trp Assign No. 8, 5 Apr 49. UNCLASSIFIED. Included as Appendix C. Additional details concerning assignment of transportation units used in airlift support at Rhein/Main and Wiesbaden may be found in other EUCOM Troop Assignments for 1949.

[13]Interv, E. S. Lay, EUCOM Hist Div, with Maj Herbert A. Smith, Adj USAASC, 28 Jul 49.

[14]For a description of the units, operations, use of vehicles and drivers, driver responsibilities, equipment, maintenance, working conditions, and training involved in providing transportation support for these airfields up to 31 December 1948, see The Berlin Air Lift - 1948, par. 18. SECRET.

[15]EUCOM Trp Assign No. 8, 5 Apr 49. UNCLASSIFIED. For text, see App. C.

[16]See The Berlin Air Lift - 1948, par. 19, for details. SECRET.

[17]BMP Trans Br, Trans Corps SOP for Tempelhof, 15 Feb 49. UNCLASSIFIED. For text, see App. H.

80. Vehicle Statistics, Rhein/Main Airfield

At the end of the air lift a detailed summary of activities
of the Transportation Corps at Rhein/Main Air Base was published
by USAASC.[18] The following figures from the report show tons
hauled by truck compared with tons lifted to Berlin and the corres-
ponding outlay in mileage, gasoline, and man-hours. Figures for
the entire airlift period are included. Airlift vehicles were driven
a total of 467,210 miles on the base during the air lift.

Month	Tons Lifted	Tons Hauled	Total Miles on Base	Miles per Gallon	Man Hours (with Tractors)
1948					
June	1,053.3	6,259	2,276	4.0	2,400
July	27,043.24	42,108	15,312	3.9	40,176
August	49,744.77	57,981	21,084	4.1	40,176
September	48,887.13	58,058	21,112	4.1	38,880
October	47,186.74	53,856	36,857	3.8	41,760
November	30,709.44	34,144	24,582	3.9	38,060
December	48,159.17	52,514	37,302	2.8	37,224
1949					
January	55,347.14	60,214	35,180	2.7	37,144
February	51,472.93	55,143	34,280	2.9	34,944
March	66,778.43	72,490	44,484	4.1	36,828
April	88,822.30	96,052	55,422	4.0	36,720
May	77,377.86	91,366	53,640	3.9	36,000
June	70,084.53	80,676	45,429	4.0	30,960
July	79,458.76	96,559	33,142	3.9	34,560
August	25,582	37,249	4,386	5.1	25,920
September	11,558.22	11,558	2,722	5.0	--

81. Vehicle Statistics, Berlin

From the beginning of the lift through 15 May 1949 inbound
and outbound tonnage hauled by TC vehicles at Tempelhof amounted
to 713,044.9 short tons, or 44 percent of the airlift total. The
April 1949 total of 99,258.4 tons marked an increase of almost 100
percent over the November tonnage. This amount was handled by

---

[18]USAASC R/M Det, Summary Report Tonnage Movements. UNCLASSI-
FIED. In EUCOM Trans Div file 88, USAASC.

TCAHT with approximately two thirds of the personnel and 60 percent of the vehicles used in November.[19]

82. Additional Rail Service

Although the German rail system had long since passed under the control of German authorities, it remained the responsibility of Transportation Division to see to it that military rail transport needs were met. Beginning 4 January 1949 extra baggage cars were added to train runs between Fassberg and Erding, three days a week.[20] A daylight train connecting Frankfurt, Marburg, Kassel, Hannover, Celle, and Fassberg, for Air Force personnel and high priority freight, began operating on 20 December 1948.[21]

83. Factors Affecting Organization

One of the lessons of Transportation Corps experience at Tempelhof was the importance of a simple and flexible organization. The TC organization at the three U.S. airfields — Tempelhof, Wiesbaden, and Rhein/Main — was based on actual lift operations, especially in regard to the types and number of planes and quantities and types of cargo to be handled. At Tempelhof the Transportation Corps was concerned with the factors of (1) supervision and organization, (2) space for and capacity to receive incoming commodities, (3) the number of vehicles available, and (4) the supply of German laborers. Space, vehicles, and laborers were adequate, and the airhead organization was flexible enough to be quickly expanded or contracted at any point.[22]

84. Costs of Transportation Support

Transportation was one of the few aspects of airlift support for which an estimate of costs was possible. At Tempelhof the cost of handling airlift cargo decreased from $5.29 per ton in November and $3.43 in December 1948 to $2.89 in January, $2.21 in March and $1.93 in April.[23] Over-all transportation costs to

---

[19]Ltr, Col Donald C. Foote, BMP Trans Off, to EUCOM COT, 20 May 49. UNCLASSIFIED. In EUCOM Trans Div file 580 (1949), Item 9.

[20]EUCOM OCOT Rept of Opns, 1 Jan - 31 Mar 49, p. 39. CONFIDENTIAL.

[21]Ibid., 1 Oct - 31 Dec 48, p. 43. CONFIDENTIAL.

[22]Interv, E. S. Lay, EUCOM Hist Div, with Lt Col J. F. Phillips, BMP Trans Off, 23 Jun 50.

[23]"Operation VITTLES" - Tempelhof, A Transportation Corps Milestone, by Col Donald C. Foote, BMP Trans Off. UNCLASSIFIED.

31 August 1949, covering TC operations at Rhein/Main, Wiesbaden, and Berlin, are given in Appendix I. Accrued costs to 31 August totaled $7,953,742.98.[24]

85. Engineer Support at EUCOM Level

In 1949 the air lift continued to require engineer support in the form of rehabilitation and construction of living accommodations, construction and improvement of airfield facilities, and the supply of engineer items and equipment. As a result of lack of an over-all airlift command, the Engineer Division of EUCOM headquarters found it necessary to coordinate the engineer planning and construction undertaken for the air lift by USAFE, the military posts, and the United States Army Airlift Support Command. The Engineer Division reviewed estimates and requirements, recommended to Logistics Division the approval of engineer projects, and allotted funds to USAFE, BMP, F&P, and other agencies for completion of approved projects.[25] Projects approved during 1949, and those approved in 1948, are listed and described in Appendix J, Parts I and II.

86. Assumption for Long-Range Planning

At the beginning of 1949 long-range engineer planning for Operation VITTLES was based on the following assumptions:[26]

(1) USAFE will use C-54's for airlift operations indefinitely.

(2) USAFE is responsible for all phases of operations, including facilities for aircraft on the ground and airborne.

(3) USAFE will effect all AF technical as well as general engineer construction (including housing and facilities required by Army supporting elements) within air installations, except in Berlin. In Berlin, AF will install navigation aids and technical facilities only.

(4) USAFE will budget for and defend all funds incident

---

[24]EUCOM Trans Div file 35, USAASC. UNCLASSIFIED.

[25]Interv, E. S. Lay, EUCOM Hist Div, with Mr. Fred G. Scherrer, EUCOM Engr Div Const Br, 25 Oct 51.

[26]IRS, EUCOM Engr Div P&C Br to C/EUCOM Engr Div, Opns Br, 24 Jan 49, sub: Construction Cost Estimates, Operation VITTLES. UNCLASSIFIED. In EUCOM Engr Div file "Operation VITTLES."

to AF responsibilities and will disburse funds budgeted by Army and allocated to AF for construction of Army facilities required on air installations.

(5) Army is responsible for all operations, including facilities, required to transport and load cargo aboard aircraft, and its discharge and distribution at airfield of destination.

(6) Army will provide required housing for USAFE outside limits of air installations and beyond capacities of facilities at such air installations within standards fixed by the Commander-in-Chief.

(7) In Berlin, Army will assume construction responsibility for all facilities except AF technical (navigation aids, communications, etc.).

(8) Army will budget for and defend funds required to carry out Army responsibilities on air installations.

(9) USAFE will continue to operate 20 planes from Wiesbaden, probably longer than one year.

(10) USAFE requires following construction in Berlin during 1949 construction season:

    (a) Tempelhof:

        1. Remove PSP from south runway; resurface with 3" of asphalt macadam.

        2. Resurface about 1,250,000 square feet of existing apron with 3" of asphalt macadam.

        3. Resurface a taxiway 60 feet wide from south runway to apron with 3" of asphalt macadam.

    (b) Tegel:

        1. Construct a second runway 200 feet wide and about 6,000 feet long, parallel to and 600 feet south of present runway using 24" brick base with 3" asphalt macadam topping.

(11) USAFE will require added housing at Frankfurt, Munich and Wiesbaden.

87. Appointment of Special Coordinator

On 30 October 1948, Col. S. E. Nortner, the Commanding Officer, 555 Composite Service Group, had been appointed Engineer Coordinator for VITTLES Projects, representing the Chief Engineer, EUCOM. On 8 November 1948 the new coordinator established a liaison office in the office of the Wiesbaden Engineer Procurement Team. Later an officer from the 555 Composite Service Group was designated Engineer Supply Expediter for Rhein/Main Air Base, to act under the immediate supervision of the Engineer Coordinator for VITTLES Projects.[27]

88. Supply of Engineer Coal to Berlin

As of 1 January 1949 the Solid Fuels Division of the Hanau Engineer Depot, located at Rheinau,[28] was supplying military coal for Berlin Military Post. Coal was sacked in 50-kilogram sacks at the rate of 250 metric tons per day, and loaded on rail cars for Rhein/Main and Wiesbaden. Normally allotted 110 German employees, the coal point required some 40 additional laborers for this operation. When air shipment of Engineer coal was discontinued, at the end of January (see paragraph 63 above), the following amounts had been shipped from Rheinau to Berlin:[29]

Year	Month	Metric Tons
1948	October	5,838
	November	4,718
	December	3,679
1949	January	7,507

---

[27] (1) Memo, Brig Gen D. G. Shingler, EUCOM C/Engr, for CO 555 Composite Service Gp, and distribution, 30 Oct 48, sub: Engineer Coordinator for VITTLES Projects. (2) IRS, EUCOM Dep C/Engr to Opns, 8 Nov 48, sub: Engineer Liaison Officer, Operation VITTLES. (3) Memo for CO 555 Composite Service Gp, and distribution, 18 Nov 48, sub: Engineer Supply Expediter, Rhein/Main Air Base. All in EUCOM Engr Div file, Operation VITTLES. UNCLASSIFIED.

[28] This installation was subsequently designated the Rheinau Coal Point.

[29] Interv, E. S. Lay, EUCOM Hist Div, with Mr. J. L. Collins, EUCOM Engr Div Opns Br, 29 May 51. UNCLASSIFIED.

89. Power Plant Equipment for West Berlin

Apart from its direct concern with housing for lift personnel and construction of lift facilities the Engineer Division had several other airlift responsibilities. One of these related to the air movement of machinery for a power plant to be constructed in the Western Sector of Berlin. Prior to the lifting of the blockade, air shipment of this cargo, amounting to 6,579 short tons, was assigned the highest priority by General Lucius D. Clay, U.S. Military Governor. The Chief Engineer, EUCOM, was charged with responsibility for furnishing equipment and technicians to assist in the solution of loading problems.[30] Wiesbaden and Schleswigland airfields were to be used for this operation, although some power-plant equipment was to be loaded at Rhein/Main.[31] Under the revised schedule prepared late in April, monthly tonnages of power-plant cargo were to rise from 400 tons in April to 650 in May, 900 in June, July and August, 800 in September and October, and close with 250 in November and 200 in December. This schedule was to allow completion of the power station by 31 December 1949. In preparation for the project a representative of the Chief Engineer, EUCOM, met with representatives of BICO, CALTF headquarters, USAASC, the Royal Air Force (RAF), and BEWAG (the German firm manufacturing the equipment) early in April, and subsequently with the flight leaders responsible for loading C-82 and C-54 airplanes at Wiesbaden. At these conferences agreement was reached on cutting various pieces of cargo by torch, disassembling other pieces, using a marking system to insure correct identification at both ends of the lift, and studying alternatives to the movement of a few items not suitable for air shipment. It was also arranged that the Berlin Post Engineer would be called on to provide necessary assistance to the Air Force in the unloading of heavy items at Tegel and Tempelhof.[32] Lifting of the blockade made it unnecessary to carry out these plans in full.

---

[30] USAASC Memo for rcd, sgd Lt Col W. B. Bunker, USAASC Actg Opns Off, 22 Apr 49, sub: West Berlin Power Station. UNCLASSIFIED. In EUCOM Trans Div file 38, USAASC, West Berlin Power Station.

[31] Memo, C. C. Eaves, BEALCOM, to Mr. Fagan, BICO, 29 Apr 49, sub: Long Range Target for Airlift of the West Berlin Power Station. UNCLASSIFIED.

[32] Memo to EUCOM C/Engr, 14 Apr 49, sub: Power Plant Shipment to Berlin. UNCLASSIFIED. In EUCOM Engr Div file, Operational Engineer Supply Matters (VITTLES).

90. Engineer Support by Frankfurt Military Post

At Frankfurt the main requirements for engineer support of
Operation VITTLES concerned the provision of housing for Air Force
personnel. Preparation of barracks in the Atterberry-Betts Area,
largely completed by the beginning of 1949, was followed by a construction program to provide the barracks with a better service club
and other facilities.[33] FMP Engineers also supported TC and labor
service units engaged in airlift operations, building a hardstand
for trucks at Rhein/Main in January and regularly performing engineer maintenance tasks for labor units at Eschborn, to the west,
and for truck companies at Edwards Area, just north of Frankfurt.[34]
Maintenance of airfields at Rhein/Main and Wiesbaden was an Air
Force responsibility. In April the Engineer work at Atterberry-
Betts Area near Rhein/Main airfield diminished, although the entire
project was not completed until 18 November (see Appendix J, Part
I). In May the end of the blockade brought an end to the work of
crating and packing household goods shipped from Berlin to Frankfurt
by air.[35] Costs of various types of support provided for Operation
VITTLES by FMP Engineer Section are shown in Table 11.

91. Engineer Support at Rhein/Main and Wiesbaden

Improvement of airlift facilities at Rhein/Main and Wiesbaden
Air Force Bases was a matter of primary concern by early 1949. Unsatisfactory operating conditions demanded certain immediate improvements, while the apparent need of continuing the air lift for
an indefinite time pointed to the necessity of expanding facilities
to meet long-range requirements. Sudden termination of the blockade
in May forced the Engineer Division to reexamine projects already
approved for construction by the Air Force. A revised program provided for many of the improved facilities needed by the Airlift Support Command, omitting construction which would not be urgently
needed during the phase-out period. Actual construction of all projects on these bases, whether runways and hardstands for Air Force
use or buildings and other facilities for airlift ground-support

---

[33](1) See The Berlin Air Lift - 1948, pars. 24 - 26. SECRET.
(2) 1st Ind, EUCOM to CC FMP, 17 Jan 49, no subject. RESTRICTED.
In EUCOM AG file 600.1 Gen Constr (1949).

[34]Interv, E. S. Lay, EUCOM Hist Div, with Lt Col C. F. Fortney,
Jr., FMP Operations, Engr Sec, 29 Jan 49. UNCLASSIFIED.

[35](1) Interv, E. S. Lay, EUCOM Hist Div, with Lt Richard L.
Moody, Jr., C/FMP Engr Sec Admin and Mgmt Br, 16 Jun 50. UNCLASSI-
FIED. (2) See The Berlin Air Lift - 1948, par. 24. SECRET.

Table 11 -- Frankfurt Military Post
Post Engineer Cost Accounting Report - Operation VITTLES

COST REPORT PERIOD: 1 July 1948 to 31 January 1950
Reports Control Symbol: Operation VITTLES -- Berlin Air Lift

Account Title	Labor		Materials		Other Costs		Grand Totals	
	DM	Dollars	DM	Dollars	DM	Dollars	DM	Dollars
Totals	412,920.23	14,524.85	1,111,512.73	264,540.02	6,568.70	1,563.35	1,531,001.66	378,903.25
Construction	363,590.67		190,185.89	45,264.24	5,593.70	1,331.30	559,370.26	133,130.12
Modifications	27,049.56		423,776.44	100,858.79			450,826.00	107,296.59
Packing and Crating			420,000.00	99,960.00			420,000.00	99,960.00
Maintenance And Repair	22,280.00	14,524.85	77,550.40	18,456.99	975.00	232.05	100,805.40	38,516.54

Source: Office of the Chief, Engineer Section, Frankfurt Military Post.

operations, was a responsibility of USAFE. The Chief Engineer, EUCOM, cooperated closely with USAFE authorities on these projects.

a. Need for Aircraft Loading Ramp at Rhein/Main. One of the most urgently-needed improvements was an aircraft loading ramp for VITTLES planes at Rhein/Main. Justification for this item was presented to EUCOM on 1 February 1949 as follows:

> The primary mission of Rhein/Main Air Force Base is to provide and support facilities required for the Berlin Air Lift. A portion of the hardstands now in use are becoming unsatisfactory from an operational viewpoint due to deterioration of the base at a rate greater than the rate of maintenance. This condition plus the wet weather have caused mud and water to cover a portion of the PSP hardstands now in use. In addition, the operating conditions and number of personnel and trucks required to load the airplanes are aggravated by the dispersion involved. In order to eliminate both of these unsatisfactory conditions, it is planned to construct a central aircraft loading ramp with proper drainage facilities, proper flood lighting, and railhead facilities in an area as indicated on the attached plot plan. Although built as a temporary structure at the present in order to gain immediate utility, the location and design of this ramp are such that it can be altered and changed into a permanent type structure in accordance with the master plan for the base. This ramp will be of sufficient size to load 20 aircraft simultaneously....In addition, the spaces of the 20 aircraft which are being loaded will permit closing of the PSP hardstands which are now unsatisfactory due to mud and water conditions.[36]

b. Board to Study Requirements. Also in February 1949, a USAFE-Rhein/Main Joint Planning Board was established by USAFE. Its purpose was "to formulate and develop plans for all major activities required at Rhein/Main Air Force Base, to enable the base to perform its current mission, and to meet future needs effectively, efficiently, and economically." On 4 April the board held a special meeting with Army personnel to decide on plans for work which would be done at Rhein/Main with funds available to the Army. The meeting was

---

[36]Ltr, USAFE to CINCEUR, Att Off of C/Engr, sub: Construction of an Airplane Loading Ramp at Rhein/Main Air Force Base, C/R No. 146, 1 Feb 49. RESTRICTED. In EUCOM AG 600.1 GEN Construction Vol. III (1949), Item 19.

attended by officers representing the Transportation Corps and EUCOM headquarters.[37] Items put forward for consideration included a new loading ramp, a scale house, to be included in the loading-ramp project, a 100-man messhall for Transportation Corps personnel, an office building for the Airlift Support Command, rehabilitation of the DP messhall, surfacing of the north access road, extension of the railhead apron, and maintenance shops for the Transportation Corps.

c. Effects of Termination of Blockade. Between 27 April and 4 May projects were approved by Headquarters, EUCOM, for construction of a road network for Transportation Corps; construction of a loading and unloading ramp for the Transportation Corps at Rhein/Main; installation of heating in the Ordnance Maintenance Shop; construction of a 100-man messhall for the Transportation Corps at Rhein/Main; and construction of a loading ramp, scale house, and access road.[38]

d. Post-Blockade Revision of Construction Program. On 17 May Col. Eugene McGinley, the Commanding Officer of USAASC, met with Lt. Col. W. E. Leonhard, Deputy Chief, Installations, USAFE, Col. Hall S. Crain, EUCOM Liaison Officer at CALTF headquarters, and Mr. Fred Scherrer of Engineer Division, EUCOM, to discuss logistical support of Operation VITTLES with relation to the approaching phase-out.[39] At these meetings it was concluded that an adequate perimeter road net and maintenance shops were needed at Rhein/Main; that runway construction at Tempelhof and Tegel should be continued to completion; that construction of a new runway at Rhein/Main, to sustain loads of transport aircraft having wheel loads of 60,000 pounds or over, should be reconsidered for continuance; and that all plans for the construction of dependent housing at Celle and Fassberg should be suspended.

e. Projects Approved as of 25 May 1949. On 25 May USAASC was notified by Headquarters, EUCOM, that eight projects had been

[37]Mins of USAFE - Rhein/Main Joint Planning Board. UNCLASSIFIED. In EUCOM Trans Div file 6, USAASC Construction.

[38]Cables SC - 19439, 27 Apr 49; SC - 20144, 4 May 49; SC - 19902, 2 May 49; SC - 19901, 2 May 49; and SC - 19589. UNCLASSIFIED. In EUCOM Trans Div file 6, USAASC Construction.

[39]Memo for rcd, F. G. Scherrer, Const Engr, EUCOM Engr Div, to C/EUCOM Engr Div Opns Br, sub: Future Status - Operation VITTLES, 23 May 49. UNCLASSIFIED. In EUCOM Engr Div file, Operation VITTLES.

approved for construction at Rhein/Main and six for construction at Wiesbaden Air Force Base. These projects, for the benefit of ground-support activities, were as follows:[40]

Airfield		Project Description	Authorized Funds (DM)
Rhein/Main	(1)	Construction of scale houses	20,750
	(2)	Messhall for DP labor	15,000
	(3)	Construction of tractor maintenance shop	15,000
	(4)	Construction of trailer maintenance shop	6,000
	(5)	Construction of Romney-hut office space for TC personnel	6,000
	(6)	Tents for aircraft loading personnel	3,000
	(7)	Truck unloading and parking area	127,700
	(8)	Construction of two buildings for Transportation Corps	93,400
Wiesbaden	(1)	Construction of facilities for railhead at Erbenheim	6,000
	(2)	Installation of flood-lighting along north apron	24,000
	(3)	Repair concrete floor Hangar #29	18,000
	(4)	Flood lighting vehicle maintenance area	3,000
	(5)	Construction of truck loading docks	36,000
	(6)	Installation of air-freight vehicle weighing scales	17,100

All these projects except the flood-lighting of the north apron at Wiesbaden Air Force Base were completed during the summer of 1949.

f. Action on Supplementary Projects. In addition to those approved, several projects were suspended. Within the next few days the Rhein/Main Detachment of the Airlift Support Command

---

[40]Cable SC - 22182, EUCOM to USAASC, 25 May 49. UNCLASSIFIED. In EUCOM Trans Div file 6, USAASC Construction. Between 20 June 1948, date of the currency reform in the three Western zones, and 29 September 1949, the official value of the Deutsche Mark, as converted for use by the Occupation Forces, was 30 cents. On 29 September, it was revalued at 23.8 cents (to be effective retroactively to 19 September).

reviewed its operational requirements and recommended further improvements in roads and parking areas. These recommendations, dated 1 June 1949, looked forward to the relocation of loading and parking areas and of the traffic control point and ready line which actually took place in August.[41] (See Map 2.) EUCOM notified USAFE on 3 June that it approved continuance of projects for construction of Transportation and Ordnance vehicle maintenance shop facilities at Rhein/Main (for 1,000,850 DM and $2,614 in depot credits), and the resurfacing of the road net at Rhein/Main with asphalt macadam (for 200,000 DM and $9,100 in depot credits).[42] Projects for a loading and unloading ramp and a 100-man messhall at Rhein/Main were canceled late in August.[43]

92. Engineer Support at Berlin

Planning for VITTLES construction at Berlin went on from mid-1948 until the lifting of the blockade. At the beginning of 1949, Engineer requirements for Berlin were estimated to include a new runway at Tegel, runway rehabilitation at Tempelhof and Gatow, and related construction on roads and taxiways. (See Appendix K.) Such construction was estimated to require 450,000 cubic yards of crushed rock, 158,000 55-gallon drums of asphalt, and 24,200,000 manhours.

a. Factors Affecting 1949 Construction Program. By comparison with the situation facing BAP Engineer Section in 1948, several factors lightened the burden of meeting construction requirements for 1949. By 1949 a sufficient number of Engineer personnel had been trained in airport building, whereas only one member of the 1948 staff had had actual experience in such construction.[44] Construction during 1949 was also aided by the arrival of fifteen 2½-ton dump trucks, ten 10-ton rollers, and two 2-unit rock crushers (combination crushing and screening plants), airlifted from the

---

[41] Ltr, 7933 USAASC R/M Det, RMAFB, to CO 7933 USAASC, 1 Jun 49, sub: Modification of Railhead Facilities. UNCLASSIFIED. In EUCOM Trans Div file 6, USAASC Construction.

[42] Cable SC - 23169, CINCEUR to USAFE, 3 Jun 49. UNCLASSIFIED. In ibid.

[43] Cable SC - 15400, CINCEUR to USAFE, 25 Aug 49. UNCLASSIFIED. In EUCOM Trans Div files.

[44] Interv, E. S. Lay, EUCOM Hist Div, with Mr. Nelson G. Greene /subsequently Lt Col Nelson G. Greene, BMP Post Engineer7, C/BMP Engr Br Opns Sec, 22 Jun 50.

Map 2

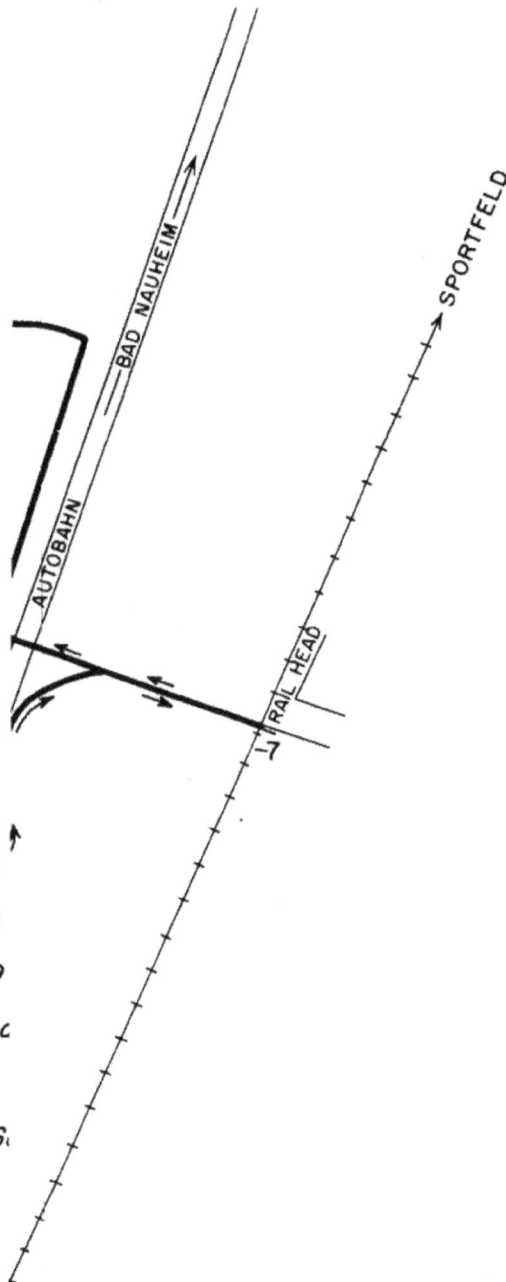

LEGEND:

1 24th TT Bn Shop

2 Base Railhead

3 Railhead Office

4 DP Mess

5 Truck Scale

6 559 Ordnance MAM Shop

7 Station Lufthafen Rhein/Main

8 Ramp Railhead   } Added in

9 24th TT Bn Park } July 1949

10 Dispatch Area TCP #1, Addec

11 Scale (Proposed)

12 Second Runway, Completed S

AUTOBAHN

BAD NAUHEIM

SPORTFELD

RAIL HEAD

7

SOURCE: Based on Rhein/Main
and Information from

U.S. Zone to Berlin.[45] By 1949 Berlin Engineers also had the benefit of progress that had been made, from a technical standpoint,
in airport construction. (See paragraph 41.)

b. Ground-Support Projects at Tempelhof. A number of Engineer projects were undertaken early in 1949 to facilitate ground-
support operations at Tempelhof. These included construction of
a wooden shelter in Hangar 5 to serve as a waiting room for German
labor crews; construction of a more adequate administrative office
for the TC headquarters; and moving of the former TC administrative
building to the ready line for use by enlisted cargo-checkers and
their German assistants.[46]

c. Major Construction Projects. The two main Engineer projects of 1949 were the new runway built at Tegel (paragraph 40)
and the resurfacing of the south runway at Tempelhof (paragraph 42).

93. Supply Aspects of Engineer Support

Engineer supply requirements arising from Operation VITTLES
were heavy. Up to the end of the blockade the expansion of airfield facilities required increasing amounts of construction supplies and equipment. Items furnished by the Engineer Base Depot
at Hanau included asphalt, rope, and emergency generator equipment.
The depot staff also handled the dismantling and reassembling of
heavy Engineer equipment shipped to Berlin by air. Because of heavy
airlift demands, some stocks previously considered adequate were
temporarily depleted.[47]

94. Signal Support

From July 1948 to January 1949 approximately 90 percent of the
supply projects processed by Signal Division, EUCOM, were for airlift support.[48] During the spring of 1949 support of Operation
VITTLES continued to be reflected in expanded communications facilities, increased traffic loads, and heavy supply requirements.[49] In
addition to its direct support of lift operations, the Signal Corps

---

[45]Ibid.

[46]BAP Rept of Opns, 1 Jan - 31 Mar 49, p. 141. RESTRICTED.

[47]EUCOM Engr Div Ann Nar Rept, 1949, par. 53a. UNCLASSIFIED.

[48]Interv, E. S. Lay, EUCOM Hist Div, with Maj E. H. Johnson,
EUCOM Sig Div Proc and Distrib Br, 20 Jan 49. CONFIDENTIAL.

[49]See The Berlin Air Lift - 1948, par. 30. SECRET.

was called on to see that communications between Berlin and the U.S. Zone were adequate in spite of conditions imposed by the blockade.

a. Traffic at Frankfurt. The lift brought Frankfurt Military Post Signal Branch an increased traffic load of roughly 20,000 words per day. The branch handled eight Air Force circuits carrying administrative (not operational) traffic and provided circuits for USAASC and air traffic control. Although two teletype channels between Frankfurt and Washington were on loan to USAFE during the lift a heavy overload of transatlantic traffic passed through tape delay at Frankfurt. Traffic on wire circuits maintained by Frankfurt Signal Branch ran to 14,000 or 15,000 messages per day. Maintenance of these circuits provided valuable training for Signal personnel. In the radio control section there was a turnover of enlisted personnel amounting to almost 70 percent during the lift, and all received solid training in radio control and wiring. Traffic decreased noticeably in June and July of 1949, and many circuits were discontinued in July and August.[50]

b. Signal Support at Berlin. At Berlin the Signal Corps handled a large volume of administrative traffic relating to the lift. Signal facilities were staffed by the 7773 Signal Service Company, with an authorized strength of 277 enlisted men and 19 officers. The BMP Signal Branch was authorized an additional 12 officers. Throughout the lift the Signal Branch stressed radio training for tactical units in Berlin.[51] One of the principal Signal projects completed in 1949 was a 200-line PAX switchboard placed in service at Tegel Air Force Base in August.[52]

c. Special Courier Service. Just prior to the blockade an Army Post Office (APO) run had been established to carry classified mail by train between Berlin and the U.S. Zone. To replace this service the Frankfurt Signal Branch created a special air courier run to handle all official written communications, including secret material, between Berlin and the U.S. Zone. The

---

[50]Interv, E. S. Lay, EUCOM Hist Div, with Lt Patrick Kearins, FMP Radio Sec, and Lt Lewis Campbell, FMP Sig Br Comm Ctl Sec; 2 Jun 50. Additional statistics on traffic at FMP are available in EUCOM Sig Div Traffic Sec file, Reports and Inspections, 1948 – 1949.

[51]Interv, E. S. Lay, EUCOM Hist Div, with Lt E. C. Kelly, BMP Signal Br, 22 Jun 50.

[52]EUCOM Sig Div, Hist Rept, 1949, p. 21. RESTRICTED.

sixteen enlisted couriers were flown by European Air Transport Service (EATS) on a number one priority. The couriers were armed and carried incendiary bombs for emergency use in destroying classified mail. Two weeks after the end of the blockade the train run was restored and the air courier service discontinued. The service had operated throughout the blockade without accident or mishap.[53]

95. Signal Communications

British airlift experience supported the view that the best possible signals system was "an essential part of any air supply operation." A highly-developed system of line and wireless communications and a special PLAINFARE telephone net made it possible for British lift agencies to conduct operations very largely through verbal communications.[54] The Department of the Army observer group reported agreement of lift units on the following minimum communication facilities to handle loading and unloading:

(1) Telephone communication from the trunk dispatching point to the Operations Control tower.

(2) A very high frequency (VHF) radio to monitor instructions given to aircraft by the control tower.

(3) A public address system to facilitate handling of labor crews.

(4) A radio-equipped 1/4-ton truck for communication with Transportation Corps dispatching office.[55]

96. Ordnance Support during 1949

The pattern of ordnance support established in 1948 was little changed during 1949.[56] At EUCOM headquarters one of the main tasks was to insure adequate supplies of vehicles and parts. By 1949 the five types of truck tractors used in the command were no longer being manufactured and no replacements were available. The most

---

[53]Interv, E. S. Lay, EUCOM Hist Div, with Lt E. T. Stanley, FMP Sig Br, 2 Jun 50.

[54]Mimeographed paper, The Rear Airfield Supply Organization. UNCLASSIFIED. In EUCOM Trans Div file 3, USAASC British Fields.

[55]DA, Observers' Report on Operation VITTLES, Annex 5, Appendix A, pp. 85 - 86, par. 3. RESTRICTED.

[56]See The Berlin Air Lift - 1948, par. 27 - 29. SECRET.

critical items, engine and power train assemblies, were being rebuilt at this time by Karlsfeld Ordnance Center at the rate of
200 per month.[57] The 1,182 ordnance vehicles supporting VITTLES
at the beginning of 1949 required 118 rebuilt vehicles, 732 rebuilt tires, and 659 tons of spare parts and supplies, above normal
per month.[58] Production of tires size 1100 x 20 at the Ober
Ranstadt Tire Rebuild Shop, for VITTLES support, was increased by
the installation of three extra molds of this size.[59] By January
1949 shop facilities for maintenance of VITTLES vehicles were excellent and tools and parts were adequate for full-scale maintenance.[60] In the Frankfurt-Wiesbaden area, field maintenance for
airlift support vehicles continued to be provided by the 559th
MAM Ordnance Company. Early in 1949 the two detachments previously servicing truck units at Mainz-Kastel and Praunheim were
withdrawn and field maintenance was concentrated at Rhein/Main
Air Force Base.[61] Weekly inspections of operations at Rhein/Main
by representatives of EUCOM headquarters, FMP Ordnance Section,
USAASC, and the 24th Transportation Truck Battalion helped make
possible the early analysis and solution of key maintenance
problems. For a full report on FMP ordnance activities in support of the lift see Appendix L. Supply of Berlin by air continued to make possible rapid delivery service from zonal depots,
allowing the Ordnance Section to continue its operations on a
comparatively normal basis.[62] Over 1,100 tons of ordnance materiel were airlifted to Berlin, including major assemblies
supplied by Karlsfeld Ordnance Center and spare parts packed and
shipped by Griesheim and Mannheim Ordnance Depots. A summary of
ordnance support at Berlin is attached as Appendix M.[63]

---

[57]EUCOM DCINC Wkly Staff Conf Notes, No. 16, 19 Apr 49, par.
18. RESTRICTED.

[58]EUCOM Log Div Rept of Opns, 1 Oct - 31 Dec 48, p. 8. SECRET.

[59]EUCOM Ord Div Rept of Opns, 1949, p. 6. RESTRICTED.

[60]EUCOM Log Div Rept of Opns, 1949, p. 6. SECRET.

[61]559th Ord MAM Co Hist of Opns, 31 Dec 48 - 31 Mar 49. UN-
CLASSIFIED. In EUCOM Hist Div Docs Br.

[62]Interv, E. S. Lay, EUCOM Hist Div, with Lt Col Martin F.
Shaughnessy, BMP Ord Off, 11 Feb 49. UNCLASSIFIED.

[63]A more comprehensive account of ordnance support is given
in European Command Ordnance Service in the Berlin Airlift, compiled under the direction of Brig Gen E. E. MacMorland, EUCOM
Chief of Ordnance, edited by Lt Col Martin F. Shaughnessy, BMP
Ord Br (1949). UNCLASSIFIED.

97. <u>Ordnance Problems at Rhein/Main</u>

Several factors made the provision of field maintenance a difficult mission at Rhein/Main. During the winter and spring most of the roads were in extremely bad condition. Inspection of eighty trailers belonging to the 68th Transportation Truck Company (Heavy) showed that the frames of thirty were either bent or cracked.[64] Long distances from the railheads (prior to August 1949) and the lack of warehousing on the base made it necessary to use trailers to hold reserve quantities of coal and flour in readiness for the lift. Steps taken to adapt tractors and trailers to meet airlift-support conditions are described in Appendix L. An additional improvement was made in June and July by adding the tarpaulin support frames or bows of 2-inch pipe to the trailers used at Rhein/Main, as already mentioned. This framework not only improved vision of drivers but gave greater structural strength to the trailer body, eliminated the side sway which had accounted for many cases of trailer damage, and provided a tarpaulin support frame which permitted loading and unloading without the removal of the tarpaulin. The pilot model for this modification was designed and manufactured at the Boeblingen Ordnance Rebuild Shop and the bows were manufactured by the 7845 Ordnance Maintenance Group.[65] Other problems at Rhein/Main related to the mission and working conditions of the unit charged with providing third echelon or field maintenance. Up to 27 October 1948 the enlisted personnel of the 559th Ordnance MAM Company had worked at Munich as supervisors of Germans who did the actual maintenance work. The unit was brought to Rhein/Main at the end of October without the benefit of an interim training and orientation period. There it was responsible for providing field maintenance for VITTLES vehicles, without any assistance from German personnel. Morale was also affected by the unsatisfactory living conditions on the base. In February 1949 the unit moved to permanent-type barracks at Atterberry-Betts Area, twelve miles from its shop at Rhein/Main. Throughout the winter and much of the spring the back-log of work orders frequently necessitated night work. Since the shop was surrounded by mud, members of the

---

[64] Ltr, EUCOM Ord Div, to CG USAASC, 19 Apr 49, sub: Damaged Trailer Frames, and 1st Ind, USAASC to C/EUCOM Ord Div, 3 May 49, UNCLASSIFIED. In EUCOM Trans Div file 6, USAASC Construction.

[65] (1) 7845 Ord Maint Gp Nar Hist, 1 Apr – 30 Jun 49, p. 11. UNCLASSIFIED. In EUCOM Ord Div files. (2) Draft cable, USAASC to CINCEUR, attn: C/Ord Div, C/Engr. UNCLASSIFIED. In EUCOM Trans Div file 6, USAASC Construction. (3) Telecon, E. S. Lay, EUCOM Hist Div, with Olive Farmer, EUCOM Trans Div Opns Br, 26 Jun 51.

unit built special approaches to the shop entrances. Special winter clothing could not be obtained through regular supply channels for the men who provided day-and-night wrecker service at the base. Some items were obtained from Air Force units on memorandum receipt and passed from one group of enlisted men to another as they came off duty. Assignment to the unit of men without training or skill in repair work tended to lower the morale of the unit while adding to the burdens of its administrative personnel.[66] On-the-job training eventually qualified this personnel to carry its part of the workload. In March, company strength was increased to four officers and 115 enlisted men. By June, better roads, improved weather, and unit maintenance had combined to make the workload of the unit appreciably lighter.[67] The parts available and the service were greatly improved. Engineer assemblies removed vehicles from deadline and the assigned ordnance companies were able to keep up requirements for ordnance work.

98. Quartermaster Support

Quartermaster (QM) support of the lift comprised subsistence and clothing for airlift personnel, equipment to serve U.S. airmen at Celle and Fassberg, laundry service, petroleum (POL) products, and the supply and rebuilding of materials-handling equipment (MHE). Support of BAP and normal support of U.S.-employed Germans in Berlin (generally supplied with dyed clothing and one meal per day), was affected by air-supply conditions, particularly with regard to the packing and handling of food products.[68]

a. Support by Frankfurt Military Post Quartermaster. In the fall of 1948 the lift had given the FMP Quartermaster a noticeably heavier workload in terms of increased requirements for rations, increased sales of officers' clothing, and increased demands for laundry and dry cleaning.[69] This type of support continued until the summer of 1949.

---

[66]559th Ord MAM Co Hist of Opns, 31 Dec 48 - 31 Mar 49. UNCLASSIFIED.

[67]USAASC, History of the United States Army Airlift Support Command, 6 Apr - 15 Oct 49, pp. 13 - 14. UNCLASSIFIED.

[68](1) Interv, E. S. Lay, EUCOM Hist Div, with Maj E. K. Buchanan, C/EUCOM QM Div Plans Br, 2 Mar 49. (2) The Berlin Air Lift - 1948, par. 31. SECRET.

[69]Interv, E. S. Lay, EUCOM Hist Div, with Lt Col Robert D. Hodge, FMP Dep QM, 31 May 50.

b. **Effect on Operations at Berlin.** Under blockade conditions the BMP Quartermaster Branch received its supplies from the U.S. Zone at irregular intervals and in varying amounts. Before each shipment the depot at Giessen informed the Berlin Quartermaster by telephone that certain commodities had left Giessen and would probably be shipped from Wiesbaden. QM representatives were on duty continually at Tempelhof to identify incoming QM cargo. Perishables, regardless of their quantity, were hauled at once to the BMP cold storage plant. Toward the end of the lift the QM Branch was working out a system whereby non-perishables would be moved by the truckload. Outstanding cooperation on the part of QM agencies in the U.S. Zone helped to make the air-supply operation successful, insuring ample food stocks for BMP throughout the blockade. Despite a great deal of small pilferage the total amount lost in this way was relatively small.[70]

c. **Handling of Food Shipments.** Food for BMP was inspected at Frankfurt QM Cold Stores, at Wiesbaden Air Force Base, and at Tempelhof. The five-man veterinary team at Frankfurt rejected approximately 3 percent of the eggs and 22 percent of fruits and vegetables because of inadequate packing or insufficient freshness. An Air Force veterinarian spot-checked food at Wiesbaden and occasionally accompanied cargo to Berlin to observe stowing and carrying procedures, temperature regulation during flights, and the condition of the food on arrival.[71]

d. **Materials-Handling Equipment.** The rebuilding of MHE for airlift use placed urgent demands on the Giessen Quartermaster Depot until April 1949. The depot extended field maintenance service to USAFE air bases and Air Force personnel came to the depot for training in the operation and lower-echelon maintenance of MHE. Sixty-one major items were rebuilt during 1949 for issue to USAFE. A conveyor-tractor manufactured experimentally by the depot was successfully tested at Rhein/Main. Designed for use in the loading of C-54 aircraft the conveyor was powered electrically from an outlet independent of the tractor; it had a maximum practical working angle of 45 degrees.[72]

---

[70]Interv, E. S. Lay, EUCOM Hist Div, with Maj James F. Fewster, Jr., BMP QM Br Exec Off, 22 Jun 50.

[71]EUCOM DCINC's Wkly Staff Conf Notes, No. 6, 8 Feb 49, par. 16. UNCLASSIFIED.

[72]EUCOM QM Div Hist Rept, 1949, Annex B, Pt. I, Giessen QM Rept of Opns 1 Jan - 31 Dec 49, pp. 16 - 19. UNCLASSIFIED.

Table 12 -- Airlift Fuel Requirements (US)
June 1948 through June 1949

	Aviation Gas (gallons)	72 Octane (gallons)	Aviation Oil (gallons)	Engine Oil (gallons)	Grease (pounds)	Kerosene (gallons)	Diesel (gallons)
Jun 48	233,444	59,321	8,050				
Jul	4,370,778	280,261	91,550	6,000	1,765	1,500	
Aug	5,649,402	312,825	5,000	29,800	1,583	2,500	
Sep	5,708,933	367,312	80,000	3,525	691	15,600	
Oct	7,122,004	362,459	53,600	2,000	1,944	53,800	24,096
Nov	7,336,438	523,151	2,000	20,088	1,159	7,000	24,096
Dec	8,342,360	430,714	122,015	6,349	1,208	43,500	24,096
Jan 49	11,306,400	751,153	181,104	40,992	12,465		
Feb	8,442,000	640,293	139,776	21,000	6,075		
Mar	11,218,200	719,993	181,650	23,646	9,254		
Apr	15,640,800	783,246	153,384	24,612	9,040		84,000
May	12,969,600	813,943	210,000	24,024	8,674		84,000
Jun	13,473,600	1,055,000					

Source: EUCOM QM Div Area Petroleum Office. CONFIDENTIAL.

- 105 -

e. <u>POL Products</u>. The task of assuring adequate supplies of gasoline and other POL products to meet airlift requirements fell to the POL Section, Supply and Procurement Branch, Quartermaster Division, EUCOM. This office also served as the Area Petroleum Office, handling all aviation gasoline for the command, the bunkering of Army transports and chartered vessels, and all tankers bringing over fuel.[73] Fuel and grease requirements for the U.S. portion of the air lift are shown in <u>Table 12</u>. Three ocean-going T-2 type tankers per month were required to move the bulk petroleum to the command and 1,500 rail tank cars per month were required to move bulk petroleum to airlift operating points. Seventy Air Force refueling units (tank trucks with pumps and filters for moving fuel from on-field storage to the airplane) plus sixty-six Standard Oil refueling units were used at the airfields.[74]

---

[73]Interv, E. S. Lay, EUCOM Hist Div, with Lt Col V. H. Moore, C/EUCOM QM Div Supply and Proc Br POL Sec, 20 Jan 49. CONFIDENTIAL.

[74]Information supplied by Lt Col E. J. Fourticq, Air Representative, Area Petroleum Office, and Col C. O. Bennett, Dep Area Petroleum Officer, Area Petroleum Office, QM Div, EUCOM, 29 Nov 51. CONFIDENTIAL.

CHAPTER VI

Phase-Out Operations

99. Discontinuance of the Air Lift

For several reasons the air lift was not discontinued immediately after the ending of the blockade. From an operational
standpoint it was not desirable to try to terminate the lift
suddenly. But apart from the practical problem of relocating
airlift personnel and equipment a more compelling reason for
not stopping the lift existed in the need for continuing to
underwrite the position of Western Berlin. Only a few days
after the end of the blockade, the rail strike at Berlin again
made air supply essential to the western part of the city. Re-
sumption of rail traffic with the Western Zones early in July
and the building up of coal stocks throughout the month removed
the last cause for delay in applying phase-out plans. In practice, scheduled reductions in the lift were accelerated and the
planned 90-day phase-out period begun on 1 August was cut to
60 days. After 14 August, cargo operations at Rhein/Main and
Wiesbaden were reduced from a 7-day to a 5-day week. On 24
September the Department of the Army expressed the view to
CINCEUR that further continuation of the air lift appeared to
be costly and wasteful, as well as unnecessary, and directed
that if he concurred with this view he should take action to
suspend the lift immediately.[1] The Air Force had concurred in

---

[1]Cable X - 94718, COFSA from Dir Plans & Opns to CINCEUR,
24 Sep 49. CONFIDENTIAL. In EUCOM SGS 094 Berlin, Vol. I (1949),
Item 93e. For reply, stating airlift would be discontinued as of
1 October, see Cable SC - 2153, EUCOM to COFSA, 29 September 1949.
CONFIDENTIAL. In ibid., Vol. I (1949), Item 93h.

this message, with the provision that its plan for the return of aircraft and personnel to the United States should continue in effect. On 28 September the Commanding General, USAFE, directed the Commanding General, 1st Airlift Task Force, to terminate the regular scheduled Berlin air lift as of 2400 hours, 30 September 1949.[2] The last load was flown from Rhein/Main to Tempelhof on 30 September 1949.[3]

100. Planning the Phase-Out

Plans for the phase-out of the air lift covered the gradual reduction of flying operations, the scheduling by BEALCOM of reduced tonnages for Berlin, and the withdrawal and disposition of equipment and personnel assigned to the United States Army Airlift Support Command.

a. Air Force Planning. The basic Air Force plan for phasing out the air lift was issued by Headquarters, USAFE, on 12 July 1949[4] in line with a United States Air Force plan drawn up in April and communicated to USAFE on 17 May.[5] The USAFE plan prescribed a gradual reduction in airlift operations over a period from D-day to D plus 130, a period divided into four phases of 30 days each and a final phase, D plus 121 through D plus 180. The USAFE directive adapted the plan to existing conditions and added a logistical annex providing for the return of certain supplies to EUCOM depots.[6] Headquarters, 1st Airlift Task Force, published

---

[2]Cable ECCG – 97082, USAFE to for action FALTF, 28 Sep 49. UNCLASSIFIED. In ibid., Vol. I (1949), Item 93g.

[3]Work sheet for 30 September 1949. UNCLASSIFIED. In EUCOM Trans Div file 53, USAASC Work Sheet Figures, August and September.

[4]USAFE, Phase-Out Plan Upon Cessation of the Berlin Airlift, 12 Jul 49. In EUCOM Log Div Plans Br files. Change No. 1 was published on 28 July. On 29 July the plan and related correspondence were downgraded from "SECRET" to "RESTRICTED." (See USAFE monograph, USAFE and the Berlin Airlift 1949, Appendix VI-E, for communication authorizing downgrading.)

[5](1) USAFE monograph, USAFE and the Berlin Airlift 1949, p. 311. In Hist Div Docs Br. (2) USAFE, History of Headquarters, USAFE, May 1949, pp. 44 – 47, gives details of the plan.

[6](1) USAFE, Phase-Out Plan Upon Cessation of the Berlin Airlift, 12 July 1949, Tab D, Logistics Plan. (2) Interv, E. S. Lay, EUCOM Hist Div, with Col Hall S. Crain, EUCOM Log Div, 16 Aug 49. RESTRICTED.

Table 13 — BEALCOM Requirements for August 1949

(All Figures in Short Tons)

Requirements							
					560	3920	8	4488

Forwarding Airport	Est. Daily Target US, UK, & Fr. Mil. Misc. & A.F.C.	Food	Coal	C & I Gas., Dies., Kero & Misc.	Mail	Daily Total	Receiving Airport
Totals	4,500	560	3,932		8	4,500	
Celle	Closed down 1200 hrs 31 Jul 49					4,500	Gatow
Fassberg	1,344		1,344			1,344	Tegel
Fuhlsbuettel	100	100				100	Tegel
Luebeck	225		225			225	Gatow
Rhein/Main	1,300		1,300			1,300	Tempelhof
Schleswigland	482		482			482	Tegel
Wiesbaden	515		511		4	515	Tempelhof
Wunstorf	534	460	70		4	534	Gatow

Breakdown of August Overall Coal Requirements. 500 tons of this total daily tonnage will be special long flame gas coal and the balance to be regular.

Note: Fuhlsbuettel will close down 2400 hours, 15 August, at which time all food lift will be flown from Wunstorf.

Source: Bipartite Control Office, August Lift Requirements. UNCLASSIFIED.

a "Vittles Phase-Out Plan" on 18 July,[7] detailing steps to be taken by units during successive phase-out periods. On 29 July, USAFE gave notice that 1 August 1949 would constitute D-day for commencement of the phase-out.[8]

b. Reductions in Tonnage Allocations. In line with Air Force planning and too-level decisions to terminate the air lift, BEALCOM reduced its inbound tonnage targets from 8,071 short tons daily, beginning 1 July (7,718 tons, effective 5 July) to 4,500 tons daily during August (see Table 13). Initial requirements for September were set at 1,305 tons daily (all in coal), and revised to 825 tons, effective 0800 hours, 6 September.[9] After 23 September the weekly total was to be 3,800 tons for the remainder of September.[10]

c. USAASC Planning. The phase-out plans of the United States Army Airlift Support Command were carefully coordinated with Air Force planning. The first detailed USAASC plan was submitted to EUCOM on 3 August 1949.[11] This plan defined the current mission of USAASC as follows: "Mission will be to phase-out Operation VITTLES over a 90-day period starting on 'D' day, 1 Aug 49. Each phase-down period to be a reduction of activity as the tonnage target of the Berlin air lift is reduced. Personnel, equipment and other responsibilities will be reduced as applicable." A revised plan calling for further reductions in personnel and equipment at Rhein/Main and Wiesbaden was published on 15 August, and on 19 August the plan was revised "to provide for a continuous reduction and final disposition of all units

---

[7]In files of EUCOM Log Div Plans Branch. This plan, originally SECRET, cited as reference a CALTF letter, sub: Gradual Phase-Out of Berlin Airlift, dated 6 Jun 49, a letter which was also cited in USAASC phase-out plans. The CALTF letter is not presently available to EUCOM Hist Div for reference purposes.

[8]USAFE carrier sheet, Div of Plans to Addressos, 29 Jul 49, sub: Cessation of Berlin Airlift. RESTRICTED. Appendix VI-E to USAFE monograph, USAFE and the Berlin Airlift, 1949. SECRET. In EUCOM Hist Div Docs Br.

[9]See EUCOM Trans Div file 53, USAASC Work Sheet Lift Figures August and September. UNCLASSIFIED.

[10]Ibid.

[11](1) USAASC Plan, Phase-Out Reductions, 3 Aug 1949. RESTRICTED. In EUCOM Trans Div USAASC File No. 26, Vittles Phase-Out Plan. (2) Ltr, USAASC to CINCEUR, 3 Aug 1949, sub: Vittles Phase-Out Plan. RESTRICTED. In EUCOM Trans Div, file 580.

assigned to, and personnel and equipment of, U.S. Army Airlift Support Command, before and subsequent to D plus 90."[12]

101. USAASC Participation in Phase-Out Planning

Following the decision to discontinue the lift, the Airlift Support Command took responsibility for releasing its subordinate units. Its first phase-out plan, detailing proposed reductions in units, personnel, and equipment, was submitted on 3 August.[13] On 12 August USAASC was directed to revise this plan to provide for the most rapid reduction in troop strength that could be achieved without sacrifice of economy in operations. The revised plan was to include target dates for the release of all assigned units and for the inactivation of the headquarters.[14] The required revision was submitted on 19 August.[15] On 31 August the Chief of Transportation, EUCOM, forwarded to Logistics Division a detailed plan to be implemented by Transportation Division "to phase out completely the ground phase of the Berlin airlift."[16] This plan provided for a final period, from 1 to 30 November, for accomplishing the reduction of USAASC personnel. Subsequent changes in planning for the phase-out of USAASC were outlined by Transportation Division on 19 and 28 September.[17] Prior to the discontinuance of USAASC on 15 October, under an accelerated phase-out schedule, the 551 Ordnance MAM Company and most of the transportation units utilized by USAASC were assigned to Frankfurt Military Post. Eight labor service companies and their respective supervision companies were inactivated

---

[12]Ltr, USAASC to CINCEUR attn Dir EUCOM Log Div, 19 Aug 49, sub: Vittles Phase-Out. RESTRICTED. This letter and the plan of 15 August are in EUCOM Trans Div file 26, USAASC.

[13]Ltr, USAASC to CINCEUR, 3 Aug 49, sub: VITTLES Phase-Out Plan. UNCLASSIFIED. In EUCOM Trans Div file 580 (1949).

[14]Cable SX - 1512, CINCEUR to USAASC, 12 Aug 49. RESTRICTED. In EUCOM Trans Div file 14, USAASC.

[15]For details see EUCOM Trans Div file 26, USAASC VITTLES Phase-Out Plan. UNCLASSIFIED.

[16]IRS, EUCOM Trans Div to Dir EUCOM Log Div, 31 Aug 49. UNCLASSIFIED. In EUCOM Trans Div file 580 (1949).

[17]IRS, EUCOM Trans Div to EUCOM OPOT Div through EUCOM Log Div, sub: Phase-Out of Ground Phase of USAASC and Reassignment of Units, 28 Sep 49. UNCLASSIFIED. In ibid.

and one labor company and one supervision company were reassigned to Frankfurt Military Post.[18] The 110th Labor Supervision Center was assigned to Wetzlar Military Post.

102. Organizational Changes During the Phase-Out

The termination of the lift was reflected in a number of major organizational changes.

a. Change in Status of USAASC. Effective 20 August the U.S. Army Airlift Support Command was relieved from assignment as a subordinate command of U.S. Army, Europe, and assigned to Transportation Division, U.S. Army, Europe.[19] The results of this move were felt mainly in the field of administration. Operationally, USAASC continued almost without change.[20]

b. Discontinuance of Headquarters, USAASC. Final disposition of all units connected with USAASC was completed on 13 October 1949, and the parent unit, the 7933 Headquarters, USAASC, was discontinued on 15 October.[21]

c. Deactivation of Headquarters, CALTF. By joint agreement of BAFO and USAFE, Headquarters, Combined Airlift Task Force, was deactivated as of 0001 hours, 1 September 1949.[22]

d. Discontinuance of Headquarters, FALTF. Discontinuance of Headquarters and Headquarters Squadron, 1st Airlift Task Force, effective 0001 hours, 1 October 1949, was directed by Headquarters, USAFE on 2 September.[23] The 61st Troop Carrier Wing took the

---

[18]USAASC, History of the United States Army Airlift Support Command, p. 24. UNCLASSIFIED.

[19]Ibid., p. 23. UNCLASSIFIED.

[20]Interv, E. S. Lay, EUCOM Hist Div, with CWO Parrott, USAASC, 12 Oct 49. UNCLASSIFIED.

[21]IRS, EUCOM Trans Div to EUCOM Log Div and EUCOM OPOT Div, 17 Oct 49, sub: Final Report on Phase-Out of USAASC. UNCLASSIFIED. In EUCOM Trans Div file 580 (1949).

[22](1) Memo, Air Hq BAFO and Hq USAFE, to CG CALTF, 12 Aug 49, sub: Deactivation of Headquarters, Combined Airlift Task Force. In USAFE monograph, USAFE and the Berlin Airlift 1949, Appendix VI-F. SECRET. (2) Stars and Stripes, Eur. ed., September 8, 1949. UNCLASSIFIED.

[23]USAFE GO 162. In USAFE monograph, USAFE and the Berlin Airlift 1949, Appendix IV-D. SECRET. In EUCOM Hist Div Docs Br.

responsibility for airlift flights made during the last ten days of the lift.[24] FALTF headquarters closed effective 0001 hours, 1 October 1949.[25]

103. Return of Equipment to Depot Stocks

Beginning in July, Logistics Division initiated action to recover for EUCOM depot stocks the equipment furnished to Air Force and Army units on a loan basis. This recovery program was completed by the end of 1949.[26] EUCOM was also concerned with the turn-in of U.S. supplies and equipment from Celle and Fassberg, the two British bases from which U.S. planes had operated during the lift. To these two bases Bremerhaven Military Post had supplied Signal Corps switchboards, lights, and cable, quartermaster refrigerators, stoves, and mess equipment, and a few other items, including medical equipment and dental chairs. Many of the items had been obtained by Bremerhaven from the depots expressly for shipment to these bases. To simplify the turn-in of such supplies, the logistic annex to the USAFE phase-out plan (as agreed by EUCOM and the services) authorized their direct return to the depots. Information copies of the shipping documents were sent to Bremerhaven to enable that headquarters to clear its accounts.[27]

104. Installations for Future Use

Although lifting of the blockade affected plans to expand airlift facilities, the Chief Engineer and the Chief of Transportation continued to be concerned with the possible need for installations to support a future air lift. A list of installations and areas considered vital to the success of such an operation, should one again prove necessary, was sent to Transportation Division by USAASC on 14 October. (See Appendix N.)[28] On 24 October Transportation Division recommended that an agreement be reached with USAFE on the use of the listed facilities.

---

[24]USAFE monograph, USAFE and the Berlin Airlift 1949, pp. 345 - 346. SECRET. In ibid.

[25]FALTF GO 9, 22 Sep 49. In USAFE monograph, USAFE and the Berlin Airlift 1949, Appendix IV-E. SECRET. In ibid.

[26]EUCOM Log Div, Rept of Opns, 1 Jan - 31 Dec 49, par. 10. SECRET.

[27]Interv, E. S. Lay, EUCOM Hist Div, with Col Hall S. Crain, EUCOM Log Div, 16 Aug 49. CONFIDENTIAL.

[28]Ltr, USAASC to EUCOM Trans Div, 14 Oct 49, sub: Desired Installations and Areas at Rhein/Main and Weisbaden Airfields. STRICTED. Included as App. N.

For this purpose a conference was held on 11 January 1950. On 14 April 1950 USAFE concurred in the agreement reached at the conference, but noted that the maintenance building and motor pool requested for use at Rhein/Main would not be available. In addition ground-support troops would be housed at Wiesbaden as in the 1948-49 lift.[29] In place of making the Transportation and Ordnance repair shops available, USAFE offered to develop project plans for replacement facilities to be furnished Transportation Corps and Ordnance during any future air lift.[30]

105. Special Shipping Requirements

The ending of the lift made it necessary for EUCOM to provide transportation for personnel, especially dependents, returning to the United States, and shipping space for certain types of aircraft equipment. As more and more C-54's returned to their original bases, quantities of spare parts were returned to the U.S. by the U.S. Army Transportation Division's marine express service, MARINEX, under priority arrangements made by EUCOM Transportation Division. Phase-out plans called for the return to the United States of two planes daily, each with a crew of eight, twelve passengers, and approximately 5,000 pounds of freight, but there was not sufficient air space for all the C-54 supplies scheduled for immediate shipment or for all the families of returning Air Force personnel.[31]

106. Reducing Flying Operations

In accordance with the USAF phase-out plan, the Naval Transport Squadrons VR-6 and VR-8 were returned to the Military Air Transport Service (MATS), the 317 Troop Carrier Group (with unit equipment less aircraft) was returned from Celle to the United States for inactivation, and 50 C-54's were returned to the U.S.

---

[29]Memo for Rcd, Major Fred L. Eaker, EUCOM Log Div Instal Sec, 23 May 50. RESTRICTED. In EUCOM AG 600.1, Vol. XVII (1949), Item 69.

[30]IRS C/EUCOM Trans Div to C/EUCOM Engr Div, 5 Jun 50, sub: Desired Installations and Areas at Rhein/Main and Wiesbaden Airfields. UNCLASSIFIED. In EUCOM Engr Div Const Br file, Operation VITTLES.

[31]Interv, E. S. Lay, EUCOM Hist Div, with Col Hall S. Crain, EUCOM Log Div, 16 Aug 49. CONFIDENTIAL. Col Crain returned to Headquarters, EUCOM, from Headquarters, CALTF, on 15 August 1949.

for cycle reconditioning during the period D-day to D plus 30.[32]
Additional units and aircraft were returned to the U.S. during
succeeding stages of the phase-out. From August to October a
reduction in USAFE airmen strength was accomplished through the
use of a roster system designed to return to the United States
all airmen who did not desire to stay and were not needed by
USAFE for further service in the European Command.[33] In the
field of supply, the closing-out of USAFE activities at Celle and
Fassberg airfields relieved a number of shortages felt at other
USAFE installations.[34] VITTLES airfields closed down as follows:[35]

Airfield	Last Airlift Flight
Celle	1200 31 July
Fassberg	0800 27 August
Fuhlsbuettel	2400 15 August
Luebeck[36]	2000 23 September
Rhein/Main (C-54 No. 7)	1845 30 September
Schleswigland	6 October
Wiesbaden	0800 2 September
Wunstorf	2000 29 August

107. Role of USAASC in Planning for Future Contingencies

When the blockade was removed, the European Command prepared standby plans based on experience gained in the air lift,

---

[32]USAFE, USAFE and the Berlin Airlift 1949, p. 311. SECRET.
In EUCOM Hist Div Docs Br.

[33]USAFE, A Short History of USAFE, 1 July - 31 December
1949, p. 108. UNCLASSIFIED. In ibid.

[34]Ibid., p. 50.

[35](1) Interv, E. S. Lay, EUCOM Hist Div, with Major Wilfred
J. McCall, C/USAASC Opns Br, Sep 1949. (2) Rhein/Main closing
time from mimeographed report, USAASC R/M Det Summ Rept Tonnage
Movements. UNCLASSIFIED. In EUCOM Trans Div, file 80, USAASC.
(3) Information Wunstorf, Luebeck and Schleswigland from BAFO,
Report on Operation Plainfare, p. 552. RESTRICTED.

[36]Stars and Stripes, Eur. ed., September 22, 1949, under
heading "RAF Chief Will Meet Last British Lift Plane," stated
that Marshal of the Royal Air Force Viscount Trenchard would
arrive in Berlin Friday /23 September/ to meet the last Dakota
of the British air lift /from Luebeck/ and would take part in
a ceremony at Gatow. The ceremony took place as scheduled.

for use in the event of a future contingency. Staff members of
USAASC shared in preparatory planning on this problem during
September and early October.[37] Prior to the discontinuance of the
Airlift Support Command, its commanding officer submitted to the
Chief, Transportation Division, a list of installations regarded
as vital to successful operations in the event the Army were required to support a future air lift from the Rhein/Main and Wiesbaden airfields.[38] Re-establishment of the Airlift Support Command was regarded as essential to any future lift, indicating
that the principle of organizing ground-support units under a
single command had won full approval during the brief half-year in
which it had been in operation.

108. Standby Arrangements

     The airlift showed the wisdom of being prepared for a simi-
lar necessity in the future. On 4 October 1949 representatives
of EUCOM, HICOG, USAFE, USAASC, U.S. Commander Berlin, and the
Transportation, OPOT, and Logistics Divisions of EUCOM met at
Heidelberg to develop an outline plan for re-establishment of the
Berlin lift.[39] Annexes to this plan were to be prepared by HICOG,
USAFE, and the U.S. Commander in Berlin. An interim plan was
held in its files by Logistics Division, EUCOM, until January
1950, when Headquarters EUCOM issued a formal "Operations Plan
for Berlin Airlift."[40]

---

[37] IRS, Dir EUCOM OPOT Div to EUCOM COFS, sub: Re-establishment of Berlin Air Lift, 5 Oct 49. CONFIDENTIAL. In EUCOM SGS
094 Berlin (1949), Item 94a.

[38] Ltr, USAASC to C/EUCOM Trans Div, sub: Desired Installations and Areas at Rhein/Main and Wiesbaden Airfields, 10 Oct 49.
UNCLASSIFIED. In EUCOM AG 600.1 (1949).

[39] IRS, Dir EUCOM OPOT Div to EUCOM COFS, sub: Re-establishment of Berlin Air Lift, 5 Oct 49. CONFIDENTIAL. In EUCOM SGS
094 Berlin (1949), Item 49a.

[40] This plan, produced in 145 copies, is on file in the Transportation Branch, BMP, in various offices at EUCOM headquarters,
and in the Documents Branch, Historical Division, EUCOM. CONFI-
DENTIAL.

BERLIN AIRLIFT

Summary by Norman L. Smith, Food, Agriculture
and Forestry Group, Bipartite Control Office.*

The Berlin airlift was initiated on 28 June 1948 by order of
the Military Governors after continuous obstruction by the Russians
had resulted in closing land and water transportation routes to
Berlin. Restrictions leading to the "blockade" are generally considered to have started in the later part of January 1948, at which
time passenger traffic to Berlin began to encounter the so-called
"technical" difficulties which accumlated until land and water
transportation were eventually at a standstill.

The airlift was started by the U.S. Air Corps using C-47's
(Dakotas) with an average daily lift of about 150 tons. C-54's
(Skymasters) were soon in action along with RAF Yorks, Haltons,
Sunderlands, and other RAF or British chartered aircraft and the
food lift was averaging over 1000 tons daily by mid-July. Airfields
at Wunstorf, Celle, Fuhlsbuettel, and Luebeck in the British Zone
and Rhein/Main and Wiesbaden in the U.S. Zone were utilized at one
time or another for the food lift. The majority of the food, however,
was flown from Wunstorf, Celle and Rhein/Main. The division of the
overall airlift between USAF and RAF was about 75 and 25 percent
respectively (however, no special effort was made to maintain this
relationship).

Following the so-called "lifting of the Blockade" on 12 May
1949, part of the Berlin food requirements were again transported by
land and water (fresh potatoes by rail and grain by barges). Approximately 24,000 tons of potatoes were sent into Berlin by rail
from the Bizone in the first few days following the lifting of the
blockade. By the time this quantity had been delivered potatoes had
become available in such quantities from the Eastern Zone that

---

*Note: This summary was furnished to the Historical Division by the
author in August 1949. Permission to use it as an appendix to this
monograph was granted by Mr. Smith, now Chief, Agricultural Production
and Extension Branch, Food and Agriculture Division, HICOG, on 24 August
1951. CONFIDENTIAL.

Berlin requirements could be fulfilled from that source at a lower
price than they could be supplied from the Bizone. This was mainly
due to the prevailing rate of currency exchange (about 4 East Marks
to 1 West Mark - by July it was 6:1). Potatoes sold for 3 West
Marks therefore actually brought an equivalent of 12 East Marks.
Eastern Zone potatoes were available to meet West Berlin needs
only during part of May and June. Potatoes to the amount of
30,000 tons were requested by Berlin during July 1949. The strike
of rail employees in Berlin in the latter part of May again halted
traffic. Barge traffic was impeded by the slowness of the Russian
authorities in signing the required permits when they were presented for their approval. This impediment threatened to reduce
barge shipment of bread grain during June from the desired 58,000
tons to 20,000 tons (less than 1 month supply in terms of flour).

Berlin Requirements:

The average daily food requirements for the approximately 2.2
million people residing in the three Western Zones amounted to
about 1305 net metric tons. This was based upon use of dehydrated
rather than fresh potatoes and vegtables, use of dried eggs as a
substitute for 1/3 of the meat ration and utilization of boneless
meat, fish fillets, and various other foods in a form which would
save airlift weight and space. The airlift was based upon the
following daily tonnage requirements (all figures in net metric
tons - 2204.6 lbs).

Flour	646	
Cereals	125	
Dehydrated Potatoes	180	
Fat	64	
Meat	109	(67 meat, 30 fish, 12 dried eggs)
Sugar	85	
Coffee	5½	
Dried Skim Milk	19	
Dried Whole Milk	5	
Yeast	1	
Salt	38	
Dehydrated Vegetables	18	
Cheese	10	
	1305½	

Dehydrated potatoes were substituted for fresh potatoes on the Berlin ration on the basis of 1 to 5 (1 dehydrated - 5 fresh) and dehydrated vegetables for fresh vegetables at a rate of 1 to 8. Dried eggs were substituted for meat at the rate of 1 to 3.

The Berlin food ration was increased on 1 July 1948 and again on 1 November 1948. A comparison of the ration for the two periods, by consumer groups, appears below.

	1 July 1948	1 November 1948
Children under 1 year of age	1786 calories	1786 calories
Children age 1 to 6	1653 "	1653 "
Children age 6 to 9	1619 "	1633 "
Children age 9 to 14	1559 "	1834 "
Employees and others	1608 "	1882 "
Laborers	1999 "	2202 "
Heavy Laborers	2498 "	2609 "

The daily requirements in tons as stated herein were based on the ration as of 1 November 1948. These requirements, with minor changes, continued until the reported lifting of the blockade on 12 May 1949. After the lifting of the blockade such goods as potatoes, vegetables, fish, and real coffee were freed from rationing.

Included under the above requirements were the following foods:

1. Flour (imported, rye, and German milled wheat flour)
2. Noodles (noodles, macaroni, spaghetti)
3. Baby food
4. Dried fruit (raisins, apricots, peaches)
5. Semolina
6. Rolled Oats
7. Rice
8. Dehydrated potatoes
9. Butter
10. Lard
11. Oil (for margerine manufacture)
12. Hard Fat (for margerine manufacture)
13. Meat (frozen beef and pork, canned meat, sausage)
14. Fish (frozen fillets and smoked)
15. Dried eggs
16. Sugar
17. Chocolate
18. Cocoa

19. Coffee
20. Tea
21. Dried Skim Milk
22. Dried Whole Milk
23. Yeast
24. Salt
25. Dehydrated vegetables (cabbage, carrots, onions)
26. Cheese
27. Knaeckebrot
28. Soups (powdered pea and bean soups)

During the period 28 June 48 – 30 June 49 there were 434,084 tons of food flown into Berlin. This is an average of about 36,000 tons monthly.

Average Daily Deliveries to Berlin
via Airlift (net metric tons)

	Food	All Commodities
June/July	1098	1560
August	958	2963
September	1281	3750
October	1176	3706
November	1128	2820
December	1461	3512
January	904	4258
February	1041	4066
March	1209	4797
April	1380	6026
May	1531	6379
June	958	6391

Procedure in Supplying Food for Airlift

Decisions as to amounts and types of food to be sent via the airlift were arrived at in the following manner:

1. A monthly request was made by the Berlin Central Food Office to the appropriate Allied Military Government Personnel of the three Western Sectors of Berlin (Allied Kommandatura Food Committee).

2. These representatives reviewed the request in light of the airlift space allocated for food during the month and the

suitability of the food for airlift and for rationing in Berlin.

3. The request in its approved form was then forwarded to the Food Supply Branch of the Bipartite Control Office, which, together with representatives of the German Administration for Food, Agriculture and Forestry, prepared a schedule indicating the kind, amount, and time of arrival of the various food items desired at each of the different airfields. The decision as to the amount of the food to be flown from particular airfields was agreed upon in monthly meetings attended by U.S. and U.K. army and air corps officials and /representatives of the/ Bipartite Control Office (Berlin Airlift Coordinating Committee). Deliveries to airfields were scheduled in accordance with the above decision.

4. Orders for delivery were given to the appropriate agencies, firm or factories by the individual commodity referats of the German Administration (VELF) in cases of food items rationed in the Bizone. The Berlin Magistrat's Frankfurt representatives of the Central Food Office arranged for purchase and delivery of food items necessary in Berlin but not rationed in the Bizone. Toward the end of the fiscal year the Magistrat's Office was contracting for all foods.

Selection of Airfields for the Food Lift

Several factors influenced the decision as to which would be utilized for airlift of food. The type and number of aircraft were an important determining factor. Certain commodities required special handling and could best be handled in certain types of aircraft (salt, for example, was carried only in aircraft which had control cables so located as not to be subjected to the corrosive action of any leakage of salt). Location of the airfields with respect to the source of food and other commodities especially coal, was important as was utilization of airfields with the best food storage facilities. A division of the food lift between the U.S. and U.K. zones was maintained mainly to reduce the effect of "weathering in" of airfields in either sector upon delivery of food to Berlin. Food was scheduled for the nearest airfield insofar as was possible considering the lift quotas established at each. Supply difficulties and the necessity of sufficient food readily available at airfields to keep all operational planes flying necessitated a departure from this system at certain times.

Handling Berlin Food at Airfields

Rhine/Main and Wiesbaden. The loading of planes at these fields was a fairly simple operation. Food arrived on rail cars and was unloaded into U.S. Army Transportation Corps trailers. Each trailer was loaded with enough food to completely load a C-54 (approximately 10 tons). Thus the operation was strictly a rail to plane movement at these airfields. No suitable storage space was available on either airfield. A constant supply of food was insured by scheduling arrivals at such a rate that approximately three days' supply for the lift was constantly on rail in Frankfurt area and available for calling forward to airfields at the convenience of the Army Transportation Corps. Storage was provided in Frankfurt by a commercial storage firm. This firm was employed by the Berlin Magistrat and its facilities used to store food as a reserve supply for the airlift at Rhine/Main and Wiesbaden and as a means of controlling the rail-pipeline which tended to become "overloaded" during bad flying and to "run dry" during good flying weather when an attempt was being made by the Air Force to make up for previous lift shortfalls.

Actual loading of planes and trailers was performed by DP's (Displaced persons) /and later by Germans/ hired by the U.S. Army and supervised by the U.S. Army Transportation Corps.

Food coming into Rhine/Main and Wiesbaden airfields was consigned to a control company who accepted the goods on behalf of the Berlin Magistrat and then transferred title to the U.S. Army for transportation to Berlin.

British Zone Airfields. The facilities for handling food at airfields in the British Zone were superior to those at Rhine/Main and Wiesbaden since most of the fields there had one or more hangars which could serve as airfield storage. In addition, each field had a British supervisor to control food movements and a German staff, including a competent warehouseman to keep stock records and to generally look after the food movements. The warehousemen were employed by the Berlin Magistrat and kept the necessary accounts in his behalf.

The hangar warehouses were excellent in that they provided for a readily available reserve food supply and provided a covered place for loading trucks and for repairing or replacing broken cases and packages.

PROBLEMS ENCOUNTERED

Procurement and operational problems were numerous and stemmed from a variety of causes including:

1. The general economic condition of Germany.

2. Reluctance of indigenous sources to provide Berlin with food.

3. Requirements peculiar to air transportation.

4. The system of financing the Berlin food supply.

5. Absence of suitable organization and sufficient cooperation on part of the German officials involved (both among themselves and with Allied personnel).

6. The number and variation in the agencies involved (both on Allied and German side).

Supply Problems

Some difficulty in obtaining desired supplies was caused by the reluctance of Laender to fulfill their Berlin food quotas. This was particularly true in the case of meat and cheese. Cooperation by the Land Ministers and the Allied Food and Agriculture representatives in the various Lands led to successful solution of this problem.

Considerable difficulty was experienced in obtaining sufficient dehydrated potatoes and vegetables to fulfill Berlin requirements. This problem was particularly acute during the latter part of 1948. Several factors were involved among which were the following:

1. Many dehydration plants in Germany were not in operating order due to the lack of business since the war.

2. Lack of trained personnel at dehydration plants.

3. Reluctance of some plants to engage in production for Berlin due to the indefinite length of time that the airlift could be expected to continue.

4. Preference of some dehydration plants to dehydrate vegetables for customers of long standing rather than to dehydrate potatoes or vegetables for Berlin consumption since this would necessarily cease with the lifting of the blockade.

5. Reluctance of many plants to change from vegetable dehydration to potatoe dehydration because of the greater returns from the former.

6. The amount of time necessary to arrange for and get delivery of imported foods.

A Military Government order directing that all dehydration plants would produce to capacity for Berlin plus active participation on the part of Land Food and Agriculture representatives and Land Ministers eventually resulted in increasing German dehydration of potatoes to a point where it equaled the Berlin requirements.

Quality Problems

Poor quality was much too common among foods delivered to airfields. Many shipments were refused because of poor quality and many more which were not detected were flown to Berlin. Shipment of poor quality food by air was a direct result of lack of proper inspection at airfields by the Berlin Magistrat since the Magistrat bought and paid for all shipments. This lack of quality check persisted in spite of numerous requests to the Magistrat to institute adequate inspection procedure. Some poor quality imported foods (usually from European sources) succeeded in passing both the loading and border inspections and yet were so inferior as to be unfit for human consumption.

Poor quality in certain instances undoubtedly arose from unfamiliarity of the processing firms with the product they were preparing (as in the case of precooked, dried pulses). A certain number of deliberate attempts on the part of suppliers to dispose of inferior products also undoubtedly occurred (but were very difficult to prove). However, more adequate supervision and inspection by the Berlin Magistrat's Office to insure that deliveries were of a quality comparable to the sample upon which the purchase was based would have reduced the amount of poor quality food transported via the airlift.

Transportation Problems

No serious transportation problems other than air transport were encountered. Bad weather during part of the winter reduced flying to such an extent that the average daily tonnage of food delivered to Berlin was less than the daily issue against the Berlin ration. In each case however there were ample stocks in Berlin to meet the ration until deliveries could be continued at the desired rate.

Storage Problems

Anticipation of possible difficulty in transporting food to airfields during the winter due to inclement weather, holidays, etc., contributed heavily toward the decision to maintain at least a 10 days' reserve of food in storage near airfields. An additional 3-day supply (based on the average daily lift) was maintained on rail as a "pipe line" to insure loads for every plane that could make the trip to Berlin.

Obtaining storage space near airfields was difficult. The nearest storage for Rhine/Main was located in Frankfurt. As a result food so stored was not immediately available to the airlift and about 24 hours was the normal time required for moving food from the Frankfurt storage to the railhead.

In the British Zone, storage presented a lesser problem than at Rhine/Main. Hangar space was available at both Wunstorf and and Celle. This space served as intransit storage and provided a reserve "cushion" which provided time to move food from main storage depots in Hannover /and other cities/.

Inclement weather during winter months, plus the emphasis placed on delivery of coal to Berlin, resulted in a backlog of food at airfields. This occurred because in such periods the actual food lift was less than the lift tonnage allocated for food upon which deliveries to airfields were based. As a result, at one time (February and March 1949), approximately a 30-day supply in terms of Berlin requirements was held in storage at airfields. This was approximately twice the necessary amount and was eventually reduced by stopping delivery from mills and factories for a period. Halting deliveries from factories was regarded as dangerous, especially during the winter, since previous experience had indicated that considerable delay and difficulty was involved before deliveries could be resumed. During late spring and early summer reserve stocks were reduced to practically nil since it was felt that a three-day supply on rail was a reasonably adequate reserve and carrying of large reserve stocks meant added cost to the Berlin Magistrat as well as added work in keeping reserve stocks "rotated" to prevent deterioration in storage.

Some minor difficulties were encountered at Rhine/Main in rate of outloading from storage necessary to supply the desired rail "pipe line." Outloading a quantity of 600 - 700 tons required at least a day. Switching and transportation to the airfield normally took most of another day. Thus a total of about 48 hours lapsed from the time orders to outload were given until the food was actually available for lifting. This was a main factor necessitating a three-day supply on rail.

Financing

Prior to the airlift, food going to Berlin was handled through normal trade channels. After initiation of the blockade and counter blockade a different method was necessary for financial reasons. Until 1 April 1949 Berlin workers were paid about 25 percent of their salary in Western DM and the balance in Eastern Zone currency. Hence food was purchased largely with East marks. However, merchants could not purchase food in the Eastern Zone nor was the Eastern Mark acceptable in the Bizone. To solve this problem a sort of "clearing house" was established by the Berlin Magistrat in that the Magistrat's Office purchased the food and was reimbursed by merchants when the food was delivered in Berlin. This, plus storage charges, etc., placed a heavy financial responsibility and burden on the shoulders of the Magistrat. This was especially true during the winter, at which time large reserve stocks in both Berlin and at airfields had to be financed in addition to making advanced payments to German dehydration plants to insure production of dehydrated goods. A monthly account of approximately 50 to 60 million DM was made available to the Magistrat through the Military Government Finance Group to finance this operation.

Political Problems

Political considerations dictated food supply policies to some extent. For example, shipment of pre-cooked, dried pulses was discontinued because of articles published in Berlin newspapers to the effect that these pulses were making the population ill. These reports may or may not have had some foundation. However, due to the unfavourable publicity given the product by the press (largely in the Eastern sector papers), no attempt was made to make further shipments. Certain types of meat products likewise received unfavourable publicity and were discontinued.

Price Problems

One of the important considerations was that of supplying a ration that could be purchased by the Berlin population. With the reduction of employment brought about by the closing of factories due to shortage of heat and power consumer prices of food became even more important. For example, considerable price resistance was encountered in the case of dried vegetables with the result that stores became somewhat overloaded and deliveries were halted.

Packaging Problems

Utilization of air transport occasioned many packaging problems. The desirability of keeping tare weights low while maintaining packages of a type that would protect the food and at the same time be of a size easily handled by hand necessitated many deviations from usual German packaging methods. For example, flour and sugar which are usually shipped in bags weighing around 100 kilos were sacked in small bags (40 and 45 kilos respectively) to facilitate handling. Due to pilferage, several items such as chocolate, meat, baby food, etc., had to be packaged in strong, banded boxes. Some imported foods had to be repackaged to provide added protection or to reduce tare and improve ease of handling.

To facilitate aircraft loading, types and weights of food packages were standardized as much as possible. Labeling was improved so that each package was marked with its weight and content. Such standardization and labeling presented problems. For example the weight change necessitated hand filling instead of machine filling of flour and sugar sacks. For some foods it meant a change in size and/or type of packaging, and in most cases a reluctance on the part of German firms to change packaging and labeling methods had to be overcome.

Shortage of bags and certain other packaging materials caused added difficulties. Sacks were returned from Berlin and reused. Because of the superior quality of the cotton bag in which flour imported from the U.S. was packed, these bags were quite popular for refilling in German mills. Since these mills were not equipped with machines for stitching the bags after filling, bags could be refilled with only 40 kilos (about 88 lbs) allowing room for tying. Sugar was filled in 45-kilo bags (the same weight as imported flour).

Personnel Problems

These problems are of two general categories -- problems involving Germans and those involving Allied organizations. Those involving the German personnel concerned with the airlift were numerous and showed great variation. They included such things as:

1. A lack of enthusiasm on the part of some German officials to make the operation as successful and as smooth-running as possible.

2. Insufficient concern for making the most efficient use of airlift space for transportation of rationable commodities (requests to transport fresh vegetables and potatoes, canned vegetables, frozen vegetables, liquid soups and other commodities of high water content and consequently uneconomical users of space were continuous throughout the blockade).

3. Attempts to transport unauthorized (non-rationable) foods.

4. Attempts to transport unauthorized commodities other than food and count it against the airlift quota for food.

5. Purchase of foods (by Berlin Magistrat) which were of poor quality, or of a type unsuitable for and previously refused for airlift.

6. Failure to purchase sufficiently in advance to insure uninterrupted delivery to airfields.

7. Countermanding delivery orders previously agreed between representatives of the Berlin Magistrat and the Allied Food Representatives in Berlin.

8. Failure to install (in spite of repeated suggestions by BICO Food, Agriculture and Forestry Group) an adequate quality check on foods delivered at airfields for transport to Berlin.

9. Failure to implement and inspect for approved packaging of foods arriving at airfields.

10. Lack of imagination and forward planning on such matters as food procurement, packaging, delivery time, etc.

11. The tendency to answer problems presented to them by the term "impossible."

Problems involving Allied organizations and personnel were usually caused by one of the following:

1. The number and variation in organizations involved and dealt with.

2. Persistent and recurring difficulties arising on the German side (as previously mentioned) and affecting Allied operations.

3. Pilferage of food items after their arrival at airfields (this involved German and DP laborers as well as Allied Military personnel and was usually confined to food items of high "black market" value).

4. The tendency of the Air Forces to "fly" in excess of their estimated quota thus causing considerable difficulty in maintaining a supply of food at airfields (this caused a supply difficulty, since daily airfields deliveries were scheduled in accordance with the daily airlift quota).

5. Orders from high military authority suddenly stopping the airlift of food for periods of a week or ten days (such orders caused much difficulty and expense since it meant that the food deliveries scheduled for airfields during that period had to be postponed by calling all the factories involved or that the food arriving had to be stored or remain on rail, all three alternatives being difficult and expensive).

Comments

The term "military operation" was often applied to the airlift. This was not a completely accurate description. Only that part of the operation extending from the time the food arrived at airfields and was loaded on Army vehicles until it was unloaded in Berlin was handled by armed forces personnel. The procurement, planning, storage, financing of supply, movement to airfields, etc., was handled by civilian components on the Allied and German side.

With much of the responsibility for implementation of food deliveries dependent upon German personnel and German facilities, actual absolute control of food procurement and control of the rate of delivery to airfields was impossible. Hence the term "military operation" was a gross misnomer and quite misleading in its implication of strict control.

It is quite evident that, from a food supply standpoint, an airlift operation of this magnitude, if under one command (as it would be in a strictly military supply operation) or jurisdiction of single agency, could be run more efficiently than the Berlin Airlift has operated. However, with the supply from many different sources and purchased by different agencies (and in many cases not originally purchased with air transport in mind) the supply system functioned remarkably well.

Lack of sufficient cooperation between German agencies concerned (especially between VELF, Berlin Magistrat, and Berlin Magistrat's Frankfurt representative) was the cause of many unnecessary difficulties and complications.

Conclusions

1. The airlift of food for a population of about 2.2 million people can be accomplished (as has been adequately demonstrated by the Berlin Airlift).

2. Storage space on airfields is advisable from the standpoint of efficiency (this storage should be large enough to provide a reserve of food to insure constant supply and have sufficient space to accommodate arrival of supplies during a period when weather prevents flying).

3. Package sizes, types, and weights should be standardized to facilitate handling, plane loading, accounting, etc.

4. Packages must be of a type which will accomplish the following:

    a) Lowest possible tare (in keeping with protection of product, etc.) to save airlift space.

    b) Prevent breakage which will lead to loss through exposure, pilferage, etc.

    c) Marked clearly as to type of contents, weight, etc.

d) Keep packaging charges as low as possible while accomplishing the above.

e) Eliminate the necessity for backloading of empty packages (paper bags can be used and offer a solution to much of this problem).

5. Continuous quality checks must be made prior to loading in aircraft to avoid loss of airlift space through transportation of poor quality products.

6. Delivery should be made at a rate equal to the daily airlift tonnage with provisions made for calling forward supplies as needed in order to avoid excessive storage of supplies. (Difficulty in renewing deliveries from factories and firms made shutting off this supply line hazardous during the Berlin operation.)

7. Handling food at airfields (loading, unloading, and storage) should be done under supervision of personnel who are competent to judge whether the handling is being properly done and who have sufficient authority over personnel doing the work to take immediate corrective action.

HEADQUARTERS
EUROPEAN COMMAND

AG 381 GSP-AGO

APO 403
30 March 1949

SUBJECT: US Army Airlift Support Command

TO: Brig Gen Philip E. Gallagher, O11249, USA
          Headquarters, European Command
          APO 403, US Army

1. With effective date 6 April 1949, in addition to your
normal assignment as Director of Posts you will organize and
assume command of US Army Airlift Support Command, with headquarters at Wiesbaden, Germany.

2. Mission. Operating as a subordinate command of US
Army, Europe, you will be responsible for all operations in
direct support of the Air Lift Force at Rhein/Main Air Force
Base and Wiesbaden Air Force Base.

3. Composition. USAASC will consist of:

a. Headquarters

b. Airlift Detachments, 7795 Traffic Regulating
Detachment, TC

c. 24th Transportation Truck Battalion, consisting of:

        67th Transportation Truck Co (hvy)
        69th Transportation Truck Co (hvy)
        70th Transportation Truck Co (hvy)
        76th Transportation Truck Co (hvy)
        83rd Transportation Truck Co (hvy)
        99th Transportation Truck Co (hvy)
        543rd Transportation Truck Co

d. 559th Ord MAM Co

e. _____ Labor Supervision Center (to be formed):

```
2958 Lbr Svc Co and  303 Lbr Superv Co
4543 Lbr Svc Co and   36 Lbr Superv Co
8957 Lbr Svc Co and  501 Lbr Superv Co
8958 Lbr Svc Co and  523 Lbr Superv Co
4052 Lbr Svc Co and   38 Lbr Superv Co
4060 Lbr Svc Co and  506 Lbr Superv Co
8512 Lbr Svc Co and   54 Lbr Superv Co
2905 Lbr Svc Co and 7880 Lbr Superv Co
7441 Lbr Svc Co and 7881 Lbr Superv Co
```

4. All elements of USAASC are attached for administration to Frankfurt Military Post under the provisions of Paragraph 9i, Circular 140, Hq EUCOM, 1948.

5. The representative of Logistics Division EUCOM at Hq CALTF will continue his function of logistic assistance to the Air Force; this function does not fall within your responsibilities.

BY COMMAND OF GENERAL CLAY:

s/ Peter Calza
t/ PETER CALZA
Lt Col, AGD
Assistant Adjutant General

Telephone: Heid Mil 02506

DISTRIBUTION: A, plus
  10 — Addressee
  50 — USAFE
  10—— CO, Rhein/Main Air Base
  10 — CG, Frankfurt Mil Post

HEADQUARTERS
EUROPEAN COMMAND

APO 403
5 April 1949

TROOP ASSIGNMENT)
:
NUMBER   8)

1. The 7934 Labor Supervision Center Headquarters, organized pursuant to General Order No. 12, Hq Frankfurt Military Post, 4 April 1949, is assigned US Army Airlift Support Command and attached for administration to Frankfurt Military Post, effective 6 April 1949.

2. The units listed below are relieved from present assignments and attachments and are assigned US Army Airlift Support Command and attached for administration to Frankfurt Military Post, effective 6 April 1949:

```
*24th Transportation Truck Battalion, Hq & Hq Det
*67th Transportation Truck Company, (Hvy)
*69th Transportation Truck Company, (Hvy)
*70th Transportation Truck Company, (Hvy)
*76th Transportation Truck Company, (Hvy)
*83rd Transportation Truck Company, (Hvy)
*89th Transportation Truck Company, (Hvy)
*543  Transportation Truck Company, (Trp)
 559  Ordnance MAM Company
 36th Labor Supervision Company, Hq
 4543 Labor Service Company (QM Labor)
 38th Labor Supervision Company, Hq
 4052 Labor Service Company (QM Labor)
 54th Labor Supervision Company, Hq
 8512 Labor Service Company (QM Labor)
 97th Labor Supervision Company, Hq
 2905 Labor Service Company (QM Labor)
 501  Labor Supervision Company, Hq
 8957 Labor Service Company (Ord Depot)
 503  Labor Supervision Company, Hq
 2958 Labor Service Company (QM Labor)
 506  Labor Supervision Company, Hq
 4060 Labor Service Company (QM Labor)
 509  Labor Supervision Company, Hq
 7441 Labor Service Company (QM Labor)
 523  Labor Supervision Company, Hq
 8958 Labor Service Company (Ord Depot)
```

3. The Airlift Detachments, 7795 Traffic Regulating Detachment, presently assigned Office of Chief of Transportation, EUCOM, are attached US Army Airlift Support Command, effective 6 April 1949.

    * Negro personnel

    BY COMMAND OF GENERAL CLAY:

                                        C. R. HUEBNER
                                        Lieutenant General, GSC
OFFICIAL:
                                        Chief of Staff

        s/ Peter Calza
        t/ PETER CALZA
          Lt Col AGD
    Assistant Adjutant General

DISTRIBUTION: G

HEADQUARTERS
US ARMY AIRLIFT SUPPORT COMMAND
APO 757   US ARMY

12 October 1949

ROSTER OF KEY PERSONNEL US ARMY AIRLIFT SUPPORT COMMAND

BRIGADIER GENERAL PHILLIP R. GALLACHER
    Commanding General until 25 April 1949

COLONEL EUGENE McGINLEY
    Deputy until 26 April 1949. Commanding Officer from 26 April
    until 10 July 1949

COLONEL LYNELL F. GORDON
    Deputy until 10 July 1949. Commanding Officer from 11 July
    until 6 September 1949

LIEUTENANT COLONEL WALTER E. SCHOENFELD
    Commanding Officer, Wiesbaden Detachment until 5 September
    1949. Assumed command of USAASC on 6 September 1949.

LIEUTENANT COLONEL JULIAN B. ANDREWS
    Chief, Plans and Movements Branch

MAJOR WILFRED J. McCALL
    Chief, Operations Branch to 27 September 1949.

MAJOR LEWIS E. MYERS
    Chief, Supply and Maintenance Branch until 31 July 1949.

CAPTAIN FRANK L. JEWELL
    Chief, Supply and Maintenance Branch effective 1 August 1949.

1st LT RICHARD A. JOHNSON
    Supply Officer

1st LT R. A. LITTLE
    PIO – Historian (Assistant Adjutant) until 10 July 1949.

MAJOR HOWARD B. SMITH
    Adjutant until 30 September 1949

WOJG CHARLES E. LANNON
    Chief, Military Personnel

LIEUTENANT COLONEL JAMES M. CLOW
    Commanding Officer, Rhine Main Detachment until 22 August 1949.

MAJOR FRANK RAYMOND
    Assumed Command Rhine Main Detachment 23 August 1949.

MR. SOL Z. BLOOMENKRANZ
    Public Information Officer and Historian (July – end).

M/Sgt. JOSEPH J. HALLINAN
    Sergeant Major

M/Sgt. DAVLIN E. GOODWIN
    Operations Sergeant

SFC JOHN F. HICKEY, JR
    Personnel Sergeant Major

ROSTER OF KEY PERSONNEL OF SUBORDINATE UNITS

110th LABOR SUPERVISION CENTER

MAJOR GEORGE E. HUDSON
    Commanding Officer until 12 May 1949

LIEUTENANT COLONEL LEONARD E. ENGEMAN
    Assumed Command 13 May 1949 until 13 August 1949

MAJOR EUGENE BERKY
    Assumed Command 14 August 1949

CAPTAIN HERMANN . STEVENS
    Executive Officer

24TH TRANSPORTATION TRUCK BATTALION

LIEUTENANT COLONEL HYMAN Y. CHASE
    Commanding Officer until 31 July 1949

LIEUTENANT COLONEL HERBERT H. NAUGHTON
Assumed Command on 1 August 1949

MAJOR RAYMOND G. HANES
Executive Officer

559TH ORDNANCE MAM COMPANY

CAPTAIN JOHN J. ONDERKO
Commanding Officer

STANDING OPERATION PROCEDURE FOR DRIVERS

1. The following Standing Operation Procedure is prescribed for drivers of the 24th Transportation Truck Battalion operating at Rhein/Main and Wiesbaden Air Force Bases:

    a. Speed limit on base, which includes to and from Zeppleinheim or Wiesbaden East, is 15 M.P.H.

    b. Drivers will place chocking blocks properly before coupling and uncoupling tractor and trailers.

    c. Drivers are responsible that tarpaulins are properly tied and lashed in place, that tarpaulins on empty trailers are carefully rolled and secured, and that the safety chains are secured.

    d. Drivers will raise or lower retractable landing gear of trailers properly before vehicle picks up or drops a trailer.

    e. Motor of parked and standing vehicles will not be permitted to idle except while a plane is being loaded.

    f. Drivers will perform <u>Driver's Daily Preventive Maintenance Service</u> as prescribed on reverse side of Driver's Trip Ticket.

    g. No driver will leave the base during a tour of duty thereat.

    h. Under no circumstances will a driver back his vehicle up to a plane or railroad car unless he is being guided by military personnel on the ground.

    i. Drivers will exercise proper precautions to safeguard loads against pilferage.

    j. Drivers will give proper hand signals and will carefully observe those of other drivers.

Source: Incl 1 to memo from Hq, USAASC, to CO, 24th TT Bn, 11 May 1949, sub: Standing Operation Procedure for Drivers.

HEADQUARTERS
24TH TRANSPORTATION TRUCK BATTALION
FRANKFURT MILITARY POST
APO 757   US ARMY

Operation Air Lift   29 December 1948

Memorandum No. 11.

Organizational Commitments for Air Lift Operations.

Provisions of Operation Air Lift Memorandum No. 2, this Headquarters, cs, are rescinded herewith and a schedule for commitment
of Heavy Transportation Truck Companies at Rhein/Main and Wiesbaden
Air Force Bases is published herein, effective at once. Commanding
Officers of 66th, 67th, 68th, 69th, 70th, 76th, 83d, and 84th Transportation Truck Companies will comply strictly with provisions of
this directive.

1. Objective: This battalion will provide transportation required for Air Lift Operations at Rhein/Main and Wiesbaden.

2. Organizational Commitments: In order to provide adequate
numbers of tractors and trailers for operational requirements at
the Air Force Bases, two plans of operation are placed in effect
as follows:

a. Rhein/Main Plan: Effective 1 January 1949 and until
otherwise ordered by this Headquarters, three Heavy Transportation
Truck Companies with one Heavy Truck Platoon (less trailers)
attached to each; will be on commitment at Rhein/Main Air Force
Base. A total of fifty-six 4 - 5 T tractors and ninety-six 10-T
semi-trailers will be in operation during any Company Tour of Duty.
This plan contemplates that personnel and tractors of any organization and attached platoon will be on duty at the Air Force Base for
twelve hours and off duty thereat for twenty-four hours. A Company
Tour of Duty will consist of either a day or a night-shift in
accordance with the Schedule of Organizational Commitments at
Rhein/Main which is included herewith.

(1) Commitment by Company: When an entire company is on
commitment at Rhein/Main, the Company Commander will control his
organization in operation and in maintenance. The Company Commander
will be present in person at the Air Force Base at the beginning of

each Company Tour of Duty and for at least two hours thereafter. He will, prior to beginning of a Company Tour of Duty, report in person to the Senior Transportation Corps Officer present and receive from him orders and instructions on the requirements for his organization. He will then proceed to the point of assembly of the officers, non-commissioned officers, other enlisted personnel, and vehicles of his command; and there issue such orders and instructions pertinent to the unit mission and essential for insuring proper individual and unit performance.

(a) Each platoon leader will be present at the Base with elements of his platoon on a tour of duty thereat. He will command and actively supervise personnel and vehicles of his platoon and he will be held responsible for proper performance thereof. In addition a platoon leader will be responsible to the battalion commander for misuse of any vehicle or damage to same by any individual under his supervision.

(b) Platoon non-commissioned officers will be present at the Base and will assist the platoon leader in the supervision of drivers and vehicles.

(2) Commitment by Platoons: In addition to the commitment of three entire companies at Rhein/Main Air Force Base, certain Heavy Truck Companies will be committed in part so as to augment the personnel and vehicles of the particular company on commitment. It is contemplated, as shown in the Schedule of Organizational Commitments at Rhein/Main, that the 1st, 2nd, or 3d Platoon of a company will be committed for duty at the Base and at the periods prescribed.

(a) The Company Commander of an organization which is committed by platoon will familiarize himself thoroughly with the schedule and assure that his particular platoon is present for duty at the Air Force Base when required. The entire commitment of his organization by platoons will be coordinated and strictly supervised by the Company Commander.

(b) When a platoon is dispatched for duty at the Base, the Platoon Leader, each non-commissioned officer, other enlisted personnel, and vehicles of the platoon will be present on the Base.

(c) A Platoon Leader will arrive with personnel /of_7 his platoon at the designated point of assembly at Rhein/Main and he will report his organization to the Commanding Officer of the company to which he is attached. He will receive from him such orders and instructions as are necessary for proper performance in connection with the company mission. In addition the platoon leader will be responsible to the battalion commander for misuse of any vehicle or damage to same by any individual under his command and supervision.

       b. <u>Wiesbaden Plan</u>: Effective 1 January 1949 and until otherwise ordered by this Headquarters, <u>one</u> Heavy Truck Company will be on commitment at the Wiesbaden Air Force Base at Erbenheim. The company on commitment will be either the 67th or 76th as directed by this Headquarters. Present Schedule of Organizational Commitments at Rhein/Main shows the 76th Transportation Truck Company relieved thereat at 0800 hours on 30 December 1948. This organization will begin its commitment at Wiesbaden at 2000 hours on 30 December 1948, relieving the 68th Transportation Truck Company thereat and remaining on duty until 2000 hours on 31 January 1949. The 67th Transportation Truck Company will begin its commitment at Wiesbaden at 2000 hours on 31 January 1949 and remain thereat until 2000 hours on 28 February 1949.

       (1) The Commanding Officer of the organization on duty at the Air Force Base will be present at the Base at the beginning of any tour of duty beginning at 0800 hours and he will insure that proper control and supervision is exercised over personnel and vehicles of his command.

       (2) The Platoon Leader of the platoon on duty at the Base will be present throughout the entire period. He will actively supervise the operation of personnel and vehicles of his command. In addition, he will be responsible to commanding officer 24th Transportation Truck Battalion for misuse of any vehicle or damage to same during his tour of duty.

   3. Each Company Commander is advised that strict compliance with the directive published herein and with the attached schedule, is required. Additional orders and instructions pertinent to organizational commitments will be published by this Headquarters as required.

                                       s/ Hyman Y. Chase
                                       t/ HYMAN Y. CHASE
                                       Lt. Col., TC
                                       Commanding.

HEADQUARTERS
24TH TRANSPORTATION TRUCK BATTALION
US ARMY AIRLIFT SUPPORT COMMAND
APO 757   US ARMY

MEMORANDUM   11 August 1949

Statistical Report on Airlift Operations
from 1 July 1948 to 31 July 1949

1. The following is a report on airlift operations of this
battalion during period 1 July 1948 to 31 July 1949.

    a. Number of vehicles involved.

        (1) 576 ten-ton stake and platform trailers
        (2) 308 tractors, 4-5 ton

    b. Vehicles by make.

        (1) Internationals - 254
        (2) Auto-Cars   - 45
        (3) Whites   -   8
        (4) Federal   -   1

    c. Mileage and tonnage for period.

Month	Mileage	Tonnage
July 1948	136,863	28,707
August	165,948	136,531
September	235,963	141,508
October	218,849	167,213
November	182,417	111,826
December	175,213	114,452
January 1949	195,708	139,162
February	129,465	131,231
March	126,743	168,380
April	128,321	174,110
May	113,184	161,549
June	92,396	132,476
July	106,744	138,072

d. Items improvised for use on tractors and trailers.

(1) Back-up lights for tractors
(2) Vapor proof plugs for tractors
(3) Special lights for loading planes
(4) Flotation plates for trailer dolly wheels
(5) Steel reinforcement braces for front upper edge of trailer bodies
(6) Bows for trailers
(7) Guards for air hose couplings on trailers

e. Modifications on vehicles.

(1) Tail gates and rear side panels removed from trailers
(2) Air and light lines removed from tractors
(3) Prefabricated cabs for tractors

f. Status of vehicles during period.

(1) Tractor status.

	Assigned	Available	PM	2d Ech.	Ordnance	Other
July 1948						
1st week	96	63	4	24	4	1
2nd week	96	63	4	21	7	1
3d week	96	64	14	11	5	2
4th week	96	56	23	9	5	3
August 1948						
1st week	192	125	16	12	20	19
2nd week	240	162	40	13	20	5
3d week	240	161	41	15	19	4
4th week	240	124	66	28	18	4
September						
1st week	192	119	31	11	31	0
2nd week	238	188	39	24	17	20
3d week	238	183	41	32	18	14
4th week	288	203	47	15	17	6
October						
1st week	238	146	90	30	15	7
2nd week	288	189	43	27	22	7
3d week	288	185	37	26	34	6
4th week	288	167	39	31	48	3
November						
1st week	302	151	74	39	33	5
2nd week	302	153	83	28	28	10
3d week	254	165	44	31	13	1
4th week	240	160	31	34	14	1

	Assigned	Available	PM	2d Ech.	Ordnance	Others
December						
1st week	288	169	63	38	17	1
2nd week	288	197	37	43	11	0
3d week	288	173	31	68	13	3
4th week	308	194	28	59	26	1
January 1949						
1st week	356	211	47	30	61	7
2nd week	356	226	40	17	68	5
3d week	308	184	43	22	53	6
4th week	308	182	37	28	53	8
February						
1st week	308	186	40	30	45	7
2nd week	308	193	43	22	48	2
3d week	308	182	49	22	54	1
4th week	308	162	43	42	60	1
March						
1st week	308	167	38	43	59	1
2nd week	308	175	37	39	54	3
3d week	308	189	36	49	27	7
4th week	308	201	52	39	13	3
April						
1st week	308	210	48	31	14	5
2nd week	308	217	48	25	17	1
3d week	308	215	45	26	22	0
4th week	308	220	47	31	9	1
May						
1st week	308	215	51	27	13	2
2nd week	308	216	53	26	10	3
3d week	308	208	50	31	15	4
4th week	308	211	51	20	21	5
June						
1st week	308	205	51	28	19	5
2nd week	308	197	55	32	15	9
3d week	260	164	63	23	19	3
4th week	260	167	52	22	17	2
July						
1st week	260	184	40	18	13	5
2nd week	268	182	43	17	20	6
3d week	308	213	47	21	24	3
4th week	308	220	50	16	17	5

(2) Trailer status.

Week Ending	Trailers in Shop (Average per day)	Average per day Repaired
9 April 1949	45	19
16 April	29	11
23 April	27	7
30 April	28	5
Average per day for April	32	10
7 May	32	9
14 May	36	11
21 May	32	10
28 May	33	8
Average per day for May	33	9
4 June	30	12
11 June	24	7
18 June	18	9
25 June	10	6
30 June	8	5
Average per day for June	18	8
2 July	17	5
9 July	13	7
16 July	8	8
23 July	6	5
30 July	9	5
Average per day for July	10	6

g. Gasoline consumption.

July 1948	44,750 gal
August	69,000 gal
September	63,000 gal
October	69,000 gal
November	57,750 gal
December	81,750 gal
January 1949	119,500 gal
February	105,000 gal
March	110,250 gal
April	106,000 gal
May	108,500 gal
June	86,250 gal
July	81,000 gal

h. Maintenance problems.

    (1) Tractors
        (a) Axles
        (b) Clutches
        (c) Fifth wheels
        (d) Engine replacements
        (e) Batteries (cold weather)

    (2) Trailers
        (a) Landing gear
        (b) Side panels
        (c) Reflectors
        (d) Safety chains
        (e) Wheel chock blocks

i. Items listed under h.(1) and h.(2) are the parts that caused the greatest problems in maintaining vehicles on a constant twenty-four hours a day operations over a period of months.

2. Vehicles, material and equipment listed below was drawn by the 24th Transportation Truck Battalion and companies assigned to the 24th Transportation Truck Battalion for use on the airlift operations. All items listed are in excess of items on TO&E's and TA's.

a. Vehicles.

NOMENCLATURE	NUMBER
(1) Truck-tractor, 4-5 ton, 2x4	20
(2) Trailer, stake and platform, 10 ton	24
(3) Truck, dump, 2½ ton, 6x6	3
(4) Truck, weapons-carrier, 3/4 ton, 4x4	6
(5) Bus, trailer type	2
(6) Bus, 6x6, 26 passengers	1
(7) Truck, heavy wrecker, 10 ton, 6x6	5
(8) Truck, tank, gasoline, 750 gal	4
(9) Semi-trailer, fuel servicing, 2,000 gal	2
(10) Semi-trailer, flat bed, 20 tons	4

b. Maintenance equipment.

	NUMBER
(1) Tool set, 2nd Echelon, set # 3 (common)	2
(2) Cleaner, chemical and steam, portable, 110 volts, 60 cycle AC., model QM 120	2
(3) Kit, cold starting aid	2

(4) Tester, battery, universal type	1
(5) Hydrometer, battery testing	3
(6) Compressor, air, portable, gasoline engine driven, 5 HP, 16 cu. ft. capacity	3
(7) Drill, electric, portable	1
(8) Charger, battery, portable, 12 volts, 2,000 watts, gasoline engine driven	1
(9) Tools	
Screwdriver, recessed screw	5
Bit, socket wrench, drag link	5
Bit, drag link	5
Chisel, hand, cold	5
Pliers, long plug crimping	2
Pliers, side cutting	1
Screwdriver, normal duty	2
Screwdriver, normal heavy duty	3
Wrench, pipe, adjustable, heavy duty	4
Wrench, 12 pt. 5/8"	1
Wrench, box, dbl. long	5
Pliers, angle nose, 10"	3
Wrench, engineer, alloy, double head, 11/16"	2
Wrench, engineer, 15° angle, dbl. head, open end	8
Bar, socket wrench, extension length 10"	5
Box, tool, steel, loose tray	3
Compressor, air, lubrication gun	2
Lubrication gun	2
Handle, socket wrench, speeder braces, type 1/2" square drive	5
Screwdriver, offset, dbl. end w/blade 3/8" length	2
Wrench, socket, detachable, 1/2", 12 point opening size 15/16"	5
Wrench, socket, detachable, 1/2" opening, size 1-1/8"	3

c. Special clothing.

(1) Caps, pile, OD	608
(2) Jacket, pile, OD	538
(3) Overshoes	590 pr.
(4) Overcoats, Parka type	560
(5) Overcoats, ski type	62
(6) Mittens, trigger finger	563
(7) Inserts, trigger finger	563
(8) Socks, wool, ski	1,286 pr.
(9) Inserts, felt, block type	723

d. Parts for trailer repair.

    (1) Steel reinforcements, front right   150
        Steel reinforcements, front left   150
    (2) Landing gear, right   427
        Landing gear, left   331
    (3) Cradle, dolly wheels   73
    (4) Wheels, dolly   147
    (5) Rack, side (long)   255
        Rack, side (short)   933
    (6) Panels, corner   265
    (7) Stakes   530

e. Tarpaulins and repair equipment

    (1) Tarpaulins   1,061
    (2) Machine, sewing, motor operated, HVY-D,
        Singer, 144 WSV – 38   3

f. Miscellaneous items.

    (1) Back-up lights for tractors   300
    (2) Vapor-proof plugs for tractors   300
    (3) Special lights for loading planes   65
    (4) Handles, crank, trailer   32
    (5) Plates, flotations   560
    (6) Rope, 1/4 inch   8,800 ft.

3. After constant observation of this operation over a period of months, the following conclusions are in order:

a. Tractors used in this type of operation should be 4x4 because of abnormal loads and road conditions.

b. Starting of motors is a great problem during cold weather. Stronger batteries are needed and some type of hot shot should be used on vehicles in the winter months.

c. Landing gear on trailers will not take the constant picking up and dropping of 10-ton loads.

d. Side panels on trailers are not strong enough for type of loads hauled on this operation.

e. Well-trained drivers and constant supervision will eliminate most of the problems encountered on this operation.

HEADQUARTERS
BERLIN MILITARY POST
APO 742   US ARMY
Transportation Branch

15 February 1949

TRANSPORTATION CORPS SOP FOR TEMPELHOF

I RESCISSIONS:

1. The following directives are herewith rescinded:

a. Transportation Corps SOP for Tempelhof dated 29 December 1948.

II TITLE

2. The Transportation Corps organization for receiving and shipping cargo by air at Tempelhof Airbase in Berlin will be known as the TC Airhead Tempelhof.

III RESPONSIBILITY

3. Transportation Officer, is charged with the overall responsibility of controlling, coordinating and supervising the TC phase of the air lift at Tempelhof. He will maintain field liasion with the Commanding Officer, Tempelhof Airbase, and administrative and technical liaison with the Commanding Officer, BMP, and with the Director, OMGBS.

4. Operations Officer, is operationally responsible to the Transportation Officer for the supervision, coordination and control of the TC phase of the air lift at Tempelhof.

5. Liaison Officer, will assist the Operations Officer by maintaining liaison with all agencies associated with the TC phase of the air lift. He also will coordinate all supply activities.

IV DEFINITIONS AND ABBREVIATIONS

6. FOIC, the TC Field Officer in Charge at Tempelhof.
Admin Off, the officer in charge of documentation and outloading.

Engineer Projects in Support of Operation VITTLES
(approved in 1949)

(1) Project No	(2) Description	(3) Amount	(4) Approval Date	(5) Starting Date	(6) Completion Date
FE-1458-VK-240-FE-22	Fritzlar Air Base – Repair of taxi runways.	DM 3,600	7-1-49	6-1-49	30-6-49
FR-350	Frankfurt – Rehabilitation and conversion of buildings for VITTLES personnel Atterberry – Betts area.	DM 487,000	14-1-49	20-12-48	18-11-49
FR-04	Frankfurt – Alteration of airweather station Hq bldg.	DM 2,400	1-2-49		
FR-07	Langen Diebach – Removal and shipment of air strip material.	DM 17,400	9-2-49	30-12-48	2-4-49
BE-472	Berlin – Rehabilitation of a building for radio station.	DM 73,800	13-1-49	1-2-49	15-4-49
BE-1476-BC-C481-FE-33	Berlin – Construction and replacement of airplane unloading equipment.	DM 7,000	6-1-49	13-1-49	1-9-49
BE-480	Tempelhof – Movement and installation of equipment, crushing and removing of rocks. Also preliminary surveys.	DM 85,000	14-1-49	18-1-49	Apr 49

Engineer Projects in Support of Operation VITTLES (cont'd)

(1)	(2)	(3)	(4)	(5)	(6)
BE-490	Tempelhof - Resurfacing south runway, Air Force Base.	DM 410,000	18-2-49	15-2-49	31-7-49
BE-510	Tegel Airfield - Construction of additional runway, connecting taxiways and warm-up apron.	DM 460,000	4-3-49	14-3-49	31-8-49
BE-501	Berlin - Construction of GCA power building, Tegel Airfield.	DM 12,000	7-3-49	16-6-49	30-7-49
1477-AF(24-135)AE	Rhein/Main - Construction of 2 huts for Navy VR 8 Sqdn. for storage.	DM 8,400	5-1-49		
AF 24-139	Rhein/Main - Erection of wood ramps and installation of facilities.	DM 16,000	15-1-49		
AF 33-44	Ober Pfaffenhoffen - construction of facilities, ramps and stands.	DM 7,500	15-1-49		
AF 21-159	Wiesbaden - Installing utilities.	DM 8,000	18-1-49		
AF-(24-137)	Rhein/Main - Temporary pickl'g shop.	DM 6,240	1-2-49		

Engineer Projects in Support of Operation VITTLES (cont'd)

(1)	(2)	(3)	(4)	(5)	(6)
AF 24-142	Rhein/Main - Construction of railroad spur.	DM 299,500	2-2-49		
AF 24-143	Rhein/Main - Construction base supply warehouse.	DM 35,500	2-3-49		
AF 1218-(24-107)	Rhein/Main - Rehabilitation and maintenance of PSP taxiways and hardstands.	DM 200,000	5-2-49		
AF 24-116	Rhein/Main - Construction of additional railroad facilities.	DM 2,254,200	1-3-49		
AF 24-115	Rhein/Main - Construction of nissen huts F/Gr operation at Hq buildings.	DM 45,500	17-2-49		
AF 6-17	Tempelhof - Construction of drainage system for new landing strips and taxiways.	DM 150,000	18-2-49		
AF 24-124	Rhein/Main - Construction of larger truck facilities.	DM 127,700	4-3-49		
1012 AF (6-14)	Tempelhof - Additional Funds - installation of high intensity approach lighting.	DM 90,000	7-3-49		

Engineer Projects in Support of Operation VITTLES (cont'd)

(1)	(2)	(3)	(4)	(5)	(6)
WU-3	Wurzburg - Removal of PSP.	DM 27,000	8-2-49		
1472-WU-2	Schweinfurt - Shipment of PSP.	DM 20,700	8-2-49		
AF 24-120	Rhein/Main - Maintenance of shops and allied facilities for Transportation Corps "Operation VITTLES."	DM 1,000,850 2,614	28-4-49		
AF 24-144	Rhein/Main - Construction of network for Transportation Corps "Operation VITTLES."	DM 291,000 5,100	26-4-49		

Source: EUCOM Engr Div Hist.

Engineer Projects in Support of Operation VITTLES
as of 10 January 1949

(1) Engr Div Proj No	(2) Construction Agency	(3) Project Description	(4) Date approved	(5) Percent Com-pleted	(6) Com-pletion Date	(7) Funds Allotted (Deutsche Marks)	(8) Manhours Allotted
	Total					8,544,539	2,339,359
1011	Berlin MP	Construction (primary phase) of runway #2 Tempelhof.	13/7/48	100	12/9/48	100,000	32,000
1012	USAFE	Completion of construction of runway #2 Tempelhof and instal-lation of lighting.	21/10/48	100	20/11/48	457,500	156,500
1017	Augsburg MP	Salvage of PSP at Gablingen for shipment to Rhein/Main.	17/8/48	100	20/7/48	42,000	14,000
1018	Wetzlar MP	Salvage of PSP at Rothwesten for shipment to Rhein/Main.	17/8/48	100	20/8/48	42,000	14,000
1067	Berlin MP	Construction (primary phase) of Tegel Airfield.	31/7/48	100	1/2/49	924,000	360,000
1068	USAFE	Construction (secondary phase) of Tegel Airfield to include the installation of lighting.	3/8/48				

Engineer Projects in Support of Operation VITTLES (cont'd)

(1)	(2)	(3)	(4)	(5)	(6)	(7)	(8)
1070	USAFE	Salvage of PSP at Eschborn and construction of 40 hardstands and connecting taxiways at Rhein/Main.	13/8/48		31/12/48	611,800	186,700
1075	Nurnberg MP	Recovery of PSP at Industriehafen for shipment to airfields outside zone.	7/9/48	100	15/10/48	10,500	3,500
1076	Regensburg MP	Recovery of PSP at Straubing for shipment to airfields outside zone.	7/9/48	100	1/10/48	40,720	14,620
1077	Nurnberg MP	Recovery of PSP at Herzo for shipment to airfields outside zone.	7/9/48	100	15/10/48	10,500	3,500
1101	Berlin MP	Construction of unloading platform at Tempelhof.	19/8/48	100	22/9/48	61,500	7,600
1106	USAFE	Remove quonset huts from Eschborn and reerect at Rhein/Main for operations buildings, and construction of C-54 nose maintenance docks at Rhein/Main.	20/8/48	100	31/12/48	120,000	40,000
1124	USAFE	Construct nose hangar washracks at Oberpfaffenhofen.	28/9/48	100	31/10/48	118,500	39,500

Engineer Projects in Support of Operation VITTLES (cont'd)

(1)	(2)	(3)	(4)	(5)	(6)	(7)	(8)
1125	Berlin MF	Rehabilitate gasoline storage tanks at Berlin.	13/10/48	100		36,200	6,000
1127	Berlin MF	Construction (primary phase) of runway #3 Tempelhof.	20/8/48	100	Dec 48	575,680	240,000
1128	USAFE	Construction of final phase runway #3, Tempelhof to include installation of runway lighting.	2/11/48	70	31/12/48	109,813	23,580
1161	USAFE	Resurface north taxiway at Wiesbaden.	2/9/48	18	1/4/49	210,000	70,000
1172	Wurzburg MF	Recovery of PSP at Schweinfurt for shipment to Rhein/Main.	9/9/48	100		53,550	17,850
1173	Wurzburg MF	Recovery of PSP at Bad Kissingen for shipment to Rhein/Main.	9/9/48	100	1/11/48	38,838	17,970
1174	Nurnberg MF	Salvage of PSP at Ansbach for shipment to Rhein/Main.	7/9/48	100		12,000	4,000
1175	Nurnberg MF	Salvage of PSP at Erlangen for shipment to Rhein/Main.	7/9/48	100		14,400	4,500
1188	USAFE	Construction of C-54 maintenance docks at Wiesbaden.	28/9/48	100	1/3/49	52,500	17,400

Engineer Projects in Support of Operation VITTLES (cont'd)

(1)	(2)	(3)	(4)	(5)	(6)	(7)	(8)
1218	USAFE	Maintenance of 40 hardstands and connecting taxiways at Rhein/Main.	4/11/48	40	31/12/48	150,000	50,000
1218	USAFE	Construction of messhall for DP labor at Rhein/Main.	4/11/48	90	31/12/48	15,000	5,000
1218	USAFE	Construction of 2d echelon maintenance shop for tractors at Rhein/Main.	4/11/48	100		15,000	5,000
1218	USAFE	Construction of 3d echelon maintenance shop for trailers at Rhein/Main.	4/11/48	100	23/11/48	6,000	2,000
1218	USAFE	Installing flood lighting along existing perimeter taxiways and hardstands at Rhein/Main.	4/11/48	10		24,000	8,000
1218	USAFE	Construction of hut for troops and office for transportation personnel at Rhein/Main.	4/11/48	15		6,000	2,000
1218	USAFE	Winterizing tents for loading personnel at Rhein/Main.	4/11/48	60	31/12/48	3,000	1,000
1219	USAFE	Installing facilities for rail-head at Erbenheim (a) access road (b) flood lighting, Wiesbaden.	4/11/48	75	1/12/48	6,000	2,000

Engineer Projects in Support of Operation VITTLES (cont'd)

(1)	(2)	(3)	(4)	(5)	(6)	(7)	(8)
1221	USAFE	Installing heating in hangar #2 and #3 at Oberpfaffenhofen.	28/9/48	98	10/1/49	39,600	13,200
1222	USAFE	Construction of aircraft maintenance shop at Rhein/Main.	9/10/48	50	1/1/49	196,000	62,000
1223	USAFE	Construction of hardstands and taxiways for C-54 aircraft, Wiesbaden.	21/10/48	70	1/4/49	303,000	101,000
1228	USAFE	Bundling and loading PSP at Neubiberg for shipment to airfields outside zone.	28/9/48	100	1/4/49	60,000	20,000
1246	Berlin MP	Construction of truck weighing scales, Tempelhof.	2/10/48	100	3/11/48	21,000	7,000
1253	Berlin MP	Construction of signal transmitter station, Berlin.	20/10/48	100		24,600	8,200
1288	USAFE	Installing central heating in FLM shop, Oberpfaffenhofen.	16/10/48	0	Indef	39,000	13,000
1289	USAFE	Construction of aircraft control room, Tempelhof.	13/10/48	35	13/11/48	17,113	6,000
1305	USAFE	Construction of temporary housing for 900 men, Rhein/Main.	4/11/48	75	31/12/48	387,000	129,000

Engineer Projects in Support of Operation VITTLES (cont'd)

(1)	(2)	(3)	(4)	(5)	(6)	(7)	(8)
1339	Berlin MP	Construction of GCA hard-stands, Tegel.	1/11/48	100	15/11/48	16,000	3,200
1351	Wetzlar MP	Construction of radio range station, Fulda.	2/11/48	100	24/11/48	7,000	1,900
1355	USAFE	Emergency repair of runways and taxiways at Wiesbaden.	3/11/48	5	1/4/49	100,000	33,000
1362	USAFE	Construction of a Swiss hut at Rhein/Main.	10/11/48			63,855	21,285
1372	USAFE	Construction of a fire station, Wiesbaden.	10/11/48	100	1/5/49	60,000	20,000
66	USAFE	Repairing existing heating system in barracks, Rhein/Main.	6/12/48	100	31/12/48	16,000	
66	USAFE	Power supply and distributing system, Rhein/Main.	6/12/48	70	1/1/49	620,000	142,280
66	USAFE	Aviation gas storage with dispensing system, Rhein/Main.	6/12/48	71	1/12/48	170,000	
452	USAFE	Hangar door for 4 butler hangars, Rhein/Main.	6/12/48	100	1/12/48	26,000	

Engineer Projects in Support of Operation VITTLES (cont'd)

(1)	(2)	(3)	(4)	(5)	(6)	(7)	(8)
453	USAFE	Repair concrete runways, taxiways and hardstands, Rhein/Main.	6/12/48	70	31/12/48	100,000	
483	USAFE	Water supply and loop distribution system, Rhein/Main.	6/12/48	96	28/2/49	96,000	85,514
1389	USAFE	Heating facilities in hangar #26, Rhein/Main.	20/11/48	100	1/12/49	8,000	1,000
1385	USAFE	High intensity approach lighting, Rhein/Main.	20/11/48	100	1/3/49	36,300	12,000
1476	Berlin MP	Construction and replacement of airplane unloading equipment, Berlin.	(5/1/49)	100		7,000	2,000
1456	USAFE	Temporary rehabilitation of second floor Columbia House, Berlin.	28/12/48			24,600	8,200
1422	Berlin MP	Rehabilitate Napoleon Bonaparte Kaserne, Berlin.	3/12/48	100	31/12/48	60,000	20,000
1403	USAFE	Installation of high intensity and approach lighting, Tegel.	26/11/48			157,800	34,000
1472	Wurzburg MT	Recovery of PSP from Schweinfurt for shipment to Celle and Gutersloh.	15/12/48	0		20,000	

Engineer Projects in Support of Operation VITTLES (cont'd)

(1)	(2)	(3)	(4)	(5)	(6)	(7)	(8)
1458	Wetzlar MP	Repair of PSP runway at Fritzlar.	(6/1/49)	0		3,000	1,000
665	USAFE	Construction of gymnasium at Rhein/Main.	6/12/48			725,000	143,200
665	USAFE	Installation of central heating in butler hangar, Rhein/Main.	6/12/48	100	31/12/48	246,000	
665	USAFE	Construction of scale house, Rhein/Main.	6/12/48	80	31/12/48	3,000	
1154	USAFE	Technical station in French Zone.	6/12/48	100	15/12/48	37,000	12,000
1388	USAFE	Erection of 20 quonset huts at Rhein/Main.	20/11/48	60	5/1/49	75,000	25,000
1396	USAFE	Installation of high intensity lighting, Rhein/Main.	20/11/48	1	20/1/49	36,300	12,000
1398	USAFE	Repair of railroad tracks from Walldorf to Rhein/Main.	2/12/48		30/1/49	25,620	8,540
1423	USAFE	Improvement of messhall at Zeppelinheim, Rhein/Main.	3/12/48	50	31/12/48	132,000	
1435	USAFE	Construction of messhall for aircraft crews, Rhein/Main.	11/12/48	25	5/1/49	21,000	7,000

Engineer Projects in Support of Operation VITTLES (cont'd)

(1)	(2)	(3)	(4)	(5)	(6)	(7)	(8)
1436	USAFE	Erection of flood lighting for 120 individual hardstands, Rhein/Main.	11/12/48			90,000	30,000
1437	USAFE	Construction of 11 portable latrine buildings, Rhein/Main.	11/12/48	5	5/1/49	16,500	5,500
1380	USAFE	Packing and banding of 6 maintenance docks for Burtenwood, England, Oberpfaffenhofen.	16/11/48			1,000	320
1477	USAFE	Construction of three nissen huts, Rhein/Main.	(5/1/49)			8,400	2,800
52	USAFE	Complete officers quarters and EM barracks, Rhein/Main.	6/12/48	95	31/12/48	72,000	
53	USAFE	Complete transient officers and EM billets.	6/12/48			6,850	
1402	USAFE	Funds for transportation services at Rhein/Main.	(8/1/49)			360,000	
1424	Frankfurt MP	Installation of lavatory facilities in 8 ronmey huts, Atterberry Barracks, Frankfurt.	6/12/48	100		23,000	

Engineer Projects in Support of Operation VITTLES (cont'd)

(1)	(2)	(3)	(4)	(5)	(6)	(7)	(8)
1465	Frankfurt MP	Recovery of PSP at Langendiebach, Frankfurt.	23/12/48	0		20,000	
FR 350	Frankfurt MP	Rehabilitation and conversion of buildings for VITTLES personnel at Atterberry and Betts areas.	(8/1/49)	0		400,000	

PRELIMINARY OUTLINE OF REQUIREMENTS, ENGINEER

I. ASSUMPTIONS:

  1. .Army will construct all added air facilities in Berlin except Navigation aids, based on plans and specifications provided by Air Force.

  2. Funds required for Berlin construction will be included in Air Force fund estimate and transferred to Army.

  3. Air Force to plan, design and construct all air installations outside of Berlin.

II. REQUIREMENTS:

  1. Army to construct following added facilities in Berlin:

  a. Tempelhof
      North Runway – 12" added macadam requiring 35,000 cu. yds. crushed rock; 600,000 gal. asphalt; 2,000,000 manhours.
      South Runway – Same as north.
      Taxiways – 12" added macadam requiring 90,000 cu. yds. crushed rock; 1,632,000 gal. asphalt; 5,000,000 manhours.
      Approach zones – Removal of apartment buildings, etc., for 2 – 3 city blocks at either end of north and south runway approach zones.

  b. Tegel
      Existing runway – extend 1,500 ft; 12" added macadam requiring 40,000 cu. yds. crushed stone; 700,000 gal. asphalt; 2,500,000 manhours.
      New runway parallel to existing runway – 150' x 7,000' requiring 52,000 cu. yds. crushed rock; 1,000,000 gal. asphalt; 3,600,000 manhours.
      Taxiways and aprons – extended and strengthened requiring 68,000 cu. yds. crushed stone; 1,032,000 gal. asphalt and 3,100,000 manhours.

  c. Gatow
      Has one runway 7-inch concrete slab, will have to be closed by spring; requires 35,000 cu. yds. crushed rock; 600,000 gal. asphalt; 2,000,000 manhours.
      Taxiways require 19,000 cu. yds. crushed rock;

330,000 gal. asphalt; 1,000,000 manhours

Apron requires 45,000 cu. yds. crushed rock; 810,000 gal. asphalt; 3,000,000 manhours.

Note: Air Force will install taxi and perimeter lighting, GCA, radio and navigation aids at all three fields.

2. Total material requirements for above:

Crushed rock, 450,000 cu. yds. - now have 18,000 cu. yds. from R.R. ballast - only source presently known for balance is Belgian paving stone used for Berlin streets; may require removal of 20 - 25 miles of street paving. Will require approximately 50 rock crushers (to maintain 25 operational) with replacement jaws, cost $35,000 each; weight 35 tons each.

Asphalt - 158,000 - 55 gal. drums (45,000 tons)

Manhours - 24,200,000

3. Transportation Corps requirements, Berlin:

    a. Warehouses
    b. Ramps
    c. Housing and messing for personnel

4. Ordnance requirements, Berlin:

    a. Shops
    b. Garages
    c. Motor Parks
    d. Housing and messing for personnel

5. Air Force desires above construction completed during 1949 construction season, say April 1949 to November.

6. List of Engineer equipment needed to accomplish above:

    a. Rock crushers (w/replacement jaws)
    b. Road graders
    c. Rollers
    d. Asphalt distributors·
    e. Bulldozers
    f. Shovels

7. Added personnel needed to accomplish above:

    a. Engineer (at each field)
    b. German (at each field)

8. Funds required for construction of each field required for FY 1950, 1951 and 1952 (divided into dollar instruments and DM for work of construction of runways, taxiways, aprons, etc; also maintenance cost on a per-day basis).

9. List of Engineer equipment needed by Air Force.

10. List of Engineer supplies and materials needed by Air Force.

11. Added engineer personnel needed by Air Force.

12. Estimate of tonnages of construction equipment, materials and supplies to be flown to Berlin.

NOTE: Further amplification of these requirements will be made at conference to be held at 1000 hours, 14 January 1949, between Air Installations Officer, USAFE, Post Engineer Berlin and Chief, Engineer, EUCOM.

Prepared by:
Colonel E. N. WALTER 04407
6 January 1949

Source: EUCOM Engr Div file, Opns VITTLES.

FRANKFURT MILITARY POST
ORDNANCE SUPPORT TO BERLIN AIR LIFT

GENERAL

With the creation of the Berlin Aiflift project on or about
26 June 1948, the Ordnance Section, Frankfurt Military Post, was
assigned through VOCG Frankfurt Military Post the mission of
providing direct automotive field maintenance support to all units
actively engaged in this project. This mission was superimposed
upon the primary mission of providing field maintenance support to
units of this post and sub-posts.

The units involved in providing this support at that time were
the 7865th Ordnance HAM Company located in Hedderheim, Germany, in
what was formerly a German aircraft motor plant, and the 565th
Ordnance HAM Company located in Oberursel, Germany, also in a
former motor plant.

In view of the importance of this assignment and the rami-
fications involved, the need for an expansion program became apparent. This is readily borne out by a study of the monthly
tonnage figures shown below.

/Cargo from Rhein/Main/

		Cargo from Rhein/Main
1948	June	3,417.58
	July	38,499.61
	August	65,231.10
	September	61,185.21
	October	61.061.67
	November	41,541.17
	December	58,726.30
1949	January	66,731.26
	February	62,492.57
	March	80,947.15
	April	102,765.31
	May	97,689.86
	TOTAL:	740,288.79

A study of the operations of the shop installations showed
the necessity for an increase in operational facilities and technical personnel in order that the additional work load commitment be
absorbed without unduly disrupting the normal operation. Additional
maintenance bays were repared, a trailer landing-gear repair and
ten-ton trailer body repair section was installed at the outset of
the airlift project at the 7865th Ordnance HAM Company, and as the
project gained momentum, this was further expanded to include an
engine and major item overhaul section. Such preparatory action
proved invaluable, as was later borne out by the type of maintenance
encountered, and contributed immensely towards the successful prose-
cution of the automotive maintenance phase of the airlift project.
Trailer landing-gear units, panel repair, engine and major items
repairs and overhaul far exceeded the other phases of automotive
maintenance.

The 559th Ordnance MAM Company was assigned to the Frankfurt
Military Post from Munich Military Post on 27 October 1948, and was
located at the Rhein/Main Air Base. The mission of the unit as
directed by the Chief of Ordnance EUCOM was to provide automotive
maintenance for all truck-tractors, International and Autocar, and
semi-trailers, 10-ton, stake and platform, of the 24th Transportation
Truck Battalion, whose mission is to provide the necessary transportation from rail heads, hauling supplies and material to the airplanes. The Battalion has six (6) Transportation Truck Companies
(heavy), each company having forty-eight truck-tractors and ninety-
six 10-ton, semi-trailers. Two of the companies are located at
Mainz-Kastel, Germany, operating at the Wiesbaden Air Base.

During the early phase of this operation, the trucking companies
serviced were on commitment in shifts of twelve hours on and twelve
hours off. This resulted in a gradual increase in vehicles being
sent to the maintenance shops for repair. Many tractors would be
driven for 48 hours or more at a time, without any driver or preventive maintenance being performed. Also two or three individuals
drove the same vehicle during that period. Lack of experienced
drivers caused a large percentage of vehicles to break down in this
difficult operation.

To insure a closely knit coordination within his organization
and to keep all abreast in the latest airlift developments, Major Eck,
of the 7865th Ordnance HAM Company, conducted weekly Commissioned
Officers and Non-Commissioned Officers calls. At these meetings,
open discussions were encouraged towards suggestions and improvements
in the methods of operation, systems to speed up production, etc.
Along with these military meetings, civilian foreman meetings were
conducted by Mr. L. Amann, the German Director. These meetings were

conducted for like reasons, as well as to encourage the indigenous personnel of this installation to keep up their good efforts and to consider themselves as part of airlift team. Such talks and discussions resulted in exceptional cooperation on the part of all concerned and conveyed a spirit of warm feeling on the part of the military towards the German employees.

All personnel of the 559th Ordnance MAM Company were military. No German of Displaced Person personnel were useed for any phase of operation.

The Company was understrength during the initial phase of this operation. Additional personnel assigned to the company did not have the proper MOS or the experience which was essential to function efficiently as a Field Maintenance Shop. On-the-job training was utilized, and this turned out to be very satisfactory in maintaining a high production level.

Field service of the 559th Ordnance MAM Company has been to provide repair teams available to the companies, making minor adjustments and repairs, in order to prevent vehicles from becoming inoperable. Inspection teams have been making spot check inspections on vehicles while they are on commitment, which has accomplished much in making the supported units more maintenance conscious.

MAINTENANCE

A continual acceleration of the Berlin airlift project presented numerous maintenance problems that demanded expeditious solutions. It can be readily comprehended that if, for example, a solution were not found to the problem of straightening trailer landing gears, such problem would have resolved itself into one of either local manufacture or procurement through established supply channels. During the airlift project, a continual critical shortage of this unit existed throughout the Command. With the time factor involved, the procurement of this unit through either of these two mediums would have had an extremely adverse effect upon the entire efforts of the supply lines of the airlift and in view of the rigid time schedule followed in the project, would in time have caused the entire project to come to a halt. This problem was temporarily solved by the 7865th Ordnance MAM Company employing a method of heating the affected parts in a forge and a blacksmith straightening the parts, or, as in the case of the leg, lathe machine to regain concentricity. However, this solution did not prove to be entirely satisfactory in that a considerable amount of time was lost in the machining operation.

Since the demand began to exceed the supply, it became evident that, if immediate corrective action were not resorted to, a definite bottleneck would result. This bottleneck in the maintenance production output was eliminated through the combined engineering skill and production "know-how" of Karl Amann, German Director, and Konrad Gertich, Plant Superintendent of the 7865th Ordnance HAM Company. They devised a method whereby the machining operation of the leg was eliminated through the use of an external die. The leg would be heated to a semi-pliable condition, then put through this die for straightening and concentricity.

Another problem encountered and successfully solved at the 7865th Ordnance HAM Company pertained to the front end of the International K-5 and K-7 passenger bus. This bus was used in the airlift operations for the purpose of transporting pilots and crew members from their quarters to the Rhein/Main Airport and return. Approximately forty such buses were assigned from the Frankfurt Military Post to the Air Forces for twenty-four-hour running schedules. Continual hard use and the fact that proper organizational maintenance could not be performed without disturbing the time schedule, caused a rapid deterioration of this vehicle. King pins, tie rods and in fact the complete steering mechanism developed such serious mechanical difficulties that the buses became unsafe for operation. Again, due to the critical shortage and practical non-existence of these parts in the Command, the problem of keeping the airlift buses rolling was becoming extremely difficult, since deadlining for the lack of parts would completely disrupt the airlift transportation system. Using his technical skill and mechanical ingenuity, D/A civilian William Malczewski, Automotive Technical Advisor for the 7865th Ordnance HAM Company solved this problem by modifying a GMC two-and -one-half-ton front-end drive to accommodate the needs of the International Bus. This modification permitted the use of GMC parts required for a bus steering mechanism. Thirty five buses were thus modified by the 7865th Ordnance HAM Company. This modification has been accepted theater-wide. For this contribution, Mr. Malczewski received an official letter of commendation from the Chief of Ordnance, Headquarters European Command.

Briefly, other maintenance problems met and solved were: side panel reinforcing by means of redesigned channels and angle iron supports; this modification has been accepted theater-wide; protective device for trailer brake hose coupling; reassembly of trailer wheel units to prevent their loss, such loss continually being experienced; manufacture of certain critical items that were not available during the early phase of the airlift project.

Weekly visits to the Rhein/Main airport, attended by the Post Ordnance Officer, EUCOM TC representative, 24th Transportation Truck Bn. Commanding Officer, were instituted with a view towards detecting any anticipated maintenance difficulties as well as to observe the ground phase of the operation as a whole. With the lack of hardstand facilities for tractors and trailers it became apparent that hitching and unhitching of trailers to tractors would eventually create a problem. With this thought in mind, arrangements were made to furnish four- and ten-ton wreckers, manned by the 7865th Ordnance HAM Company and 565th Ordnance HAM Company personnel, to raise loaded trailers bogged down in mud and soft ground, so that tractors could be hitched to them. Sgt. Hyle, a member of this detachment, was awarded the Army Commendation Ribbon for volunteering his services as Wrecker Chief at the Rhein/Main Airport for approximately 45 days of 24-hour continual duration. Major Unger, who at this period was Commanding Officer of the 7865th Ordnance HAM Company, designed a set of hooks to be used on the wrecker for this purpose, thereby lessening the danger of damaging the trailer. Though this method proved effective in assisting the Transportation Corps, it was only a temporary expedient, and gradually lost its effectiveness as the number of operational trailers continued to increase. The wrecker operations were later taken over by the 559th Ordnance HAM Company with a crew of 13 men, who assisted in 1,274 hitching operations.

Since wreckers were not available in sufficient quantities to satisfy the needs of the operations at the airport, some other means had to be resorted to in order to meet this operational difficulty. Realizing the necessity, Major Unger, together with his Operations Officer, Capt. John J. Zober, designed a set of flotation plates to be mounted on the lower end of the trailer landing gear unit. These plates so mounted permitted the front end of the trailer to be set in mud or soft stand without sinking to a point where difficulty would be experienced in hitching the trailer to the tractor. This modification has been accepted for theater-wide use.

Night loading and unloading operations presented individual problems, namely, the flood lighting of trailers and preventing collisions when trailers are backed to planes. A study of these problems suggested permanent lighting installations at the loading railhead ramps and at the loading plane ramps. This suggestion proved to be impracticable in light of the ever increasing operational facilities at the airport. An alternate solution of

designing a flood light to be mounted directly on the tractor and
to use the circuits of the vehicle was accepted. This was accomplished by designing a universal mount with a G.C head lamp to
be mounted to the rear of the tractor cab in a manner such that the
light would completely flood the interior of the trailer and the
surrounding area, thereby eliminating possible damage to the plane
when the tractor was being backed to it or eliminating possible
injury to loading and unloading personnel. A total of 250 of the
floodlights were installed by the 7865th Ordnance HAM Company.
For this and the flotation plate design Major Unger of the 7865th
Ordnance HAM Company was awarded the Army Commendation Ribbon. On
or about 28 August 1948, Major Unger received orders transferring
him to the Zone of Interior for reassignment and was succeeded by
Major Harry L. Eck presently commanding the 7865th Ordnance HAM
Company.

Body repair, including trailer stake and panel section, and
landing gear repair was consolidated and placed in one building.
This removed the congested working condition from the maintenance
shops and at the same time allowed more bays to be opened. To
accelerate the return of trailers, a system of repaired panels for
unrepaired panels and repaired landing gear units for unrepaired
units was instituted. This eliminated the "down time" experienced
in towing a trailer to the shop for repair. To forestall any
developing "dead lines" at the airport, and at the time to keep
abreast of maintenance difficulties, spot check inspection teams
were formed. Their mission was to conduct semi-weekly spot checks
of the vehicles at the airport and to report their condition.
Analysis of these reports indicated the general maintenance requirements. These timely operational changes as instigated by
Major Eck proved their worth, as evidenced by the fact that as the
airlift project continued at its unabated pace and the maintenance
work load required a seven-day work-week schedule, all the commitments of this unit were met at all times.

At the time the 559th Ordnance HAM Company was ready to begin
its maintenance activities, a shop was in the process of being
built at Rhein/Main/ Personnel of this unit were to expedite construction. This shop is 32' x 144' in size, has 10 bays, and
accommodates ten vehicles. No other space is available in this
shop for other functions. Portable Nelson heaters were obtained
from the Air Corps to provide heat for personnel. Electricity was
furnished by a gasoline generator because power was not available
from the Air Base. Several maintenance tents were erected for
personnel in the inspection and welding sections. Planking was
laid down in front of both entrances of the shop, to facilitate
moving vehicles in and out, due to the muddy conditions which

prevailed during the months of January through March 1949.

Total number of job orders completed by the 559th Ordnance MAM Company on selfpropelled vehicles from 4 November 1948 to 25 May 1949 was 789. A breakdown of this figure is: Major repairs 439, which included 125 engine assemblies replaced; 157 clutch assemblies and 38 rear axle assemblies; 171 governors were set and sealed and 159 parts were issued on emergency job orders including 51 rear axle shafts.

All trailers were evacuated for repair or replacement by this maintenance shop to Ordnance Service Center of Frankfurt Military Post, due to inadequate facilities. A total of 75 trailers were evacuated.

Vehicles were received by the 559th Ordnance MAM Company maintenance shop regardless of organizational deficiencies. This reflected in the total field maintenance production of the shop which normally would have been higher. Vehicles were rejected only when it was found that parts were missing and showing evidence of cannibalization.

The 559th Ordnance MAM Company shop operated on a seven-day workweek schedule, and whenever necessary, worked nights. The most common breakdown of the truck-tractor vehicles were: engines, clutches, and axle shafts, and carburator governor seals were broken on at least ninety percent of vehicles received by this organization.

Top overhaul was attempted by the 559th Ordnance MAM Company maintenance shop, by obtaining parts such as pistons, rod-bearing-inserts, and valves. Difficulty was experienced in obtaining sufficient quantities of these parts, so this procedure to assist in relieving the high backlog was discontinued.

A modification design to prevent air brake connections on the front of the trailers from being broken when backing Tractor-Trailer together was welded on all trailers used in the airlift operation by the 559th Ordnance MAM Company.

The shop foreman of the 559th Ordnance MAM Company designed a frame for the trailers which would both protect and strengthen the side-racks and the tarpaulins used. A model has been made and production approved. At present the model is in actual operation to determine its merits. This model was designed specifically for this airlift operation, but would not be practical for general use.

The personnel of the 559th Ordnance MAM Company gave all assistance possible to the truck companies being supported. Instances where vehicles were received, and it was determined the failure was not fair wear and tear but vehicle abuse, facts were reported through channels, and action initiated. Frequent inspections of the operation, and recommendations given, alleviated the mortality rate of vehicles being sent to the shop for repair. A procedure was set up on 15 April 1949 to evacuate a vehicle if it was not completed in seven working days. Thereupon the unit was reissued a vehicle from the stock of the Ordnance Section, Frankfurt Military Post.

The 565th Ordnance MM Company performed Ordnance Field maintenance support on a total of two hundred and forty-nine vehicles, for the air lift. These included the sedans and vehicles to 1½ ton.

To expedite the repair of vehicles assigned for operation to the air lift, first and second echelon deficiencies were not considered grounds for refusal of vehicles into the Field Maintenance Shop of the 565th Ordnance MAM Company.

The 565th Ordnance MAM Company also developed and produced special equipment needed for the airlift. For example:

The first samples for the landing plates to be used on semi-trailers on soft ground during inclement weather were designed in conjunction with the 7865th Ordnance HAM Company, and the most practicable method of manufacturing was developed.

The specially designed spotlight for unloading semi-trailers at night was manufactured by the 565th Ordnance MAM Company from material on stock and material ordinarily used on vehicles. This method was found to be more practicable, cheaper, and faster than using contractors.

A similar type of spotlight connected with the electrical system of the vehicles to be used inside the airplane for loading and unloading during the time the airplane was being refueled, was developed and produced in this field maintenance shop. Approximately three hundred plugs, to be used for the special light equipment, were installed on semi-trailers by the 565th Ordnance MAM Company.

The total number of airlift vehicles processed at the 7865th Ordnance MM Company were as follows:

1. Tractors: (4-5 ton type):
   Inter. Harvest   85
   Autocar   26
   White   8
   Wrecker (10 ton)   17
   Prime Mover   1

        TOTAL: 137 vehicles

2. Trailers:
   a. Landing gear units rebuilt   250 sets
      Field Maintenance   236 "

        TOTAL: 486 vehicles

   b. Individual side and stake panels rebuilt 785 each.

3. Buses, passenger:
   IHC-K-5   100
   IHC-K-7   98
   GMC   32
   Chevrolet   5

        TOTAL: 235 vehicles.

4. Emergency transit repair, 138 vehicles

5. Vehicles prepared and airshipped to Berlin, 18 each

6. TOTAL: 1,014.

   The Maintenance Branch of the Ordnance Section, Frankfurt
Military Post, performed 30 motor pool inspections of airlift
support units. Also, 393 airlift support vehicles were inspected
by Ordnance Road Block teams.

SUPPLY FUNCTIONS

   The Ordnance Service Center, Frankfurt Military Post,
furnished all supplies for units and Ordnance companies connected
with the airlift.

Engines supplies (all types)			423
Transmissions supplies (all types)			281
Axles assemblies	"	"	610
Transfer cases	"	"	"	308
Clutch assemblies supplied (all types)			551
Tires	"	(all sizes)	1,771
Tubes	"	"	"	1,293
Paint	"	(all types gals.)	2,500
Anti-freeze		"	1,409
Batteries	"	(all sizes)	.504

From 21 June 1948 to 12 May 1949, 1,398 requisitions, classified as deadline, emergency, or special, were submitted to Ordnance depots.

The Allied Trades section of the 7865th Ordnance HAM Company was divorced from Field Maintenance, and top engine overhaul and power train repair, formerly a part of Field Maintenance, was placed under operational control of Allied Trades. This move enabled Depot Supply to receive critical parts manufactured in Allied Trades as well as overhauled engines and power trains with the least amount of downtime.

The following is a list of vehicles issued by the Frankfurt Military Post Ordnance for airlift:

Truck, wrecking, heavy, 10-ton	4
Truck, 1/4-ton, 4x4, C&R	11
Truck, 3/4-ton, 4x4, W/C	24
Truck, 2 1/2-ton, 6x6, Cargo	49
Truck, tractor, 4-5 ton	218
Trailer, semi, 10-ton, 2,000 gal fuel	8
Trailer, semi, 10-ton, stake, platform	163
Bus, 2 1/2-ton, 6x6, converted	40.

The supply section of the 559th Ordnance MAM Company furnished parts only to vehicles undergoing repair in the shop. Parts were issued to using units only on emergency job order requests, when they could not be filled on requisitions submitted to the supply section of Frankfurt Military Post, their normal channel of supply.

The 559th Ordnance MAM Company is supplied by the Ordnance Service Center, Frankfurt Military Post. Parts for the International 4x2 COE Truck-Tractors, and the Auto-Car 4x4 COE Truck-Tractors, had not been anticipated in quantities necessary to maintain the above vehicles on this operation. This condition created a large back-log of vehicles awaiting parts before they could be put in the shop. During the months of December 1948, January, February and March 1949, this back-log reached seventy truck-tractors awaiting repair. The average during this period was approximately fifty-five.

The 565th Ordnance MAM Company acted as a processing agency in the evacuation of vehicles which had been flown in from Berlin for repairs. This unit was responsible for receiving the vehicles at the air field, unloading and storing until ready for shop inspection section, performing technical inspections before evacuating vehicles to higher echelons. The total number of vehicles thus handled amounted to one hundred and ninety one.

All requisitions for material for airlift vehicles were given special attention by this unit. They were further expedited by being hand-carried to supply depots.

In addition to the foregoing, approximately fifty cranks to be used for raising the dolly wheels on semi-trailers, were produced by the 565th Ordnance MAM Company for the airlift vehicles.

8 June 1949

Source: Lt Col Walter H. Freeman, Exec O, Ordnance Section, FMP

HEADQUARTERS
BERLIN MILITARY POST
ORDNANCE BRANCH
APO 742   US ARMY

23 June 1950

REPORT FOR HISTORICAL SECTION EUCOM

The stock level of Ordnance supplies at the beginning of the critical period, 1st of April 1948, was approximately 27 days on hand. This stock level was steadily increased throughout the air lift until in February 1949 it reached approximately 130 days, and remained at that level for the remainder of the blockade period, the target being 180 days.

The total unit vehicles assigned as of November 1948 were 2,497. This is not taking into consideration the vehicles in depot stock which would add approximately 10 percent to that figure. Additional vehicles flown in for use in the air lift were 24 trucks, tractors, 4 - 5 ton, issued to the 7807th Motor Transport Battalion and 18 trucks, 2½ ton, 6x6, dump, issued to the 7826th Engineer Service Company. The only decrease in vehicles in Berlin during this period was an outshipment by air of 28 sedans and 124 trucks, ¼ ton.

The maintenance on vehicles supported during the air lift increased considerably, mainly due to their being subjected to continuous operation and overloading. This was evidenced by broken trunnion shafts on 2½ ton trucks, and a high mortality on hoist assemblies and swivel pins on dump trucks, and the springing of bodies and frames on semi-trailers.

The main problems of Ordnance as far as maintenance was concerned was in conservation of parts because of tonnage restrictions or allocations to Ordnance on the air lift. This tonnage allocation was limited to 105 tons per month. This was met by enlarging the rebuild section of the Automotive Shop and devising means of repairing such items that normally would be thrown away. A method was devised whereby manufactured journals were welded to broken trunnion shafts, wheels were straightened, propeller shafts were welded, transmissions and transfer cases were reinforced and rebushed, and frames were reinforced and straightened. Other repairs included reinforcement of steering apparatus, building-up and refinishing clutches and brake-shafts and brake-housings, modification of GMC axles for K-7 27-passenger busses, complete overhaul of tractors, five wheels, and the utilization of metal spray to build up worn parts so that they could be subjected to another tour of duty. In addition the Machine Shop was utilized to augment items in short supply or zero balance by manufacturing such items.

In May and June of 1949, 120 vehicles of all types were evacuated for base maintenance, and 29 trucks, tractors, and 19 trailers were brought in to Berlin for replacement of like items that had become practically worn out during the air lift. Ordnance felt at that time that with the supply situation and rebuild facilities on hand we would be able to carry on an indefinite period of time.

The maximum total number of Ordnance personnel at this Post employed at any one time was 602, broken down as follows:

Officers	19
Warrant Officers	1
Enlisted Men	233
D. A. Civilians	3
Allied Civilians	1
German Nationals	302 for OSSA
	43 on GARIOA

The 43 on GARIOA represented an additional allocation to take care of the extra Ordnance load imposed by the air lift. In this respect it must also be noted that due to imposition of training schedules the Enlisted Men had less than 50 percent efficiency in terms of hours spent on the job.

At present there remain in Berlin 178 vehicles allocated to a blockade reserve. All but three (3) of these are of the cargo type, those three being ¼-ton trucks (jeeps) for use of liaison personnel in case of a reimposition of the blockade. The transportation authorized Berlin has been reduced by approximately 800 vehicles. Thus Ordnance has evacuated 625, and 212 yet remain in Berlin and are in the process of being rebuilt by Ordnance personnel at this Station.

JAMES G. KLEESE
Maj   Ord
Executive Officer

Tel: BERLIN 44 392

- 190 -

US ARMY AIRLIFT SUPPORT COMMAND   14 Oct 49

SUBJECT: Desired Installations and Areas at Rhein-Main and Wies-
           baden Airfields

TO   :   Chief, Trans Div, Hq EUCOM

1. In the event the Army is required to support an Airlift
from the Rhein-Main and Wiesbaden airfields, the following installations will be vital to the success of the operation:

        a. PLM and Ordnance Repair Ships.
        Description: See attached Planviews 7390 Air Force
Eng Group Nos 363 AFO and 364 AFO. Project No. 24-120.

        b. Mess Hall (Laborers). Description: 1 floor, 4312
sq ft. See attached real property record Bldg T-154, for construction and installed property. Project No. 24-101.

        c. Ready Line Offices (3 Niessen Huts). Description:

        Bldgs T-181   1 floor   2304 sq ft
              T-172   1 floor   1152 sq ft
              T-173   1 floor   1152 sq ft
        See attached real property record for construction
and installed property. Project No. 24-110.

        d. Scale House w/33' x 12' scale. Bldg T-164. See
attached real property record for construction and installed property. Project No. 24-50.

        e. Railroad Spurs, Rhein-Main:

Location	Length in ft	Track Designation
AC Warehouse Area	2000	8W
Extension Gasoline Farm	180	6A
Walldorf to Perimeter	4144	-
RR Spur Runway	34594	6 N 7 5 & 10
Storage Spur	1600	7
SW Corner of Field	6700	9W

Location	Length in ft	Track Designation
To AC Warehouse	1350	8 E
RR Spur to New Runway	19000	11 & 12 & 13
Track and Double Cross-over switch		7 & 8
Warehousing Area	7312	1 & 2 & 3

f. Road Network. To include all installations and areas to be used by the Army and the road networks necessary to connect same. Project No. 24-144.

2. The above listed projects were constructed from Appropriated Army Funds 821.99.

3. One (1) ready-line latrine should be requested from Air Force for use by ready-line personnel (Bldg T-175). See attached real property record (Bldg T-175) for construction and installed property.

4. Two installations built from Army Funds 821.99 will be desired if the lift should be revived at the Wiesbaden Airfield:

    a. Loading Dock - Project No. 20-31   Location: Adjacent to Hangar 29, Wiesbaden Airfield

    b. Truck Scale - Project No. 20-33

Walter E. Schoenfeld
Lt Col   TC

Source: AG Restricted file 600.1 Vol. XVII (1949) Item 96, title "Construction." RESTRICTED. Map cited is in USAASC files in Transp Div, EUCOM.

4th Ind

SUBJECT: DESIRED INSTALLATIONS AND AREAS AT RHINE MAIN AND WIES-
           BADEN AIRFIELDS

Headquarters, European Command,

TO   :   Commanding General, United States Air Forces in Europe

        1. A conference was held in the office of the Deputy
Commander, Rhine Main Air Base, on 11 Jan 50, between representatives of USAFE and EUCOM. The purpose of the conference was to
determine what facilities at Rhine-Main and Wiesbaden Air Bases
would be utilized by the US Army in the event of a future airlift.

        2. It was decided what existing facilities would be made
available for use by the US Army; and that facilities, not now
existing would be constructed for use of the US Army. These are:

        a. Rhine-Main Air Base (see inclosed map, Incl #1.)
            (1) Existing and available facilities

		Bldg. No.	Map Code
(a)	Office building for detachment head-quarters US Army Airlift Support Command, and Traffic Control Points	T 171	A
(b)	Shelter for truck operating personnel	T 172	B
(c)	Shelter and office building for labor	T 173	C
(d)	Base Railhead, single track, capacity 26 cars		D
(e)	Truck platform scale and house, capacity 25 tons	T 164	E
(f)	Labor mess hall, capacity 200 men	T 154	F
(g)	Railhead, double spur, capacity 48 cars		G

	Bldg. No.	Map Code

(h) Truck and trailer park and dispatch
    area, capacity 200 vehicles   H

(i) Transportation Corps Maintenance Shop
    and Ordnance Field Maintenance Shop,
    with adjoining hardstanding capacity
    250 vehicles   T 180 & 181   I

(j) Troop messhall, capacity 500 men
    (to be used jointly with air force
    personnel)   T 300   J

(k) Troop Housing facilities for US Army
    personnel capacity 400 men   T 401 to
                                 402 Incl   K

(l) Railroad Marshalling Yard (not shown
    on map), capacity 350 cars   see note
                                       on map

   (2) Approved projects, the construction of which is suspended
        indefinitely

(a) Railroad unloading and truck loading
    ramp (1603' x 110') partly covered
    and with office space (Project 24-146,
    and cost 1,090,500 DM)   L

(b) Truck platform scale and house, cap-
    acity 50 tons, with concrete access
    road (Project 24-121, cost 22,000 DM)   M

       b. Wiesbaden Air Base (no map inclosed)
         (1) Existing and available facilities:

(a) Aircraft Hanger (for bulk in-transient stor-
    age) and office space for Det Commander
    and traffic control point.   Bldg No 29

(b) Truck platform scale and house, cap-
    acity 25 tons.   next to 29

(c) Truck unloading and loading dock
    (40' x 85')   next to 29

(d) Troop housing facilities for US Army
    personnel capacity 100 men

(2) No projects are required which do not now exist at Wiesbaden Air Base.

3. The following points are submitted for your concurrence, or comment:

a. The facilities, listed in par 2a (1) and 2b above at Rhine-Main and Wiesbaden Air Bases will be made available for immediate use by the US Army, in the event of reinitiation of the airlift.

b. Sufficient ground space will be retained at Rhine-Main Air Base on which to construct facilities, listed in par 2a (2) above, which are not now existing, but which will be required by the US Army.

c. All new construction required by the US Army to support a Berlin Airlift at either Rhine-Main or Wiesbaden Air Bases will be coordinated with, and supervised by, the Chief, Engineer Division, this headquarters.

4. In the event of a future airlift, there are a number of air base installations planned for utilization of the Ground Forces. Some of these facilities at Rhine-Main were dependent upon completion of projects during GFY '51. It is therefore requested that any projects which affect the facilities listed in this letter, not be cancelled and a substitution made therefore, until it has been coordinated with EUCOM.

/sgd/

Noce

Source: AG Restricted file 600.1 Vol. XVII (1949) Item 96, title "Construction." RESTRICTED. Map cited is in USAASC files in Transp Div, EUCOM.

- 195 -

Glossary

This glossary contains all abbreviations and foreign words used in this volume except those listed in SR 320 - 50 - 1, dated 28 October 1949, and Change 1 thereto, dated 22 August 1950.

AAF	Army Air Force
AATO	British Army Air Transport Organization
a/c	Aircraft
Allied Kommandatura	Supreme commission of army commandants representing the victor powers in Berlin
ALREP	Air Lift Report
BAFO	British Air Forces of Occupation
BEALCOM	Berlin Air Lift Coordinating Committee
BEWAG	German manufacturers of power-plant equipment
BICO	Bipartite Control Office
BMP	Berlin Military Post
C/	Chief
CALTF	Combined Air Lift Task Force
C and I	Consumer and industrial
CBR	California bearing ratio, a unit of compaction employed in engineering
C/N	Carrier note
COT	Chief of Transportation
Ctl	Control
DCINC	Deputy Commander in Chief
Dep	Deputy

DM	Deutsche (German) Mark
Doc	Document
DP	Displaced person
EATS	European Air Transport Service
EUCOM	European Command
FALTF	1st Air Lift Task Force
FMP	Frankfurt Military Post
GCA	Ground control approach
Gp	Group
HICOG	High Commissioner for Germany
HICOG BE	High Commissioner for Germany, Berlin Element
Hist	History, Historian, Historical
H/S	Hardstand
Interv	Interview
IRS	Internal Route Slip
Lbr	Labor
LS	Labor Supervision
LSD	Labor Services Division
Magistrat	Supreme executive organ of the West Berlin city government
MHE	Materials-handling equipment
Oberbuergermeister	Chief Mayor of Berlin, head of the Magistrat
OCOT	Office of the Chief of Transportation

OMGBS	Office of Military Government (Berlin Sector)
OMGUS	Office of Military Government, United States
OPOT	Operations, Plans, Organization and Training
p.	Page
P&A	Personnel and Administration
P&C	Planning and construction
PLAINFARE	British code name for the Berlin Airlift
POL	Petroleum and petroleum products
PSP	Pierced steel plank
Pt.	Part
RAF	Royal Air Force
RASC	British Rear Airfield Supply Organization
R/M	Rhein/Main
RMAFB	Rhein/Main Air Force Base
sgd	Signed
sub	Subject
Supv	Supervision
TC	Transportation Corps
TCAHT	Transportation Corps Airfield Tempelhof
TRD	Traffic Regulating Detachment
TT	Transportation Truck
USAASC	United States Army Airlift Support Command

USAFE	United States Air Forces in Europe
USAREUR	United States Army, Europe
USMA	United States military attache
VHF	Very high frequency
VITTLES	U.S. code name for the Berlin airlift
Vol.	Volume
Wkly	Weekly

Chronology

Date	Event	Paragraph Reference
27 Jul 48	Conference held at Heidelberg to clarify airlift responsibilities.	11
1 Oct	Military coal shipments to Berlin began.	63
12 Jan 49	BEALCOM decided to use airlift space beyond approved daily targets to carry coal.	63
31	VITTLES Board appointed.	30
1 Feb	Military coal shipments to Berlin discontinued.	63,88
	Operations Manual for Transportation Officers on VITTLES Air Lift, published by Transportation Division, EUCOM.	45
14 Mar	BMP Engineers began building second runway at Tegel.	40
30	Brig. Gen. Philip E. Gallagher, Director of Military Posts, EUCOM, directed to organize and assume control of USAASC.	14
6 Apr	U.S. Army Airlift Support Command established.	14
	7934 Labor Supervision Center established in Frankfurt.	14,16c
13	Effective date for organization of 7933 Headquarters, USAASC.	14
15 – 16	Combined airlift planes carried 12,940.9 tons to Berlin in an operation termed "Easter Parade."	2,74
4 May	Big Four agreement on lifting of blockade signed.	2
	A Stratocruiser C – 97A joined the lift.	6

Date	Event	Paragraph Reference
10 May 49	7934 Labor Supervision Center discontinued and replaced by 110 Labor Supervision Center.	14
12	Berlin blockade lifted.	2
21	West Berlin rail workers began rail strike.	2
24	The Stratocruiser C-97A withdrawn from lift.	6
21 Jun	Resurfacing of south runway at Tempelhof completed.	42
1 Jul	Rail freight between Berlin and western zones restored.	2
	8-hour day established for truck units in support at Rhein/Main.	28
	USAFE issued Air Force plan for phasing out air lift.	100
31	Last airlift flight from Celle to Berlin.	106
1 Aug	Airlift operations reduced from 24-hour to 8-hour work day at Rhein/Main.	27,37
	D-Day for commencement of airlift phase-out.	100a
4	Second runway at Tegel became operational.	41
14	Airlift operations at Rhein/Main and Wiesbaden reduced from 7-day to 5-day week.	99
15	Last airlift flight from Fuhlsbuettel to Berlin.	106
20	USAASC relieved from assignment as subordinate command of USAREUR and assigned to Transportation Division, USAREUR.	102a

Date	Event	Paragraph Reference
27 Aug 49	Last airlift flight from Fassberg to Berlin.	106
29	Last Airlift flight from Wunstorf to Berlin.	106
1 Sep	Headquarters, CALTF, deactivated.	102c
	USAASC published revised airlift operations manual.	45
2	Last airlift flight from Wiesbaden to Berlin.	106
23	Last airlift flight from Luebeck to Berlin.	106
28	USAFE directed FALTF to terminate air lift as of 2400 30 September 1949.	99
30	Last airlift flight from Rhein/Main to Berlin.	2,99
1 Oct	FALTF headquarters closed.	102d
6	Last airlift flight from Schleswigland to Berlin.	106
15	7933 Headquarters, USAASC, discontinued.	102b

Distribution

No. of Copies		Copy No.
10	Office, Chief of Military History	1 - 10
5	Berlin Military Post	11 - 15
5	Historical Division	16 - 20
3	Director, Logistics Division	21 - 23
2	Chief, Engineer Division	24 - 25
1	Chief, Transportation Division	26
1	Director, Personnel and Administration Division	27
1	Director, Operations, Plans, Organization and Training Division	28
1	Adjutant General Division	29
1	HICOG	30
1	USAFE	31

www.ingramcontent.com/pod-product-compliance
Lightning Source LLC
Chambersburg PA
CBHW050457110426
42742CB00018B/3285